Twentieth-Century French Women Novelists

Twayne's World Authors Series

French Literature

David O'Connell, Editor

Georgia State University

TWAS 813

Twentieth-Century
French Women Novelists

By Lucille Frackman Becker

Drew University

Twayne Publishers
A Division of G.K. Hall & Co. • Boston

Twentieth-Century French Women Novelists
Lucille Frackman Becker

Copyright 1989 by G.K. Hall & Co.
All rights reserved
Published by Twayne Publishers
A Division of G.K. Hall & Co.
70 Lincoln Street
Boston, Massachusetts 02111

Book production by Janet Z. Reynolds
Book design by Barbara Anderson

Typeset in 11 pt. Garamond
by Williams Press, Inc., Albany, N.Y.

Printed on permanent/durable acid-free paper
and bound in the United States of America

Library of Congress Cataloging-in-Publication Data

Becker, Lucille Frackman.
    Twentieth-Century French women novelists / by Lucille Frackman
Becker.
        p.   cm.—(Twayne's world authors series ; TWAS 813. French
    literature)
    Bibliography: p.
    Includes index.
    ISBN 0–8057–8251–6
    1. French fiction—Women authors—History and criticism.
2. French fiction—20th century—History and criticism. 3. Women
and literature—France—History—20th century.   I. Title.
II. Series: Twayne's world authors series ; TWAS 813.   III. Series:
Twayne's world authors series. French literature.
PQ673.B43   1989
843'.91'099287—dc19   88-33372
                                                            CIP

Contents

About the Author

Lucille Frackman Becker is a professor of French at Drew University. She received a B.A. from Barnard College, where she was elected to Phi Beta Kappa, a Diplôme d'Etudes Françaises from the University of Aix-Marseilles, where she studied under a Fulbright grant; and an M.A. and Ph.D. from Columbia University. Her articles and reviews have appeared in the *Nation, Collier's Encyclopedia, Yale French Studies, Romanic Review, French Review, Modern Language Journal, Romance Notes, World Literature Today, Encyclopedia of World Literature in the 20th Century, Major World Writers,* and *Contemporary World Writers.* She contributed a chapter to the book *Montherlant vu par des jeunes de 17 à 27 ans* (La Table Ronde, 1959) and edited a critical text of Henry de Montherlant's play *Le Maître de Santiago* (D.C. Heath & Co., 1965). Her books include *Henry de Montherlant* (Southern Illinois University Press, 1970), as well as *Louis Aragon* (1971), *Georges Simenon* (1977), and *Françoise Mallet-Joris* (1985), which were published in Twayne's World Authors Series. Dr. Becker has lectured on modern French literature at universities in Thailand, Australia, New Zealand, Hong Kong, People's Republic of China, Sri Lanka, India, and Nepal. She was the keynote speaker at the National Press Club and at the International Monetary Fund during the 1987–88 Georges Simenon Festival in Washington, D.C.

Preface

Man and his world have been the bedrock on which the Western novel has been built. One of the primary goals of twentieth-century French women authors has been to broaden the scope of the novel in order to examine the world from the female perspective. In their works, whether shown as heroines or as victims, women are defined through their own awareness. Male prototypes are rejected, as women reframe and redefine their situation and their selves on their own terms, and as they forge new definitions of women from a woman's point of view.

The novel, which is essentially grounded in social reality, proved the best outlet for the expression of women's experience. Because the novel is the freest and most representative of literary genres—"the most independent, most elastic, most prodigious of literary forms," according to Henry James—it provides a medium through which important, controversial ideas can be disseminated or criticized. It enables women to expand literature to include their visions, dreams, and experiences. Writing from firsthand experience, they trace the stages in their development and tell of their search for fulfillment; they speak of the divorce between what they think they should be—according to the dictates of society—and what they are. They inscribe in their works the changing nature of female awareness; they speak about communication and responsibility, about freedom and the obligation to define themselves.

In this work, I analyze the oeuvre of fifteen major French women novelists to show how they have brought the elements of women's inner world into consciousness and given them shape in the novel. This study does not pretend to be exhaustive; it is an attempt to examine what appear to be the main tendencies of the twentieth-century French women's novel. While I have tried to deal with those authors who seem to me representative and significant, I have been forced to eliminate others to preclude a simple enumeration of authors and titles. Similarly, a choice had to be made among the works of these authors; those that do not figure in the text are mentioned in selected bibliographies at the end of each section.

In the first chapter, I trace the decisive influences on twentieth-century French women's literature of two writers who inspired a completely new vision of woman: Colette redefined in her novels the traditional relationship between men and women and proposed in its stead one in which women are subjects and men objects; and Simone de Beauvoir laid the base of all modern feminist inquiry in her theoretical work of 1948, *The Second Sex,* where she explained that society rather than biological destiny was responsible for woman's inferior status. Chapter 2 is centered around the work of Marguerite Yourcenar—the only woman ever elected to the French Academy—whose approach to language and literature is fashioned by masculine social and cultural values, and whose work underlines the difference between the traditional novel and the new novel of female awareness.

Chapter 3 examines the novels of Elsa Triolet and Zoé Oldenbourg whose works bear the mark of the doubly exiled, the foreigner and the female. In these novels, we find the woman alone, witness not only of her own evolving concept of self but also of women's situation in general. Chapter 4 is devoted to the work of Geneviève Gennari, who was among the first women writers in France to document the situation of French women, torn between the imperatives of a male-dominated society and the desire and need for self-realization.

Chapter 5 deals with the works of three women of the post–World War II generation. In the novels of Françoise Mallet-Joris and Françoise Sagan we find a woman who is no longer prey to the guilt arising from the conflicting demands of freedom and crippling traditional values that tortured Geneviève Gennari, and who seeks personal fulfillment in a society that provides no models for women. Claire Etcherelli writes the bildungsroman of the working-class woman whose development is threatened by the dehumanizing factor of poverty.

Chapter 6 traces the movement toward a new language and a new vision in the works of Nathalie Sarraute and Marguerite Duras, who have redefined and extended the scope of the novel. Breaking free from the confines of traditional structures and language, they have centered their fictional exploration around previously unexplored mental and emotional states. Finally, in Chapter 7 I discuss the feminist visions of liberated sexuality and female transcendence set forth in the novels of Christiane Rochefort, Violette Leduc, Monique Wittig, and Hélène Cixous. Their prescriptions for rebellion and alternate life-styles, as well as their visions of utopia, represent the culmination of the movement by twentieth-century women novelists away from male-ordered language and literature toward the realization of the female transcendent subject.

Lucille Frackman Becker

Drew University

Chronology

1873   Sidonie-Gabrielle Colette born in Saint-Sauveur-en-Puisaye.

1880   Enactment of the Camille Sée law extends secondary school education to girls.

1884   Divorce reestablished in France.

1892   First international women's congress to call itself "feminist."

1896   Elsa Triolet (Elsa Kagan) born in Moscow.

1897   *La fronde,* first feminist daily created uniquely by women.

1900   Nathalie Sarraute (Nathalie Tcherniak) born in Ivanovo-Voznessensk, Russia.
Claudine à l'école (signed by Willy). Colette's first published novel.

1903   Marguerite Yourcenar (Marguerite de Crayencour) born in Brussels.

1907   Married women acquire the right to dispose of their own salary.
Violette Leduc born in Arras.

1908   Simone de Beauvoir born in Paris.

1914   Marguerite Duras (Marguerite Donnadieu) born in Phnom Penh, Indochina.

1916   Zoé Oldenbourg born in Saint Petersburg, Russia.

1917   Colette Reynaud starts feminist, socialist, pacifist, and internationalist paper, *La voix des femmes.*
Christiane Rochefort born in Paris.

1919   Colette appointed literary editor of *Le matin.*

1920   Colette named Chevalier of the Légion d'Honneur.
Law bans sale of contraceptives.
Geneviève Gennari born in Italy.

1925   Nathalie Sarraute admitted to the Paris bar.

1928   Colette named Officier of the Légion d'Honneur.

1929   *Alexis ou le traité du vain combat,* Marguerite Yourcenar's first published novel.

1930   Françoise Mallet-Joris (Françoise-Eugénie-Julienne Lilar) born in Antwerp, Belgium.

1934   World Congress of Women against Fascism.
Claire Etcherelli born in Bordeaux.

1935   Colette elected to the Académie Royale de Langue et de Littérature Françaises de Belgique.
Françoise Sagan (Françoise Quoirez) born in Carjac, France.
Monique Wittig born in the Haut-Rhin region of France.

1937   Girls' and boys' secondary schools begin to offer identical programs.
Hélène Cixous born in Oran, Algeria.

1938   Married women become legal majors.
Bonsoir Thérèse, Elsa Triolet's first published novel in French.

1939   *Tropismes,* Nathalie Sarraute's first published work.

1942–1944   Many women, among them Elsa Triolet, active in the French Resistance during World War II.

1943   *L'Invitée,* Simone de Beauvoir's first published novel.
Les impudents, Marguerite Duras's first published novel.

1944   French women obtain the vote.

1945   Colette elected to the Académie Goncourt.
Le premier accroc coûte deux cents francs by Elsa Triolet awarded the Prix Goncourt.

1946   French Constitution recognizes equality of women in most areas.
Argile, Zoé Oldenbourg's first published novel.
L'Asphyxie, Violette Leduc's first published novel.

1949   Colette elected president of the Académie Goncourt.
Publication of *Le deuxième sexe* by Simone de Beauvoir.
Les cousines Muller, Geneviève Gennari's first published novel, awarded Prix International du Premier Roman.

1951   *Mémoires d'Hadrien* by Marguerite Yourcenar, awarded the Prix Fémina-Vacaresco.
Le rempart des béguines, Françoise Mallet-Joris's first published novel.

1953   Colette named Grand Officier of the Légion d'Honneur. *La pierre angulaire* by Zoé Oldenbourg awarded the Prix Fémina. The English translation, *The Cornerstone*, a Book-of-the-Month-Club selection in the United States.

1954   *Les mandarins* by Simone de Beauvoir awarded Prix Goncourt.
Bonjour tristesse, Françoise Sagan's first published novel, awarded the Prix des Critiques.
Death of Colette.

1956   *Les mensonges* by Françoise Mallet-Joris, awarded Prix des Libraires de France.
Nathalie Sarraute publishes *L'Ere du soupçon*.

1958   Geneviève Gennari publishes *Simone de Beauvoir*.
L'Empire céleste by Françoise Mallet-Joris, awarded the Prix Fémina.
Le repos du guerrier, Christiane Rochefort's first published novel, awarded Prix de la Nouvelle Vague.

1961   *Les petits enfants du siècle* by Christiane Rochefort, awarded the Prix Populiste.

1962   *Massacre at Montségur*, translation of Zoé Oldenbourg's *Le bûcher de Montségur* (1959), a History Book Club selection.

1963   *Lettre à moi-même* by Françoise Mallet-Joris, awarded Prix René Juillard.

1964   *Marie Mancini, le premier amour de Louis XIV* by Françoise Mallet-Joris, awarded Prix de Monaco.
Les fruits d'or by Nathalie Sarraute, awarded International Prize for Literature.
La bâtarde by Violette Leduc and *L'Opoponax*, Monique Wittig's first novel, published.

1965   Law revokes most anachronistic aspects of Napoleonic code.
Geneviève Gennari publishes *Le dossier de la femme*.

1966   Evelyne Sullerot publishes *Histoire de la presse féminine en France des origines à 1848*.

1967   Neuwirth law authorizes sale of contraceptives.
Formation of feminist groups "Féminin-Masculin-Futur" and Féminisme-Marxisme.

Elise ou la vraie vie, Claire Etcherelli's first published novel, awarded Prix Fémina.

Le prénom de Dieu, Hélène Cixous's first published text.

1968 *L'Oeuvre au noir* by Marguerite Yourcenar, awarded the Prix Fémina.

Lettre ouverte aux hommes by Françoise Parturier.

The group "psychanalyse et politique" formed.

1969 *Les guérillères* by Monique Wittig published.

Françoise Mallet-Joris elected to Prix Fémina jury.

1970 Marguerite Yourcenar elected to the Académie Royale de Langue et de Littérature Françaises de Belgique.

Françoise Mallet-Joris elected to Goncourt Academy.

Death of Elsa Triolet.

MLF (Mouvement pour la Libération des Femmes) adopted as name of women's liberation movement in France.

1971 Founding of "Féministes révolutionnaires," a group of radical feminists whose goal is to destroy patriarchal order.

By law "paternal" authority replaced by "parental" authority within the family.

Manifesto of the 343, signed by 343 women who admitted that they had had abortions, includes Simone de Beauvoir, Christiane Rochefort, and Françoise Sagan.

Women's march from the Bastille to the Nation for contraception and free abortion on demand.

"Choisir" (free reproductive choice movement) formed.

Le torchon brûle, radical feminist paper, published.

The Heirs of the Kingdom, translation of Zoé Oldenbourg's *La joie des pauvres* (1970), a Literary Guild selection.

1972 Death of Violette Leduc.

1973 Françoise Mallet-Joris elected vice-president of the Goncourt Academy.

Gisèle Halimi publishes *La cause des femmes.*

MLAC, a movement for freedom of abortion and contraception founded.

Establishment of the des femmes bookstore, run by the group "politique et psychanalyse," which sells and publishes only women's works.

Monique Wittig publishes *Le corps lesbien.*

1974   Repeal of law forbidding abortion.

Luce Irigaray publishes *Speculum de l'autre femme.*

Special issue of *Les temps modernes,* "Les femmes s'en-têtent."

Government creates Secretariat of State for the Status of Women headed by Françoise Giroud.

Founding of the "Ligue du droit des femmes," presided over by Simone de Beauvoir.

Le quotidien des femmes, newspaper of "politique et psychanalyse," established.

1975   Hélène Cixous publishes "Le rire de la méduse" and *La jeune née,* the latter written in collaboration with Catherine Clément.

Divorce by mutual consent law passed.

1976   Monique Wittig publishes *Brouillon pour un dictionnaire des amantes.*

1977   Publication of *Histoires du MLF, Histoire du féminisme français* by Maïté Albistur and Daniel Armogathe, and *Ce sexe qui n'en est pas un* by Luce Irigaray.

Journal *Questions féministes,* edited by Simone de Beauvoir, founded.

1978   Publication of journal *des femmes en mouvements,* edited by des femmes publishing house.

Publication of *Le fait féminin.*

"Choisir" presents the *Programme commun des femmes.*

Monique Pelletier named Minister for the Status of Women, becomes the third woman minister of Barre government.

1979   *Les écrits féministes de Simone de Beauvoir* published.

1980   Marguerite Yourcenar decorated with the rank of Officier of the Légion d'Honneur and elected to the Académie Française.

1982   Marguerite Yourcenar elected to the American Academy of Arts and Sciences.

1984   *L'Amant* by Marguerite Duras awarded Prix Goncourt.

1986   Death of Simone de Beauvoir.

1987   Death of Marguerite Yourcenar.

Chapter One

"In the Beginning":
Colette and Simone
de Beauvoir

Colette and Simone de Beauvoir exerted a decisive influence on French women writers of the twentieth century, one that led to a completely new vision of women. They are, however, very different from one another. Colette's work is characterized by a complete absence of intellectualism or ideology; it reflects her subjective view of reality, one in which women are subjects and men objects. Not only did she redefine the traditional relationship between men and woman, but she also presented a new type of woman, one who assumed her sexuality and proclaimed her joy in her body. Her female is the precursor of "la mère qui jouit"[1] (the mother who experiences sexual pleasure), the orgasmic mother celebrated in the works of contemporary French feminists. Simone de Beauvoir's work, on the other hand, is built on an intellectual foundation and is centered around ethical and sociopolitical preoccupations. Her theoretical work of 1948 *Le deuxième sexe (The Second Sex)* is the basis of modern feminist inquiry. And yet in her novels we still find the traditional portrayal of women as objects; her objective view of reality dictated her portrayal of these women not as they should be, but as they are, immanent in a world of male transcendence.

Colette (Sidonie-Gabrielle Colette)

Colette (1873–1954) is one of the few twentieth-century French women novelists to have been included in literary anthologies before, and even after, the Second World War. Her novels seemed to fit into established patterns—depicting the female in the role of naughty adolescent or slave of love—and, as such, did not overtly challenge patriarchal society. Germaine Brée speaks of Colette's "lucid and meditative acceptance of life with its servitudes and inequalities," and adds

1

that Colette was always aware of the time-honored, traditional conflict between a woman's career and her needs and role as a woman in regard to her male partner.[2] If Colette shows that it is difficult to be a woman, this difficulty is not the result of social injustice, but of love, and therefore is in the nature of things and not subject to change.

It is precisely because Colette's novels appear to be conventional that traditional criticism has often misjudged them. Henri Peyre remarks that Colette was "antideluvian" in the subject of her stories—childhood, roots, and love. He adds that she entertained our grandmothers through her insolent boldness and the audacity with which she dealt with what she termed "the pleasures that are lightly called physical." He maintains that her implicit ideals never endangered those of the bourgeoisie.[3] Marguerite Duras continues in the same vein: "There are many women who write as they think they should write. Colette wrote like a little girl, a turbulent and terrible and delightful little girl. So she wrote 'feminine literature' as men wanted it. That's not feminine literature in reality. It's feminine literature seen by men and recognized as such. It's the men who enjoy themselves when they read it."[4]

It is only recently that scholars have reconsidered Colette and her novels in the light of new feminist inquiry, recognizing that she reversed the traditional view of the male as subject, the female as object. Woman is at the center of Colette's novels and man becomes the erotic object of her vision. He has lost his autonomous existence and exists only in the woman's eyes, defined by his external attributes. Colette gives to woman the opportunity to look at man as he has always looked at her; he is relegated to a state of passivity, called forth from nothingness by woman who, by looking at him, creates him. Man's place in Colette's work is that of a carnal being, limited to his purely erotic function and serving as an instrument of pleasure for a woman whose sexual pleasure is even greater than his. What Colette did was to present woman's point of view without seeking male approbation and without dreading male condemnation. And the story she told was diametrically opposed to the old tale of woman's angelism. Rather, it was situated in a female-centered universe and focused on a subtle investigation of female sexuality, an integral part of which is the lesbian story. That is why Elaine Marks insists on the decisive influence of Colette in modern portrayals of female homosexuality. She remarks that "the preponderant role played by women, alone and together, in her writings, as mothers and daughters, as sisters, as friends, as lovers, received less recognition than the more obvious but fundamentally less important relationships between men and women."[5]

Colette's work comes out of her own life and belongs to a hybrid genre consisting of autobiography that slides into fiction and fiction that slides into autobiography. The use of this hybrid genre characterizes all of Colette's writing; she weaves herself (or a fictionalized version of herself) into her observation of other characters. It is this trait, above all, that marks her modernity. It also makes it imperative to create another type of mixed genre when discussing Colette's works, one that moves back and forth between biography and literary criticism.

Gabrielle-Sidonie Colette was born in 1873 in the village of Saint-Sauveur-en-Puisaye in Burgundy. Her father, Captain Jules-Joseph Colette, was forced to give up his military career when he lost a leg in Louis Napoleon's campaign in Italy. He became tax collector in Saint-Sauveur, where he met and married Sidonie Robineau, a wealthy widow and mother of two children. Together they had two other children, a boy and Gabrielle-Sidonie, her mother's favorite. Colette's youth was marked particularly by her mother; she returns repeatedly in her work to images of her idyllic childhood reigned over by the maternal presence. Her relationship with her mother was the most important in Colette's life. In her work, portrayals of female homosexuality are sanctified by comparisons to the mother-daughter relationship; "all of Colette's empathetic attitudes toward women loving women are contained within this image and will also be repeated in non-lesbian situations between all those who love passionately and exclusively in a relationship between a young person needing protection and an older person offering refuge and caring."[6] Many contemporary feminist writers, among them Hélène Cixous, are now in the process of exploring the maternal influence on the female unconscious and, by extension, on the woman writer.

Colette's childhood and adolescence is one of the two periods in her life to which she returns repeatedly in her work. The other is that of her first marriage, at the age of twenty, to Henry Gauthier-Villars (Willy), a jaded, sophisticated Parisian who was fifteen years her senior. The bohemian life she led with Willy provided the characters and setting for many of her works. "Heavens, how young I was and how I loved that man! And how I suffered!" she had Renée Néré, the most autobiographical of her heroines, exclaim.[7] Years after it had ended, Colette attributed her love for Willy to a burning sensuality. The emotional distress caused by Willy's constant infidelities and the stresses of a life so different from that of her youth made Colette violently ill. To distract her during her convalescence, Willy suggested that she write down her girlhood memoirs, which he published two years later under the title *Claudine à l'école (Claudine at School)*, 1900. As he had done with his other works, all of which were ghostwritten, he published Colette's first novel under his name.

Claudine at School is presented as a diary written by a fifteen-year-old heroine who recounts the events of her last year in school. It is an original and satirical view of growing up and acquiring knowledge. The novel contains two main lines of development. One is centered around the jealous love of the ugly, red-headed headmistress, Mlle Sergent— who is also having an affair with the school doctor Monsieur Dutertre— for the young teacher Aimée Lanthenay. The second concentrates on the classroom and the incidents that take place in and around it, culminating in an account of the final examinations. These are followed by the end-of-the-year dance in the last scene, during which the headmistress is discovered in bed with the school doctor.

In *Claudine at School,* we find for the first time in French literature a woman who looks at another woman as an object of pleasure and describes her pleasure without any excuses. When Claudine observes Aimée Lanthenay, she exclaims: "Her nature is like a demonstrative cat's; she is delicate, acutely sensitive to cold, and incredibly caressing in her ways. I like looking at her nice pink face, like a fair-haired little girl's, and at her golden eyes with their curled up lashes."[8] Marks notes that "from Claudine to Violette Leduc's Je and Thérèse,[9] to Monique Wittig's J/e,[10] female voyeurism gains in intensity as it focuses on the relationship between the self and the other. The movement from Colette's heroine to Wittig's J/e is one from self-consciousness in culture to self-consciousness in writing, from an attempt at portraying new attitudes in an old language to an attempt at creating a language capable of speaking the unspoken in Western literature—female sexuality with woman as namer."[11]

Claudine, who is the prototype of Colette's subsequent heroines,[12] appears in three more novels, all signed by Willy. *Claudine à Paris (Claudine in Paris),* 1901, continues Claudine's journal and is made up of a series of brief scenes that show Claudine's entrance into Parisian society. It focuses more than the first novel on female awakening to sexuality. Colette also creates here a young male homosexual, Marcel. At the end of the novel, Claudine falls in love with Marcel's forty-year-old father, Renaud, and the novel ends with their engagement.

The next novel, *Claudine en ménage (Claudine Married)*, 1902, continues Claudine's diary fifteen months after her marriage to Renaud. The first sentence, "Definitely, there is something wrong with our married life,"[13] sets the tone for the remainder of the novel. Before her marriage, Claudine had hoped to find in Renaud a master who would dominate her both physically and mentally. Her desires reflect the traditional assumption, which Flaubert mocked in *Madame Bovary* (1856), that a husband should know everything and dispense bits of this knowledge to his childlike, adoring wife. Claudine finds that, while Renaud is an admirable lover, he fails utterly as a figure of authority. Her relationship with Renaud prefigures all heterosexual relationships in Colette's work, which pit a strong, superior woman against an inferior man, and which lead inevitably to the bitter disillusionment of the woman when she discovers that the man she thought superior is mediocre. The hero of whom she dreamed is seen objectively as an ordinary human whose defects usually outweigh his virtues.

The failure of the marriage of Claudine and Renaud also results from the basic incompatibility of female and male sexuality,[14] a basic theme in Colette's work that is explored and developed by contemporary feminist writers. For Colette, sex, far from uniting two people, proves that such union is illusory and incapable of eliminating solitude. "It would seem that for him," Claudine states, "—and I feel that this is what separates us—sexual pleasure is composed of desire, perversity, lively curiosity and deliberate licentiousness. To him pleasure is something gay and lenient and facile, whereas it shatters me and plunges me into a mysterious despair that I seek and also fear."[15]

Claudine then meets Rézi, the beautiful wife of a retired English colonel. Her description of Rézi's physical attributes is reminiscent of the young Claudine's celebration of Aimée Lanthenay's beauty: "I noticed almost at once one of the most definite sources of her charm: all her movements, the turn of her hips, the arching of her neck, the quick raising of her arm to her hair, the sway of her seated body, all described curves so nearly circular that I could see the design of interlacing rings, like the perfect spirals of sea shells, that her gentle movements left traced on the air."[16] Claudine and Rézi become lovers, but Colette does not describe this relationship in a libertine manner; she does not focus on lovemaking or celebration of the female body. Rather, she insists in *Le pur et l'impur (The Pure and the Impure)*—a discourse on all forms of sexual pleasure which Colette wrote in 1932—that it is not passion that fosters the love of two women, but rather a feeling of kinship, a recognition of the similarities between them. In *La vagabonde* (*The Vagabond*), 1910, she writes that women who love women are fleeing from a painful experience with a man and are looking for solace: "They are two weak beings who have perhaps taken refuge in each other's arms, to sleep, to weep, to flee from man who is often cruel, and to taste, better than any pleasure, the bitter happiness of feeling that they are alike small, forgotten."[17] Renaud perversely encourages Claudine's affair with Rézi, which comes to an end when Claudine discovers that Rézi is also Renaud's mistress. Hurt by their betrayal, Claudine flees this unusual ménage à trois and goes back to her childhood home, a flight that is repeated by many of Colette's heroines, who seek escape from the enslavement of sexuality in the return to childhood, to the mother's garden of love and security. Claudine has proved herself Renaud's physical equal—they shared the same lover—and now, by her flight and refusal to compromise, she proves herself his moral superior.

In the next volume in the series, *Claudine s'en va* (*Claudine and Annie*), 1903, Claudine, reunited with Renaud, has left Paris with him to live in bucolic peace in the village of Montigny. Her friend Annie, who has always been a perfect, submissive wife, discovers that her husband has a mistress. This discovery prompts her to reassess her life, and she decides to assume responsibility for herself and no longer live in her husband's shadow. The same characters reappear in *La retraite sentimentale* (*The Retreat from Love*), 1907, which takes place five years later. Renaud is ill in the hospital, and Claudine is living in the country with Annie, who now devotes her life to satisfying her sexual desires. Annie debunks the flowery euphemisms that adorn sexuality, for, she exclaims, love is neither spiritual nor emotional; love is purely and simply physical. By reducing love to pure physical pleasure, Colette destroys here the male-created mythology of spiritual love surrounding the sexual act. She also upsets the traditional dichotomy between male/strength and female/weakness in this novel. Renaud dies at the end of the novel, a death that prefigures the deaths of many of Colette's male characters, who succumb because they are weak, while the women, "such solid creature[s],"[18] survive and prosper without them. Woman is so strong, Colette writes, she would seem to be "made of steel," but she is in truth "merely made 'of woman,' and that is enough."[19] Colette believes that women have an infinite capacity to adapt and adjust, to face reality and to cope with it.

In 1906 Colette broke with Willy, from whom she was divorced in 1910, and became a music hall performer in order to support herself; she still, however, continued to write. Her experiences in the music hall and on tour inspired *L'Envers du music-hall (Music-Hall Sidelights)*, 1913, a series of vignettes that provide the background for three novels: *The Vagabond;* its sequel *L'Entrave (The Shackle)*, 1913; and *Mitsou ou comment l'esprit vient aux filles (Mitsou)*, 1919. *The Vagabond*, which was written at the same time as the events it recounts, is the most personal of all of Colette's novels. It is particularly modern in its preoccupation with female sexuality and work and its treatment of a woman's discovery and affirmation of self.

Renée Néré, the protagonist, is thirty-three years old. She has been earning her living as a music hall mime since her divorce from the famous portrait painter Adolphe Taillandy, a notorious womanizer whom Colette patterned on Willy. Renée chose her profession not only because she needed to earn her own living but also because the theater offered a way of life that permitted a withdrawal from society and freedom from emotional attachments. Renée finds on stage the only space in which she feels fulfilled, secure, and forgetful of male tyranny and betrayal; it is her "room of her own,"[20] in which she is "protected from the whole world by the barrier of light."[21] Despite this, her solitude begins to weigh on her, and when the novel opens she has just realized that she is in truth waiting for something to change. Her dissatisfaction leads her to accept the attentions of the Marquis de Fontanges (Max). Despite her fears of finding herself again in a situation that could lead to betrayal and renewed suffering, her sensuality gains ascendency over her reason and, little by little, she permits Max to insinuate himself into her life. At the end of the first part of the novel, Renée leaves on tour, in a reversal of the typical Odysseus/Penelope dynamics, while Max waits patiently in Paris for her to return to start a new life together.

The second part of the novel is Renée's account of the tour, interspersed with her letters to Max. Although Max proposes marriage, Renée remains torn between her desire for him and her need to remain independent. She finally decides to reject Max to attain emotional independence and professional autonomy. Renée's sublimation of her sexuality takes on feminist dimensions when she concludes that she cannot live as a dependent creature created by masculine needs. By her writing and her dancing, Renée has succeeded in creating her own order instead of one imposed by a male. She must, therefore, reject Max because he threatens all the gains she has made. Like all Colette's heroines, Renée is a reflection both of the author and of the modern woman who knows that her life rests in her own hands and that she no longer can rely on a man to give it form and meaning.

Unlike Renée, Colette did marry again. In 1912 she married Henry de Jouvenel, coeditor in chief of the newspaper *Le matin,* with which she was affiliated from 1910 to 1923. Their daughter Colette de Jouvenel, whom she nicknamed "Bel-Gazou,"[22] was born a few months after the marriage. Her maternity distinguishes Colette from her heroines, all of whom are childless. The refusal of maternity is perhaps linked to a desire to assign an episodic role to man; it is as much a refusal of the subjugation of marriage as it is of the fetters of maternity. In what was perhaps an effort to make peace with her own marriage, Colette wrote a sequel to *The Vagabond, The Shackle.* Renée, now three years older, has received a small inheritance and has left the music hall. She has also given up writing. It is the lack of meaningful, productive activity that makes her vulnerable to a young man, Jean; she becomes his mistress, deluding herself into believing that their relationship can be purely sexual. Little by little, however, she confirms her initial intuition that sexual pleasures involve submission to a master. At the end of the novel—and for the only time in her work—Colette sets forth the traditional view of woman, which equates female sexuality with submission and defines woman as an object reflected in a man's mirror.

Mitsou, like *The Vagabond,* is concerned with woman's discovery and affirmation of herself. Half-dramatic, half-epistolary, it is Colette's only experimental novel. The first part, in dramatic form, shows how Mitsou, a music hall girl, meets a handsome bourgeois lieutenant, dressed in blue. She falls in love with this "blue lieutenant," but he looks upon her merely as a passing fling. The second part of the novel is made up of their letters and clarifies the meaning of the subtitle "How Girls Grow Wise." Mitsou finds her identity by means of her correspondence; she learns to write as her love grows and her letters become increasingly well written and elegant. When she realizes that her lover is never coming back, she writes to him in her final letter that she is going to become his illusion. Mitsou saves herself, rising through love above her corrupt, demimondain milieu. Like Colette's other heroines, she is not destroyed by abandonment, but finds in suffering the strength that comes from self-knowledge. The lieutenant is but another of Colette's two-dimensional males, reduced to his role of erotic object and source of sexual pleasure unrelated to love. To conceive of the possibility of purely sensual pleasures, as Colette does, is an important step toward the liberation of women from the role of passive sexual object.

Like Mitsou, Chéri, the beautiful sexual object, is redeemed through love. In both *Chéri* (1920), which has been called a hymn to masculine beauty, and its sequel, *La fin de Chéri (The Last of Chéri)*, 1926, love and suffering give a certain dignity to characters who would otherwise remain unredeemedly mediocre. When the first novel opens, Chéri, the extraordinarily handsome twenty-five-year-old son of a courtesan, has for six years been the lover of Léa, a well-preserved forty-nine-year-old demimondaine. Chéri has found in Léa not only a lover, but also, for the first time in his life, a caring, maternal figure. The relationship between a mature woman and a young man appears with regularity in Colette's work. Loving someone who is younger or weaker than herself permits a woman to play a dominant role in a heterosexual relationship. Léa and Chéri, the narrator and Vial in *La naissance du jour*, the woman in white and Phil in *Le blé en herbe*, and Julie de Carneilhan and Coco Vatard or Toni in *Julie de Carneilhan*[23] are among the couples who prefigure or mirror the relationship between Colette and her third husband Maurice Goudeket, in which an older, maternal woman uses the authority conferred on her by her age to dominate a submissive younger man.

When *Chéri* opens, the protagonist is about to be married to a beautiful young heiress, Edmée, who is also the child of a courtesan. Neither Chéri nor Léa view the marriage as a threat to their relationship since they have not yet realized that they are bound, not only by passion, but by love. It is only after the marriage, when Chéri and Edmée leave Paris for an extended honeymoon trip, that Léa discovers her overwhelming loneliness without Chéri, and she also leaves Paris. Chéri, too, has become aware that something is wrong; his marriage is not going well, for Edmée fails to give Chéri the image of himself as all-important that he derived from Léa's love. When the young couple returns to Paris, Chéri finds that he is unable to live without Léa. Unlike the women in Colette's work, who actively work to remedy an unsatisfactory situation, Chéri can only retreat from life. He leaves Edmée, moves into a hotel, and seeks forgetfulness in an opium den. When Léa returns to Paris, Chéri bursts into her bedroom, they fall into one another's arms, and make plans to leave together. But, in the harsh morning light, Chéri observes an aging woman. Léa notices his reaction and has the courage to send him back to his wife and youth.

As she looks into her mirror, she sees what he had seen, a fat old woman. Her acceptance of this image of herself is a lucid acceptance of life, a gift that Colette grants to her women, even as she denies it to her men.

The Last of Chéri takes place in 1919. Chéri has returned from the war, an aimless drifting veteran. During his absence, Edmée and his mother have increased his already appreciable fortune by skillful management. They are now busy, efficient administrators in a military hospital. Only he is unable to find a place for himself in life. The usual malaise of the returning veteran is exacerbated in his case by his highly irregular background. Léa is particularly responsible for his alienation, since she kept him in a protected world for six years, a world in which he was the beautiful, adored, spoiled child. Remembering this magical existence, Chéri returns to Léa, hoping to recapture the childhood security of what was, in effect, the mother's house. When he enters Léa's new apartment, however, he sees a fat old woman with gray hair whose appearance proclaims her abdication of femininity. Even more distressing than her physical transformation, for Chéri, is her calm acceptance of it. While Léa has been liberated by age from the bondage of sexuality and is now invulnerable, Chéri cannot go on without her. He finally kills himself, for he was the creature of a Léa who no longer exists; he had no independent existence.

Le blé en herbe (The Ripening Seed), 1923, like *Chéri* and *The Last of Chéri*, is a love story in which very ordinary young people momentarily transcend their mediocrity through love. Like all of Colette's plots, this one is simple. Phil and Vinca have spent their summers together for fifteen years on the Breton coast where their parents share a villa. This summer, however, their relationship has changed, for they have become aware of their sexuality. Their awakening has brought them to the brink of crisis, particularly after Phil is seduced by Madame Dalleray, an older woman who introduces him to the mysteries of sex. Unlike Léa, Madame Dalleray is not a woman in love, but merely one who wants to seduce and dominate. Vinca waits until the older woman leaves before obliging Phil to share his new knowledge with her. The next morning, Phil discovers to his amazement that Vinca has reacted to their night of love, not with the tears he was taught to expect, but with a song, as she comes to the window and calmly waters the flowers.

La naissance du jour (Break of Day), 1928, again involves an older woman and a younger man. It is a hybrid genre, part autobiography and part fiction. Colette herself appears in a house she owned near

Saint Tropez, then a sleepy Mediterranean fishing village, a house she named "La Treille Muscate." Friends of Colette appear in the work and she speaks at length of her mother, using Sido's letters and her own commentaries on them. The fictional part of the work concerns the love of a much younger man, Valère Vial, for the author. But she, like Léa, accepts the fact that she is growing old and rejects the youthful love being offered to her; she redirects it instead toward a young woman, Hélène Clément. According to Maurice Goudeket, the young man with whom she was then living and who was to become her third husband in 1935: "If ever a novel appears to be autobiographical, it is that one. Everything is in it, 'La Treille Muscate,' the garden, the vineyard, the terrace, the sea, the animals. Our friends are called by their real names. Colette puts herself into it, describing herself in minute detail. Never has she pushed self-analysis so far. . . . Everything is there, except that *La naissance du jour* evokes the peace of the senses and a renunciation of love, at the moment when Colette and I were living passionate hours together, elated by the heat, the light and the perfume of Provençal summers."[24] While the work may not have mirrored Colette's life of the moment, it did announce her future acceptance of the inevitability of old age, so diametrically opposed to Simone de Beauvoir's rebellion against the humiliation of old age and death.[25]

Colette's last five novels and *Gigi*, her most important novella, are written in the third person and all center on the theme of woman's adaptability, endurance, and superiority to men. The first of these novels, *La seconde (The Other One)*, 1929, provides a most unusual denouement to the story of a traditional ménage à trois. Thirty-seven-year-old Fanny has been married for twelve years to Farou, a playwright eleven years her senior. His adolescent son, Jean, lives with them as does his English secretary, Jane. Fanny has accepted Farou's many mistresses, but becomes angry when she learns that his infidelity is also taking place under her roof with Jane, who has become her friend. When Fanny confronts Jane, the latter explains that her real attachment to the family is Fanny, whom she prefers: "You, Fanny, are a much finer person as a woman, than Farou is as a man. Much, much finer."[26] Fanny, too, finds Jane superior to Farou and decides not to send her away. While Farou could easily find another mistress, Fanny concludes, she would not be able to find another friend like Jane. The two women recognize that there is a deep bond between them; they are united against Farou in a female alliance. After all, they conclude, "a man isn't so important. . . . A man is . . . a man is only a man!"[27] The theme of female friendship and bonding, new in literature, is developed by later feminist writers and will find its ultimate realization in the feminist utopias of Christiane Rochefort and Monique Wittig.[28]

The love triangle in *La chatte* *(The Cat)*, 1933, is unique, its resolution even more unusual than in *The Other One*. Alain Amparat, still another of Colette's immature and passive young men, marries Camille Malmert, the modern, aggressive daughter of a nouveau riche family. When Alain brings his beautiful cat, Saha, to live with them, Camille becomes jealous of their relationship, particularly when Alain leaves their bed, in which he feels threatened by Camille's overwhelming sexuality, to sleep on a divan with Saha. One day, during Alain's absence, Camille pushes the cat off the balcony. The cat's fall is broken by a canopy, and it is brought back into the apartment by Alain. The cat's accusing stare reveals the truth to Alain. He leaves the modern apartment and his dynamic, threatening wife to return to his old family home with Saha, who represents childhood and innocence. Like Chéri, Alain refuses to adapt to change, and retreats.

Even weaker than Alain and Chéri is Michel, the protagonist of *Duo* (1934), who is the prototype of the inferior male in Colette's work. The novel covers a period of eight days in the lives of Alice and Michel, who have been married for ten years. They have come from Paris to spend their Easter vacation in their country home. Michel surprises Alice as she is rereading a letter, which reveals that she had an affair the year before with one of Michel's business associates. In a role reversal typical of Colette's characters, Alice explains to Michel, with masculine aplomb, that the affair was purely physical and that she was never emotionally involved with her lover. Colette traces here Michel's suffering in minute detail, underlining the physical ravages of jealousy. Michel retreats to bed as he will retreat from Alice and, ultimately, from life. In a final effort to save their marriage and to placate Michel, Alice shows him three letters she received from her lover to prove that the affair was purely physical. But, when Michel sees corroboration of the affair written by a man, for it is the word of the male that carries weight, he gives way to complete despair and kills himself. Once again, it is the man who disappears and the woman who emerges with even greater strength than before.

In the sequel to *Duo*, *Le toutounier* (1939), which takes place after Michel's suicide, Alice returns to the Paris apartment where she grew up with three sisters, and where two of them still live. The principal pieces of furniture there are a piano and a large leather sofa, which the sisters have nicknamed the *toutounier*. It is the heart of the apartment, an exclusively female sanctuary from which the male is excluded. It is not a permanent refuge, however, for in Colette's world the male is, unfortunately, a sexual necessity. The *toutounier* offers a temporary refuge to which they retreat periodically in order to find the strength provided by female communion, which permits them to return to the social fray. When her two sisters leave Paris to follow their new lovers, Alice remains behind. She will keep the apartment ready for them in case of need, just as it was there for her after Michel's suicide. But any return, she knows, will be only temporary, for there will always be another man somewhere beckoning to them. This traditional expression of the need for the male is counterbalanced by the depiction of female bonding and solidarity, as well as of the antagonism and lack of communication inherent in heterosexual love.

The strong female and the weak, contemptible man again occupy center stage in *Julie de Carneilhan* (1941). Julie, a forty-five-year-old, twice-divorced aristocrat, has been living in a small studio apartment since her divorce from her second husband, Herbert d'Espivant. She has a twenty-five-year-old lover and a few female friends, but her life is basically empty and boring. Her daily routine is interrupted one day when she receives an urgent call from d'Espivant, who has just had a heart attack. Julie rushes to his bedside in the home she had once occupied before her divorce and d'Espivant's remarriage to a wealthy woman, Marianne. Although Julie had thought she was over her infatuation, she finds that d'Espivant still has a hold over her. He asks Julie to help him to obtain money from his present wife to enable him to escape her sexual demands, which he fears threaten his weak heart. Like so many of Colette's males, emasculated by woman's strength or sensuality, d'Espivant prefers retreat to confrontation. He asks Julie to send Marianne an IOU for one million francs, which he had written to her in jest when they were married. He knows that Marianne will feel obliged to honor her husband's obligations. Still mesmerized by Herbert and still believing that he also loves her, Julie sends him the paper. Two days later, she receives a visit from Marianne, whom he has sent with the money after having secretly removed nine hundred thousand francs from the envelope. In a scene that calls to mind the confrontation between Fanny and Jane in *The Other One,* Julie becomes aware of the superiority of her rival to her husband and decides to keep secret the account of d'Espivant's treachery, stoically accepting full responsibility for the scheme.

Julie's suffering and humiliation are, according to Colette, the inevitable consequences of heterosexual love. After Marianne's visit, Julie returns to her ancestral home to find peace. Her retreat, however, is not like that of the males in Colette's work, for it does not imply a refusal to face reality. She has struggled, she has loved, and now she seeks the inner tranquility that comes from the renunciation of love. The novel conforms to a pattern that is often repeated in the author's works. There is a principal action involving a loss; if the character who has suffered the loss is able to survive, then the loss is transformed into a gain, a gain in lucidity and a gain in self-knowledge.

Colette's major collections of short stories, like many of her novels, have filiations with both fiction and autobiography. Two other works, *La maison de Claudine (My Mother's House)*, 1922, and *Sido* (1929), belong to the same intermediary genre. In these works, considered by many to be her masterpieces, Colette celebrates what is to her the most important human relationship, the one existing between mother and daughter, and emphasizes the transmission of female wisdom from generation to generation. Here, as throughout the author's fictional world, it is the female element that is transcendent. While traditional novels pose the question of whether there is such a thing as a woman without a man—whether father, husband, lover—Colette shows that there is no woman without a mother.

A final work by Colette, in the combined autobiographical-fictional genre, striking in its modernity, and significant in a consideration of twentieth-century women's literature, is *The Pure and the Impure*.[29] In this discourse on sexual pleasure, written during a period when such discussion was taboo, Colette presents examples of various forms of sexual relationships and deals with a broad range of problems relating to sexuality, particularly various aspects of homosexual experience. The author listens to and transcribes the confidences of a group of men and women, reaching conclusions similar to those of present-day women authors, among them Monique Wittig and Hélène Cixous.[30] While women who love women play the central role in this work, the author attacks those among them who attempt to imitate men and reproduce the male-female relationship, playing solutions of the straight heterosexual institution. Colette has "Amalia X"—a down-at-the-heels old actress she knew from her early days in the theater—say: "You see, when a woman remains a woman, she is a complete human being. She lacks nothing, even insofar as her *amie* is concerned. But if she ever gets it into her head to try to be a man, then she's grotesque. What is more ridiculous, what is sadder, than a woman pretending to be a man?"[31] What Colette emphasizes here is that it is a feeling of identification that makes women love each other. "In living amorously together, two women may eventually discover that their mutual attraction is not basically sensual. . . . In no way is it passion that fosters the devotion of two women, but rather a feeling of kinship. . . . I have written 'kinship' when perhaps I should have used the word 'similarities.' The close resemblance even sets at ease sensual desire. A woman finds pleasure in caressing a body whose secrets she knows, her own body giving her the clue to its preferences."[32] It is through the experience of Eros with other women "that women experience themselves for the first time, not as others but as essences, reaching that place in their consciousness where they can tap the sources of their own libidinal energy."[33]

In Colette's work, we see a first step in woman's search for self. Modern feminists admire and emulate her acceptance of herself as a woman who experiences herself not as Other, but as subject, as a distinct, autonomous being. Her heroines are strong, free, dominating, and unvanquished. While her aggressiveness never assumes the proportions of a feminist ideological system, as with later feminist writers and theorists, she influenced all of them by her unconscious revolt, in which man becomes the anonymous and interchangeable object of sexual pleasure, as woman was before him.

Simone de Beauvoir

Simone de Beauvoir (1908–86), unlike Colette, did not pattern her female characters on herself. The women in her novels exemplify the central thesis of *The Second Sex,* that "one is not born, but rather becomes, a woman. No biological, psychological, or economic fate determines the figure that the human female presents in society; it is civilization as a whole that produces this creature, intermediate between male and eunuch, which is described as feminine."[34] Beauvoir's fictional women are thus reflections of what women are, not of what they should be; none reflect the author's life as a successful female in a male-dominated world. Beauvoir never suffered from the humiliations and setbacks experienced by the women in her novels; her life, as described in her autobiographical works, was one of freedom and self-realization. For years, she writes, she was a "femme alibi,"[35] a spurious example of what all women purportedly could accomplish if they tried. The women in Beauvoir's novels confirm, on the contrary, that women are denied self-realization by society. Her theoretical work *The Second Sex* explains why and how this occurred.

Simone de Beauvoir was born into an upper-middle-class family and raised in the Catholic faith. When she reached adolescence she rejected Catholicism and other values of her family. Horrified by the subservient position of women, she vowed never to do domestic work, to become independent financially, and to reject the crippling effects on women of marriage and children. She received her *agrégation de philosophie*, with distinction, in 1929 and taught from 1931 to 1943, when she abandoned teaching for writing. In 1929 she met Jean-Paul Sartre who, she wrote in *Mémoires d'une jeune fille rangée (Memoirs of a Dutiful Daughter)*, 1958, was "the dream companion [she] had longed for from the age of fifteen . . . the double in whom [she] . . . found all [her] . . . burning aspirations raised to the pitch of incandescence. . . . [She] would always be able to share everything with him."[36] Throughout her life, Beauvoir remained the intimate and intellectual companion of Sartre, but always rejected the servitude of marriage. Still, it was Sartre's work that received fame and reviews, while Beauvoir's was relegated to a few lines of criticism in anthologies and critical works. Often it was snidely insinuated that it was Sartre who actually wrote her works, and it is, therefore, not unusual to find in a work on Beauvoir—in one written as late as 1979, for example—that the first item in her chronology is the birthdate of Jean-Paul Sartre.[37] It is only now that full recognition has been accorded to Beauvoir's work, fictional as well as theoretical, as well as to her role as the intellectual forerunner of the women's movement.

Simone de Beauvoir has explained the difference between her theoretical works, where she is discussing woman's condition or defending feminist theses, and her novels. In the autobiographical *La force des choses (Force of Circumstances)*, 1963, she writes: "My essays reflect my practical opinions and my intellectual certainties; my novels reflect my astonishment at the human condition."[38] In an interview with Madeleine Chapsal she stated that she was interested in ideas as well as in people. When she thought something, she explained, she wrote an essay in which she attempted to draw conclusions. But in a novel, on the contrary, she sought neither to convince nor to prove, but rather to reproduce life in all its ambiguity.[39]

When Simone de Beauvoir wrote *The Second Sex*, which was to become the intellectual foundation of the feminist movement, she intended to write a theoretical rather than a polemical work. She was motivated less by a desire to demand women's rights than by the need to understand and account for women's inferior place in society. In the introduction to *The Second Sex*, Beauvoir gives an account of the condition of women throughout history in an effort to explain how men have transformed women's biological destiny into a condition of social, political, and existential inferiority. Man thinks of his body, she writes, as a direct and normal connection with the world. Humanity, thus, is defined as male, and woman is defined as relative to him, not as an autonomous being. Woman is "defined and differentiated with reference to man and not he with reference to her; she is the incidental, the inessential as opposed to the essential. He is the Subject, he is the Absolute—she is the Other" (xvi). Because woman is the inessential facing the essential, she has been condemned by men to stagnation. Those who are condemned to stagnation, Beauvoir writes, are described as happy, on the pretext that happiness consists in being at rest. She, however, rejects such a concept in the light of her existentialist ethics, which maintains that such stagnation is not happiness but rather the reduction of the person to the state of being an object. She writes:

There is no justification for present existence other than its expansion into an indefinitely open future. [This expansion, or transcendence is the move of the individual projecting himself or herself toward freedom. But every time transcendence is condemned to fall uselessly back upon itself because it is cut off from its goals], every time transcendence falls back into immanence, stagnation, there is a degradation of existence into the *"en-soi"*—the brutish life of subjection to given conditions—and of liberty into constraint and contingence. This downfall represents a moral fault if the subject consents to it; if it is inflicted upon him, it spells frustration and oppression. In both cases, it is an absolute evil. Every individual concerned to justify his existence feels that his existence involves an undefined need to transcend himself, to engage in freely chosen projects. (xxix)

And she continues:

what peculiarly signalizes the situation of woman is that she—a free and autonomous being like all human creatures—nevertheless finds herself living in a world where men compel her to assume the status of the Other. They propose to stabilize her as object and to doom her to immanence since her transcendence is to be overshadowed and forever transcended by another ego *(conscience)* which is essential and sovereign. The drama of woman lies in this conflict between the fundamental aspiration of every subject (ego)—who always regards the self as the essential—and the compulsions of a situation in which she is the inessential. (xxix)

Beauvoir then asks how a human being in woman's situation can attain fulfillment, a question that would be meaningless if one were "to believe that woman's destiny is inevitably determined by physiological, psychological, or economic forces" (xxix).

To prove the contrary, Beauvoir considers, in part 1, book 1, of *The Second Sex*, how woman is viewed by biology, psychoanalysis, and historical materialism; why woman has been defined as the Other; and the consequences for both the male and the female (xxix). In part 2 Beauvoir traces the way in which man has transformed woman's biological dependence into a condition of permanent social, political, and even existential dependence and inferiority. Not only is it man who has determined the values of the tribe and imposed them on woman, but it is also he who has deemed his functions to be superior to those of woman. It has always been man who invented and created while woman was limited to generating life. While childbearing only perpetuates life, constantly repeating the same action in an apparently absurd cycle, man exists by what he has done, his experience transcends life. It is his superior strength and physical daring that establish values: "Man's power and transcendence make him fully 'existent,' while woman, doomed to immanence and passivity, is not really 'existent' or even as fully human as the male."[40] The opposition Simone de Beauvoir describes in *The Second Sex* between subject and object, between transcendence and immanence, can be found in all her novels.

In part 3, book 1, "Myths," Beauvoir demonstrates that, after having reduced woman to an inferior position, man convinced her to accept her status by weaving a series of myths around her throughout the ages. While these myths express man's ambivalent attitude toward woman, they all, nevertheless, define woman in terms of man's needs and desires, with the result that woman appears always as the Other, the nonessential. To combat his feelings of helplessness in the face of the mysteries of the universe, man created the myth of the eternal feminine, which is in effect meaningless. By means of this myth, man projected on the Other his fears, his guilt, and his ignorance. His greatest victory, however, has been to have made woman accept for so long the idea that there is an irreversible fatality governing her life.

In book 2 of *The Second Sex*, Beauvoir considers woman today and the situation that is the key to her deliverance. Here Beauvoir makes the critical assertion that "one is not born, but rather becomes a woman" (267). To prove that there is no predetermined female essence and that woman is created by cultural influences and by her education and situation in life, Beauvoir traces the physiological and psychological itinerary of woman from the beginning to the end of her life. The section on the formative years demonstrates that the young girl learns that she must please in order to exist, that she must transform herself into an object, and that she must accept the subsidiary role society imposes on her. In the last chapter of this section, Beauvoir deals with the lesbian. Lesbianism, according to Beauvoir, who echoes here Colette's views, is not of physiological origin but can stem from causes as varied as disappointment over male sexuality, difficulties in finding a man, or a search for affection. The lesbian is "no more an undeveloped woman than a superior one. . . . Woman's homosexuality is one attempt among others to reconcile her autonomy with the passivity of her flesh" (406–7). Beauvoir concludes: "The truth is that homosexuality is no more a perversion deliberately indulged in than it is a curse of fate. It is an attitude *chosen in a certain situation*—that is, at once motivated and freely adopted. . . . It is one way, among others, in which woman solves the problems posed by her condition in general, by her erotic situation in particular" (424).

The next section of book 2, "Situation," presents a detailed analysis of woman's traditional occupations—marriage and motherhood. Beauvoir concludes here that marriage as a career for woman and motherhood as a justification for her existence are insufficient. In accepting the economic support of a man, a woman remains dependent and lives through another. Childbearing and domestic chores are not transcendent activities, but merely a continuation of life. After treating marriage and motherhood, Beauvoir deals with woman's social life, including that of prostitutes and hetairas. She then traces woman's progress from maturity to old age and concludes the section with a consideration of woman's situation and character. "It is evident," she states, "that woman's 'character'—her convictions, her values, her wisdom, her morality, her tastes, her behavior—are to be explained by her situation" (624). Woman must reject the limitations of her situation. Resignation is only abdication and flight—she must work for her liberation. "This liberation must be collective and requires first of all that the economic evolution of woman's condition be accomplished. There have been, however, and there are [still] many women trying to achieve individual salvation by solitary effort . . . attempting to justify their existence in the midst of their immanence . . . to realize transcendence in immanence" (627–28).

Beauvoir describes such pathetic solitary efforts, made by the narcissist, the woman in love, and the mystic, in the following section, "Justifications." Narcissism, Beauvoir explains, "is a well-defined process of identification, one in which the ego is regarded as an absolute end and the subject takes refuge from himself in it. . . . [The narcissist] gives herself supreme importance because no object of importance is accessible to her. . . . If she can thus offer *herself* to her own desires, it is because she has felt herself an object since childhood" (629–30). The woman in love was educated to believe that being loved is somehow equivalent to transcendence. This being the case, woman must valorize love above all else, and it is for this reason, according to Beauvoir, that love becomes a religion. It also results in woman's accepting existence as the Other, a relative being, striving to find her identity in the male fantasy of what she should be. "Love has been assigned to woman as her supreme vocation, and when she directs it toward a man, she is seeking God in him; but if human love is denied her by circumstances, if she is disappointed or overparticular, she may choose to adore divinity in the person of God Himself" (670). While we find the narcissist and the woman in love in Beauvoir's novels, we do not find examples of the mystic.

In the concluding section, "Toward Liberation," Beauvoir discusses the obstacles to women's liberation, principal among them the psychological conditioning of both the sexes, which produces preconceptions of what constitutes femininity as well as the collusion of society to make women accept their supposed inferiority and passive role. Beauvoir maintains further that it is only through gainful employment that woman can achieve liberty. Once she has ceased to be a parasite, the system based on her dependence crumbles. But Beauvoir demonstrates in her novels that even economic emancipation is insufficient without a change in psychological conditioning. While many of her female protagonists are gainfully employed they still remain psychologically dependent on the men in their lives.

At the end of the final chapter, "The Independent Woman," Beauvoir writes: "The free woman is just being born; when she has won possession of herself perhaps Rimbaud's prophecy will be fulfilled: 'There will be poets! When woman's unmeasured bondage shall be broken, when she shall live for and through herself, man—hitherto detestable—having let her go, she, too, will be poet! Woman will find the unknown! Will her ideational worlds be different from ours? She will come upon strange, unfathomable, repellent, delightful things; we shall take them, we shall comprehend them' " (715). Beauvoir remarks, however, that it is not certain that women's "ideational worlds" will be different from those of men, since it will be through attaining the same situation as men that women will find emancipation. Beauvoir repudiated this idea, however, in 1976 when she expressed a thought that is shared by contemporary feminist writers: "The recent evolution of feminism has made us understand that we occupy a unique position in this universe and that, far from denying this uniqueness, we must assert it."[41]

Beauvoir's novels illustrate one of the central theses of *The Second Sex,* which is that a woman who accepts her femininity as it is defined by a male-dominated society gives up any claim to being a subject and initiator of action and thus finds it impossible to justify her existence as an autonomous human being. Furthermore, if she attempts to deny her femininity and become a man, she is then reduced to being an incomplete human being. This impossible choice faces Beauvoir's female characters as they struggle to affirm themselves as essential subjects, even as they adopt attitudes, options, and ambivalences that lead to failure. "I identify with women who have assumed responsibility for their lives and who struggle to make them successful; but that does not prevent me . . . from being interested in those who have failed to a greater or lesser degree and, in a more general way, in that element of failure that there is in every existence."[42]

In an interview with Pierre Viansson-Ponte, Beauvoir states, "I never wrote so-called militant works, except for essays, prefaces, but even though I think that literature should be *engagé* [committed], I do not think that it should be militant because then it winds up as socialist realism with positive heroes, with lies. [Because] I have always tried in my books to remain close to real life. . . . certain women have reproached me for having depicted broken, unhappy women rather than positive heroines. I did so because that is the way I see women's lives now, and I do not feel like portraying militant, heroic women who do not exist."[43] Beauvoir expressed the same idea in *La force des choses:* "The writer must not promise 'des lendemains qui chantent'[44] [a brighter future] but, by portraying the world as it is, create the will to change it."[45]

There is a basic pattern that is repeated in the novels *L'Invitée (She Came to Stay),* 1943; *Les mandarins (The Mandarins),* 1954; *Les belles images (Les Belles Images)*, 1966; and *La femme rompue (The Woman Destroyed)*, 1968. At the beginning of each work, the female protagonist is involved in a relationship with a man. Her life is centered around this relationship so that, whatever her profession or occupation, she does not derive fundamental satisfaction from it but subordinates it to her affective life. During the narrative, she becomes enmeshed in a love triangle, which threatens her emotional relationship as well as her work, her mode of life, and even her life itself. In each novel, the resolution of the love triangle changes the course of the heroine's life. As she wrestles with the problem, she is forced to take stock of her life and grapple with the meaning of her existence. Either she succeeds, finally confronting her existence and assuming responsibility for it, or she fails, refusing responsibility for her life and remaining forever condemned to the reified state of inessential Other.

Beauvoir's first published work, *She Came to Stay*, is both a philosophical and a psychological novel in which new philosophical ideas blend with a classical study of jealousy. It is a philosophical novel in that it serves to illustrate the Hegelian concept that "each conscience seeks the death of the other"; each one seeks to be recognized by the Other while refusing recognition to the Other. It is this concept that underlines Beauvoir's view of the situation of women. In *She Came to Stay*, the author attempts to work out the fundamentally irreconcilable relationship between one's self and the Other, the inability of one consciousness to come to grips with the fact that all other consciousnesses also consider themselves absolute and essential.

She Came to Stay takes place in Paris. Françoise, a writer, lives with Pierre Labrousse, a stage director. They are an ideal couple, united in mind, body, and mutual respect. Despite Pierre's infidelities, Françoise knows that she has the best, the essential part of him. Françoise corresponds in many ways to the ideal, emancipated woman posited in *The Second Sex*. She is a liberated woman who has renounced marriage and children; she writes novels and also collaborates with Pierre in his theatrical ventures. Yet, despite the fact that she is financially self-sufficient, an absolute prerequisite for woman's liberation according to Beauvoir, she is emotionally dependent on Pierre and considers her career secondary to his work and to their relationship. While Pierre accepts the responsibility for creating and justifying his life through his work, she seeks justification through outside sources, particularly Pierre, for she has no inner sense of self. She depends almost entirely on the confirmation she finds in him.

Pierre and Françoise decide to "adopt" Xavière Pagès, a young woman from the provinces, becoming a joint Pygmalion to her Galatea. But Xavière is lethargic; she refuses to be molded or educated and choses to assert herself by refusing to play the role assigned to her by Françoise. She is able to do so when Pierre begins to take her seriously and recognize her as subject. Since Pierre has always dictated the terms of their relationship, Françoise is forced for the first time to really see Xavière instead of the image she has projected on her. She is forced to recognize this hostile and foreign consciousness, which refuses, in turn, to recognize her, for Xavière has also learned the power of recognition. She and Françoise become locked in a Hegelian struggle: Françoise attempts to overcome Xavière's resistance, Xavière refuses; Françoise demands to be recognized, Xavière again refuses. Nor will she confirm the image Françoise and Pierre have projected of themselves as the embodiment of the ideal couple. Xavière is the absolute Other. "She did nothing and she was Xavière: she was so in an indestructible way. . . . It wasn't even that she preferred herself to others, she was absolutely not aware of their existence."[46]

Françoise triumphs, however, when Pierre breaks with Xavière, with whom he has had an affair, and returns to her. Not only is Françoise once again sure of Pierre's love, but she is also preferred by Gerbert, Xavière's other lover. Thus, paradoxically, she is completely victorious at the very moment she decides to rid herself of Xavière. She murders her because she cannot bear the monstruous image Xavière has of her and must free herself from it forever; she must annihilate this hostile consciousness. Her destruction of another as a means of achieving an identity may be called a philosophical crime. But the murder of Xavière is a false solution, which never satisfied Beauvoir; while Françoise may have eliminated Xavière as a consciousness, she was never able to gain the victory of recognition from that consciousness, and that is the only victory possible in a Hegelian philosophical contest.

Like *She Came to Stay*, Beauvoir's second published novel, *Le sang des autres (The Blood of Others)* of 1945, is a philosophical novel. Its epigraph—"Each of us is responsible for everything and to every human being"—is taken from Dostoevski and announces the existentialist thesis of the novel that responsibility arises not only from our acts and their consequences but also from the mere fact of our existence.[47] *The Blood of Others* is also a problem novel, since its aim is to serve as an arena for the clash of those ideas that preoccupied Beauvoir at that time. It is, in effect, an intellectual quest for self-discovery.

While *The Blood of Others* is centered around a male—Jean Blomart—he remains, according to Beauvoir, more or less an abstraction and has less "life blood" than the female protagonist Hélène, to whom she gave more of her own traits.[48] This affirmation is surprising since throughout most of the novel Hélène conforms to the unflattering description we find in *The Second Sex* of the woman in love who expects her love affair to provide justification for her existence. It is only at the end of the novel that she acts to create her own essence instead of waiting to be defined by others. Her metamorphosis, however, is flawed, since it seems to result more from the author's didactic intention than from any truly believable transformation on her part. Jean Blomart, on the other hand, has spent his life trying to assuage his existential guilt through choice and action. Yet, he has succeeded only in producing suffering and tragedy for those around him. He alienated his mother, when he abandoned his class to join the Communist party, and he caused the death of his friend Jacques, whom he led into a demonstration in which he was killed. When he rejected Hélène, she turned to a man she did not love, became pregnant, and almost died from a painful, illegal abortion. Every time Jean has accepted responsibility, he has exposed those around him to mortal danger. Finally, he permits Hélène to leave on a dangerous Resistance mission, which costs her her life. But it is precisely this act, her own action, her assumption of responsibility for her own life, that at last transforms her into a subject. She realizes that it is her "own life that [she] . . . is finally living."[49] As she lies dying, she demonstrates to Jean that one must act, that silence is a crime, and that it is impossible to withdraw without leaving a void to be filled by evil, suffering, and death. Consequently, as the novel ends, Jean decides to send a friend out on a dangerous Resistance mission. Although the decision may have fatal consequences, it will in the long run be a decision that will lead to freedom.

The Mandarins, Beauvoir's most successful novel and winner of the Prix Goncourt, is a fictional effort to work out the insights she gained in her study of women in *The Second Sex*. It is also an evocation of Parisian intellectual life in the postwar period of 1944–47. The novel traces the political activity of a group of Parisian left-wing intellectuals, the mandarins of the title, after the liberation of Paris in 1944, as they cope with the problems presented by the realities of Stalin's regime, the cold war, and the punishment of the wartime collaborators. The novel conveys their preoccupation with moral and political issues and their foredoomed attempt to remain both morally pure and effectual.

It shows how one's compromises affect the very things one is attempting to change.

The political and intellectual component of the novel, true to the reality it portrays, centers around and is told from the viewpoint of a man, Henri Perron. Henri, who is in his late thirties, is a journalist and editor of the independent newspaper L'Espoir, which he established during the war with a friend in the Resistance. His close friend is Robert Dubreuilh, a sixty-year-old writer and political organizer. Dubreuilh always believed in socialism, and the Liberation offers him the possibility of building an independent socialist movement, which he names the S.R.L. Since he is convinced that his new movement needs its own newspaper, he tries to persuade Henri to join the S.R.L. and to make L'Espoir the official organ of the movement. Henri has taken advantage of the Liberation to leave Paris to travel to Spain and Portugal. On his return, he writes a series of articles for L'Espoir that describe the poverty and repression underlying the United States–supported fascist dictatorships of Franco and Salazar. When the article appears, a United States agent comes to his office and offers financial help to the paper if Henri will avoid publishing articles inimical to U.S. interests. At the same time, the paper is attacked by the French right wing, which accuses it of being a Communist party organ. Henri now finds that his idealistic dream of an independent newspaper without the backing of any party is impossible, and agrees to join the S.R.L.

The central plot of the novel, according to Beauvoir, is the breaking of the friendship between Robert and Henri over disagreements about the newspaper, and the subsequent mending of that friendship.[50] Problems first arise when the newspaper faces financial difficulties and Robert is willing to accept funds from questionable sources. Matters become even more serious when news reaches them about the Soviet slave labor camps and Robert wants to suppress the news; he feels that such information would threaten the French Communists, who represent the only hope of the proletariat, in the next election. Henri, however, does publish an article on the camps, while pointing out at the same time that the ills of communism do not in any way mitigate or justify those of capitalism. The next day, Henri receives a letter from Robert expelling him from the S.R.L. and severing its relationship with his newspaper. Their disagreement ends a fifteen-year friendship.

Both men discover simultaneously that there seems to be no role for the independent, left-wing intellectual to play, as positions polarize around their disagreement—the right wants to turn L'Espoir into an anticommunist journal, while the left wants the S.R.L. to affiliate with the Communist party. Theirs is the tragedy of the intellectual who strives to found a new world in which, by the nature of things, he can have no place. In the meantime, Henri has been drawn into a moral controversy. His current lover, Josette, collaborated with the Germans, as did her mother. A man who is to be tried for collaboration will give Henri the documents that incriminate the two women if he, in turn, will testify that the man was a double agent. Although Henri until now has represented the uncompromising moral point of view, he does provide testimony to protect Josette, which contradicts even that of two survivors of the Dachau concentration camp. Henri's failure is the result of sexism. He never would have spent time with a male collaborator, but he simply does not have the same moral standards for a woman. Besides, although he has been her lover for several months, he has never taken Josette seriously enough to be outraged by her past. Henri's action does produce one positive result, however. It leads him to resign from the newspaper—since he now questions whether there is such a thing as morality—and to a reconciliation with Robert and a new collaboration on an independent political magazine. Their break had been caused by a differing response to the problem of whether the truth should be revealed if it might damage a cause judged worthy of sacrifice. Now, while they realize that there is no clearcut solution to this problem, they will still continue to work for truth as best they can.

The Mandarins is not only an account of the problems faced by the French Left after the Liberation, it is also a working out of theses presented in *The Second Sex,* as illustrated by the lives of three women: Anne Dubreuilh, Robert's wife; Nadine, their daughter; and Paule, Henri's lover. While Anne, a psychiatrist, is the strongest of all of Beauvoir's female characters, she is still a dependent woman in that she lives for others and has modest ambitions. When asked whether she had put much of herself into Anne, Beauvoir replied that there is an enormous difference between them:

I lent her tastes, feelings, reactions and memories that were mine; often I speak through her mouth. Yet she has neither my appetites, nor my insistences, nor, above all, has she the autonomy that has been bestowed on me by a profession which means so much to me. Her relations with a man almost twenty years older than herself are almost like those of a daughter and, despite the couple's deep understanding, leave her solitary; she has only tentatively committed herself to her profession. Because she does not have aims and projects of her own, she lives the "relative" life of a "secondary" being. It was mainly the negative aspects of my experience that I expressed through her: the fear of dying and the panic of nothingness, the vanity of earthly diversions, the shame of forgetting, the scandal of living. The joy of existence, the gaiety of activity, the pleasure of writing; all those I bestowed on Henri. He resembles me at least as much as Anne does, perhaps more.[51]

While Anne lives in an intellectual and political milieu, and while she is party to the discussions between Robert and Henri, she is only a witness and does not participate. It is only through her interior monologues, and not through her actions, that her political understanding is presented. In everything, her husband is her referent. Anne's life is so fused with her husband's that even her career is played out against his ideas and goals. It is her interpersonal relationships, not her work or ideological/political commitments, that sustain her. This, as Beauvoir indicated in *The Second Sex,* is as typical of female behavior as is Anne's self-deprecation.

Anne goes to the United States to attend a psychiatric convention. In Chicago, she meets and falls in love with Lewis Brogan, modeled on the writer Nelson Algren, with whom Beauvoir had an affair and to whom the novel is dedicated. Anne's passionate affair with Lewis changes her image of herself from that of an old, sexually defunct and, therefore, worthless female, into a desirable human being.[52] Nevertheless, in her relationship with Lewis, Anne continues to function as a relative being, subordinating her needs to his moods. He dictates the terms of the couple and makes all the decisions. Their affair comes to an end because he will not permit her to do the same, he will not accept her on her terms. It is then that Anne realizes that by existing always as a function of others, she has disappeared as a subject, a realization that provokes suicidal depression. But, just as she is about to commit suicide, she hears the voices of her daughter and grandchild and decides to live. Ironically, this decision is Anne's first act as a subject. The novel ends as she reflects, "Either one founders in apathy, or the earth becomes repeopled. I didn't founder. Since my heart continues to beat, it will have to beat for something, for someone. Since I'm not deaf, I'll once more hear people calling to me. Who knows? Perhaps one day I'll be happy again. Who knows?[53]

Anne assumes responsibility for her own life at the end of the novel, but Paule, Henri's mistress, cannot even conceive of doing so, for she is the woman in love, *l'amoureuse* of *The Second Sex*, who lives only through a man. When *The Mandarins* opens, Paule has been living with Henri for ten years. While she has defied convention by choosing love outside of marriage, she is still caught in the traditional trap of devoting her entire life to love. She sacrificed her singing career to their relationship without realizing that she was using it as a pretext to avoid professional competition. Now Paule is in a completely dependent position financially, without means of survival should Henri abandon her. By making her life solely a function of Henri's love for her, Paule has refused freedom and rejected responsibility, and, in doing so, has also impinged on Henri's freedom. Finally, by fabricating an imaginary world in which Henri still loves her, Paule deviates from reality and has a nervous breakdown.

Nadine, Anne and Robert's daughter, exemplifies another type of woman described in *The Second Sex*. She is torn by the conflict between her unconventionality and rebellious spirit and her femininity, which she seeks to prove in unsatisfactory and often painful ways. Her awareness of the limits placed on women leads her to take refuge in these limits rather than seek transcendence through achievement. Nadine illustrates Beauvoir's contention that anyone who has the necessary lucidity and ability to escape societal limitations consumes his or her freedom in denying them. For Nadine, as for all the women in Beauvoir's work, it is men who constitute the meaning and establish the values of this world, and it is to this male world that they feel they must relate. They stand by and stagnate, while the men, the "mandarins," create.

Les Belles Images deals with the victimization of all people, but particularly of women, by the mass-media-dominated, capitalist society of the sixties. The effect of consumerism and its ability to limit women solely to the role of purchaser, which we find here, is an important theme in the works of many feminist writers, particularly Elsa Triolet and Christiane Rochefort.[54] Another problem considered in the novel, one that is central to feminist thought, is the role played by mothers in transmitting patriarchal values and preparing their sons for transcendence and domination, their daughters for immanence and subjection. The role of the mother, which was also considered in *The Mandarins,* will be worked out in the novels of Hélène Cixous.

Beauvoir wrote that she chose as a witness of this sixties society a young woman who was so much a part of it that she was unable to judge it objectively, but who felt, nonetheless, that something was amiss.[55] The witness is Laurence, an advertising executive. It is she, among others, who creates the "beautiful pictures" of the advertising industry that transmit bourgeois ideology and values. But Laurence begins to feel a vague discontent as she becomes increasingly aware of the discrepancy between these images and reality. Her malaise finally deepens into existential anguish, precipitated in part by her daughter Catherine's questions about the world and the horrible images of it that Laurence has not been able to screen entirely from the girl's awareness. As she awakens to reality, Laurence finds that she has abdicated responsibility for her life. Even worse is her discovery that the husband and father to whom she assigned this responsibility are lacking in moral values. When her husband faults her for wrecking their car by swerving to avoid hitting a cyclist, she is appalled by the idea that he is the man she had chosen as her moral guide. The analogy Lawrence perceives increasingly between the superficiality of her milieu and the beautiful, false images she creates in her work makes her despair. To combat her feelings of hopelessness she would have to act, but nothing in her life has prepared her to do so, and so her revolt takes one of the accepted, traditionally favored routes open to women—a nervous breakdown. While she is unable to transcend the constraints of her situation, which is a result of both her class and her sex, she determines, as she slowly recovers, that she will attempt to save her daughter. She will not permit her to be conditioned, as she was, to see only the pretty pictures; she will assume responsibility for giving her daughter an authentic way of living. "Bringing up a child does not mean turning it into a pretty picture,"[56] she tells her husband.

In the three stories of *The Woman Destroyed* Simone de Beauvoir portrays crucial moments—old age, solitude, and the brutal end of love—in three women's lives. The stories are linked by the themes of failure and of time, the greatest enemy of women, who must remain young and sexually attractive in a male-dominated society. The woman in "The Age of Discretion" refuses to grow old, while Murielle in "Monologue" has frozen time into a perpetual present of hatred and anger. Finally, Monique, "the woman destroyed," cannot admit that people and feelings change with time. All three women, according to Beauvoir, experience the difficulty, even the impossibility of human communication.[57]

The female protagonist in "The Age of Discretion," like Anne in *The Mandarins,* appears to have made a success of her life. She is a sixty-year-old professor who has had a career in teaching and has published two highly acclaimed critical works. Her husband, André, is a well-known scientist and her son, Philippe, is working on his doctorate. Her life is a model of professional, affective, and familial success. But Philippe's decision to abandon his teaching position and to use his father-in-law's influence to enter the Ministry of Culture has shaken the couple, whose relationship has already been strained by André's old-age crisis. It is summer, and he has left to spend his vacation in his native Provence. She has broken with her son and closes herself up in her apartment where she rereads all her critical works, only to discover that her last work is a rehash of what she has already said. When she decided to write the study, which she now perceives to be "useless," she did so in the hope of starting afresh, something a man can always do with a younger woman.

One of the strains that had recently been placed on their marriage had been André's acceptance of the limitations of old age. She originally had been unable to see what one lost in growing old. "Well, I could see now, all right," she remarks. "I had always refused to consider life as . . . [a] process of dilapidation. I had thought my relations with André would never deteriorate, that my body of work would grow continually richer, that Philippe would become every day more and more like the man I had wanted to make of him. As for my body, I never worried about it. And I believed that even silence bore its fruit. What an illusion!"[58] At the end of the story, however, the woman is obliged to accept her situation:

We had always looked far ahead. Should we now have to learn to live a short-term life? . . . [and] not look too far ahead. Ahead there were the horrors of death and farewells: it was false teeth, sciatica, infirmity, intellectual barrenness, loneliness in a strange world that we would no longer understand and that would carry on without us. Shall I succeed in not lifting my gaze to those horizons? Or shall I learn to behold them without horror? We are together: that is our good fortune. We shall help one another to live through this last adventure from which we shall not come back. Will that make it bearable for us? I do not know. Let us hope so. We have no choice in the matter.[59]

In the second story, "Monologue," a woman vents her hatred and misery in a tormented monologue in which she attempts to exculpate herself for her daughter's suicide, for which she knows herself responsible. Her rage and refusal of responsibility, her bad faith and evasions stem from a desire not to be alone, not to be the only one blamed. Condemned and shunned by all, she seeks to convince her invisible auditors to reflect back the image of innocence that will assuage her guilt by absolving her of responsibility.

"The Woman Destroyed," the title story of the collection, is an illustration of the plight of the married woman, of which Beauvoir spoke in *The Second Sex,* and a summing up of the condition of all Beauvoir's female characters, crippled and then destroyed by a patriarchal society. Like the other women in Beauvoir's work, Monique's total conditioning by male-dominated institutions has blinded her to the truth of her very unequal and inferior place in society. Beauvoir does not gloss over Monique's complicity in the making and development of her situation, even as she details her agonies at the loss of her husband to another woman.

The pages of Monique's diary, which make up the novella, reveal the social forces that induce an intelligent, educated woman to choose to give up everything, including her self, for marriage and a family. The consequences of this abdication gradually become clear to Monique. First, she denies the reality of the situation; then, she justifies her abdication of responsibility for her own destiny, to exist as a relative being in the role of ideal wife and perfect mother; and, finally, she retreats into a breakdown when all her justifications are stripped away and she realizes that she is the victim of an education that promised her a life of fulfillment and transcendence through living and doing for others. Now, those for whom she has lived no longer need her—her daughters are grown and her husband has another woman. She has nothing left since she has lost her dual role of beloved wife and indispensable mother, and she must face the fact that, outside of these roles, she does not exist. In reality, it is due to her "sacrifice," which has made her dependent on her husband and children, that she becomes a burden to them. As she never tried to develop her personality, she has nothing to offer them and no resources with which to struggle against her difficulties. Monique sacrificed her own career to live according to society's imperative that the female's place is in the home, entirely dependent on the male for sustenance, protection, and thought. Yet, at the end of the story, the "woman destroyed" is perhaps a woman on the verge of being created. "The door to the future will open. Slowly. Unrelentingly. I am on the threshold. There is only this door and what is watching behind it. I am afraid. And I cannot call to anyone for help."[60] Monique stands alone before an unknown future, but she will finally attempt to create her own essence. She may be afraid, but she asserts her existence and her readiness to assume her situation.

Beauvoir leaves those of her fictional heroines who are not totally destroyed by society on the threshold of the future, which later novelists, among them Rochefort, Wittig, and Cixous, will cross. But they are able to do so primarily because Beauvoir showed them the way, establishing the itinerary for their journey toward a future in which woman will be subject, not object, transcendent, not immanent.

Chapter Two

The Law of the Father: Marguerite Yourcenar

Considered one of the great writers of the twentieth century, Marguerite Yourcenar (1903–87) was the first woman named to the Académie Française in its four-century history. Her oeuvre, which remains within the great French classical tradition, differs from that of the majority of contemporary French women authors both in themes and language. Unlike her contemporaries, who insist that language is sexually biased because it is structured according to oppositions—male/female, mind/body, intellect/emotion—which are ordered by a patriarchal society and which work to the detriment of women, she has always maintained that language and logic are universally valid and are generally the same for both sexes.

The aristocratic values expressed in Yourcenar's work also place her within the French classical tradition, as does her passionate interest in history, particularly Roman history. Her novels, other than *Denier du rêve (A Coin in Nine Hands),* 1934, have no connection with contemporary reality because she believes that our preoccupation with the present obscures the eternal truths to which history provides the key. What she seeks instead is to rediscover and reaffirm traditional values. In keeping with the classical doctrine that maintains that art must be impersonal and that the peculiarities and excesses of the individual are not valid unless they touch universal experience, Yourcenar provides no autobiographical details in her novels. Neither she, nor her milieu, nor her background, nor her country, nor her time figure in them. As a result, while Yourcenar, like many contemporary French women authors, is a lesbian, she does not speak of it, nor does it constitute for her, as it does for them, a positive value, which affirms the rejection of a male-dominated society and provides a basis for the construction of a new, or even utopian society.[1] Later writers, Monique Wittig in particular, write about lesbian woman as subject in a world in which all women are subjects. But Yourcenar retains the traditional male/subject–female/

object dichotomy and always sacrifices the female and heterosexual love to male homosexuality.

Marguerite Yourcenar's background is as anachronistic as her values and ideals. While nothing of her own life is revealed in her oeuvre, her two-volume autobiographical work, *Le labyrinthe du monde* (The labyrinth of the world) does trace her maternal and paternal heritage, which are the key to her work. *Souvenirs pieux* (Holy memorial cards), the autobiography's first volume, published in 1974, evokes the history of her maternal lineage, while the second volume, *Archives du nord* (Northern archives) of 1977, tells about her father and his ancestors. The author's father, Michel de Crayencour, from whose name she devised the imperfect anagram Yourcenar, was of northern French ancestry. He led an adventurous life, which included an adolescent fugue to Antwerp and later enlistment in the French army, which he deserted twice (once to pursue a married woman). His unorthodox life was marked by the death of his first wife and her sister in the Crayencour apartment within hours of each other after "surgery" performed by a shady doctor. His second wife, Fernande de Cartier de Marchienne, Marguerite Yourcenar's mother, descended from a long line of wealthy Belgian landowners and industrialists. After their wedding in 1900, Yourcenar's parents traveled throughout Europe to various spas and casinos, and Marguerite was born in Brussels during one of their trips. She never knew her mother, who died of puerperal fever, and was raised by a series of women, many of them her father's mistresses. Yourcenar was educated largely by tutors under the direction of her father. Although he gambled away the family property and fortune, Yourcenar seems to have borne him no grudge. In fact, it was on her father that she modeled the only important heterosexual character in her fiction, Henri-Maximilien Ligre, the sixteenth-century Flemish freebooter in *L'Oeuvre au noir (The Abyss)*, 1968. But Henri-Maximilien dies halfway through the novel, leaving the field to Zeno, the prototype of Yourcenar's clever, homosexual men.

Marguerite continued to travel with her father to the fashionable European gambling centers until his death in 1929 and traveled alone thereafter. In 1939 she came to the United States on a lecture tour and remained when war broke out in Europe. In 1947 she became an American citizen, but her French citizenship was restored in 1981 to permit her to be elected to the Académie Française. In 1950 she moved to Mount Desert Island, Maine, with Grace Frick, her companion and translator. They lived there together until Frick's death in 1979, and Yourcenar then lived there alone until her own death in 1987. While

Yourcenar began her literary career by writing poetry, and while her oeuvre contains a body of nonfiction prose as well as several theatrical works, she excelled in her novels and short stories, particularly *Mémoires d'Hadrien (Memoirs of Hadrian),* 1951, her most celebrated work. Although her novels do not contain autobiographical details, they do constitute an intellectual and moral autobiography.

Yourcenar's first novel, *Alexis ou le traité du vain combat (Alexis),* 1929, whose subtitle translates, "the treatise of vain struggle," was written when the author was nineteen and published when she was twenty-six. It sets forth the story of a man's escape from his wife and child in search of the possibilities he imagines contained in a world of men. This novel, according to Yourcenar, "like every story written in the first person, is the portrait of a voice."[2] It is a confession in the form of a letter written by Alexis to his wife to explain why he is deserting her and their infant son for a life of homosexual freedom. He is not seeking to justify his actions, he maintains, but wishes only to be understood. Proceeding in chronological order, Alexis speaks of his life, starting with his fatherless childhood surrounded by protective, loving women. The child's veneration for women made him incapable of associating them with physical pleasure. In addition, his sensitivity and musical talent served to reinforce his homosexual tendencies. And then one day, he writes, he understood what differentiated him from other men: "on this particular morning, I encountered beauty."[3] Homosexuality is not mentioned by name—Alexis leaves it to his wife to understand what he means by beauty. While it was possible for Colette to speak openly about female homosexuality a generation before Yourcenar, because women and their affairs were not taken seriously, male homosexuality was a forbidden subject.

To flee from this new discovery about himself, Alexis leaves his family and settles in Vienna where he gives music lessons. Like Gide's "immoraliste,"[4] he becomes gravely ill, an illness that symbolizes society's view of homosexuality. When he throws off this repressive illness, he is able to come to terms with his body and its needs. Shortly thereafter he meets his future wife and believes that marriage will solve his sexual problems. But, like both Gide and Gide's hero, he succeeds only in having another share his torment. When he finally is able to fulfill his marital obligations and gives his wife a son, he feels free to leave her. He is no longer willing to fight against his nature; the only solution left to him is to go away. "Not having known how to live according to common morality, I endeavor, at least, to be in harmony with my own: it is precisely when one rejects all principles that one must arm oneself with scruples. I undertook imprudent obligations toward you to which life refused to subscribe. With the utmost humility, I ask you now to forgive me, not for leaving you but for having stayed so long."[5]

We see then in *Alexis* that from the very start of Yourcenar's career the sexual dynamics of her stories and novels, where the woman is sacrificed to homosexual love, are already in place. While in the first novel the wife's rival is man in general, the identity of the beloved is particularized in Yourcenar's second novel, *La nouvelle Eurydice* (The new Eurydice, 1931), as it is in all subsequent novels. In addition, *Alexis* lacks the sadistic component that appears in later works. Despite these differences, however, Alexis's homosexuality and aristocratic nature illustrate and confirm the author's consistently antiexistentialist attitude, which further sets her apart from the majority of contemporary women authors. Her homosexual protagonist prefers to be the victim of his nature rather than of his milieu or upbringing. He prefers to be fundamentally, not accidentally, homosexual, to be set apart from the herd by his race, his inner being, or his destiny.

The original version of *A Coin in Nine Hands* appeared in 1934. The author reworked it completely in 1958 and published a definitive edition in 1971. Although the second version was modified substantially, the characters as well as the primary and secondary themes remain unchanged in the final version. Yourcenar also published a theatrical adaptation of the novel entitled *Rendre à César*. The play is less successful than the novel, which was better able to express the thoughts of the characters by means of interior monologues rather than by the continual soliloquies and asides which impair the dramatic qualities of the play. In the 1971 preface to the novel, the author explains her predilection for this work, stating that it was one of the first French novels to portray honestly the ugly reality hidden behind the pretentious facade of fascism at a time when most writers visiting Italy were still enchanted with the picturesque customs of the Italians and the punctual departure of Italian trains. She adds that the realization that life is even more tragic and stranger than she suspected when she first wrote the book was perhaps her strongest reason for rewriting it.

The plot centers around the activities of a small group of Italians plotting to assassinate Mussolini in 1933, the eleventh year of the fascist dictatorship. It presents the members of a clandestine antifascist group and describes their revolt, which they know to be doomed, just as Marcella, who will become one of their martyrs, knows intuitively that her attempt to assassinate Mussolini will fail. Around Marcella and three other heroes of the principal episode, in this modern "tragedia dell'arte,"[6] are grouped characters who, consciously or unconsciously, are affected by the political climate of the time. The "denier" of the title is a coin, an ordinary ten-lira piece, which passes from hand to hand, and which symbolizes the superficial nature of all human contact and the fundamental isolation and solitude of all human beings.

Marcella, an ardent antifascist, is separated from her successful physician husband, Alessandro Sarte, because their ideal marriage struck her as a criminal attachment that sidetracked her from the antifascist conspiracy. She then took a lover, a writer, Carlo Stevo, who was arrested for antifascist activities. He had been denounced by a magnificent young Russian exile, Massimo Iacovleff, whom he loved with an unacknowledged homosexual passion. Massimo now lives with Marcella and has become her lover, but she knows that Carlo preferred Massimo to her. That, rather than her antifascist beliefs, precipitates her ultimate suicidal action; she dies as she attempts to prove her superiority. Here, as everywhere in Yourcenar's work, the woman is sacrificed to masculine love.

In a final conversation with her estranged husband, Marcella learns that she has been protected from the fascist police by his connections, that Stevo died in prison after divulging several names, and that Massimo is a double agent. She, in turn, reveals that she will try to kill Mussolini that evening. When Alessandro leaves her, he goes into a darkened movie theater where he initiates an anonymous exchange of masturbation with a woman. "Despising her, and at the same time grateful to be able to despise all women in her, he nevertheless respected the pleasure she had just dispensed."[7] Alessandro seems to sum up the bitterness of the closet homosexual, but it is not clear whether this is Yourcenar's intention or whether he is meant as a representation of what men turn into after the hopelessness of trying to live with women who, like Marcella, transmit nothing but death and the void.

Yourcenar writes in the preface to *Le coup de grâce (Coup de Grâce)*, 1939, that the novel relates a true story derived from the oral account of the principal character and that the three protagonists remain true to the real-life characters. What she wished particularly to present was a self-portrait of a certain type of modern international soldier of fortune. She adds that she also wished to portray, "through this episode of civil war, a group of young people surrounded by violence and danger and struggling with destitution and solitude, but involved even more in the ardors and upheavals of youth itself."[8] Like many of Yourcenar's other novels, it is written in the first person and narrated by the protagonist, a technique that obviates the need for third-person commentary. *Coup de Grâce* is constructed in the manner of the traditional French novel, and has many of the characteristics of classical French tragedy, in particular, unity of time, place, and action. The action, which is limited to three characters, leads inexorably to the tragic denouement.

Eric von Lhomond, wounded in the Spanish Civil War where he fought on Franco's side, tells his story as he awaits repatriation to Germany. The events he recounts take place in 1919 after the Russian Revolution and during the anti-Bolshevik fighting in the German Baltic states. After an absence of several years, Eric returns as a volunteer anti-Bolshevik fighter to the Castle of Kratrovitsy, the home of his boyhood friend Conrad de Reval and his sister Countess Sophie. Sophie falls in love with Eric, and is willing to sacrifice everything to win his love. Eric, who does not return her love, takes sadistic pleasure in encouraging and then rejecting Sophie's advances, setting up a relationship he describes prophetically as one between victim and executioner. Sophie finally discovers that Eric's coldness is caused by his homosexuality, and, in particular, by the love he has always felt for her brother Conrad. In desperation, she flees him and the class he represents to join the ranks of the Bolsheviks. In the course of a battle between Eric's troops and the Bolsheviks, in which Conrad is killed, Eric's troops manage to encircle the Bolsheviks. Among the prisoners, whom they will execute, Eric recognizes Sophie. She, who will be the last to die, insists that Eric himself be her executioner. Eric remarks that he thought at first that her request was motivated by a desire to give him "final proof of her love, the most conclusive proof of all. But . . . [I] understood only later that she did it to take revenge, leaving . . . [me] prey to remorse. She was right in that," he continues, "I do feel remorse at times." His final words sum up the misogynistic leitmotif of Yourcenar's works: "One is always trapped, somehow, in dealings with women."[9] His remarks reveal that he completely ignores the fact that Sophie has been his victim from the moment he returned to carry out the anti-Bolshevik struggle until the moment he shoots her, even bungling the execution so that her agony is prolonged, forcing him to finally administer the coup de grâce of the title.

Memoirs of Hadrian and Reflections on the Composition of Memoirs of Hadrian, considered Yourcenar's greatest work, was inspired by a sentence she read in a volume of Flaubert's correspondence: "Just when the

Gods had ceased to be, and the Christ had not yet come, there was a unique moment in history, between Cicero and Marcus Aurelius, when man stood alone."[10] A large part of her life, according to the author, was to be dedicated to an attempt to define and then to portray this man, both isolated and at the same time closely bound with all being. The novel consists of a 295-page letter from the emperor, who sees that his death is approaching, to his heir Marcus Aurelius. In it he sets down the important events of his life as well as his meditations on all aspects of human existence. "Like everyone else I have at my disposal only three means of evaluating human existence: the study of self, which is the most difficult and most dangerous method, but also the most fruitful; the observation of our fellowmen, who usually arrange to hide their secrets from us, or to make us believe that they have secrets; and books, with the particular errors of perspective to which they inevitably give rise."[11] He says he will use these three means to shape his narrative.

First, Hadrian tells about his childhood, his education, and his accession to power. The diversity of his aptitudes and skills brings him to the attention of his cousin, the emperor Trajan. At the same time, he becomes the protégé of Trajan's wife, the empress Plotine, an admirable, asexual woman, the antithesis of Hadrian's wife, who is sacrificed to his love for young boys. Hadrian shares with Yourcenar's other protagonists an overwhelming contempt for women. Women's love "seemed to me sometimes as light as one of their garlands; it was like a fashionable jewel, or a fragile and costly fillet, and I suspected them of putting on their passion with their necklaces and their rouge" (63). Conversely, "A man who reads, reflects, or plans belongs to his species rather than to his sex; in his best moments he rises even above the human. But my fair loves seemed to glory in thinking only as women: the mind, or perhaps the soul, that I searched for was never more than a perfume" (64). Hadrian's disgust stems from his conviction that woman's love is artificial, built on a specious difference. Without women, the world becomes infinitely more comprehensible. Monique Wittig, too, postulates a world freed of the other sex in *Les guérillères* (1969), but hers is a lesbian world without males.

Hadrian's sexual life centers around two beautiful young men: the Roman Lucius and the young Greek-Asiatic boy, Antinous. He tells of the idyllic years he spent with Antinous in the fourth part of the *Memoirs of Hadrian*, "Saeculum aureum," the Golden Age. This section of the work could be read as a separate novella of homosexual love.

Happy in his personal life, the emperor embarks on ambitious political and artistic projects, always accompanied by Antinous for whom he is both God and master. But, little by little, Hadrian seeks to defile in order to escape from this love, which is crushing him. Finally, Antinous commits suicide, sacrificing himself—in a ritual reenactment of the death of Osiris—in the hope of passing on his youth and strength to his master, while at the same time taking on to himself any disaster that might await Hadrian. Hadrian overcomes his despair and decides that, unlike Alexander the Great "who had celebrated the funeral of Hephaestion with devastation and mass slaughter of prisoners," he would "offer to the chosen one a city where his cult would be forever mingled with the coming and going on the public square, where his name would be repeated in the casual talk of evening, where youths would toss crowns to each other at the banqueting hour" (218). The cult of Antinous spreads rapidly over the eastern world and his image is preserved by numerous statues erected at Hadrian's bequest.

The fifth part of the book, "Disciplina Augusta," follows the terrible death of Antinous. Hadrian's thoughts now turn away from the pleasures of this world to thoughts of immortality. He builds libraries and universities, constructs his mausoleum and his villa. He does not renounce war, however, and brutally crushes a revolt in Judea led by Bar-Kochba, striking Judea from the map and renaming it Palestine. The last part, "Patientia," is a meditation on death, with the final words: "Let us try to enter into death with open eyes . . ." (297).

Memoirs of Hadrian has been classified as a historical novel, but it is basically a hybrid. On the one hand, relying on Yourcenar's extensive research about the second-century emperor, it relates what happened. On the other hand, it deals with the fictional and psychoanalytical elements, which are the realm of literature. Yourcenar, here, in the manner of the historical novelist, is both the historian who tells us what happened, and the novelist who tells us how it felt. Since the present in which the historical novelist writes, as well as the novelist's interests and preferences, are reflected in the selection of his or her subject, Yourcenar's predilection for secretive, bitter, clever homosexual men informed her choice of Hadrian, as it did that of her other heroes, including the protagonist Zénon of the historical novel *The Abyss*. Completely dissimilar in every way, Hadrian and Zénon share only their profound contempt for women.

The Abyss was a reworking of one of the stories in the author's early collection of 1934, *La mort conduit l'attelage* (Death drives the team of horses). The three stories in this collection were inspired by the work of three artists: Dürer, El Greco, and Rembrandt. *The Abyss* was based on the story written "D'après Dürer" (In the manner of Dürer). The French title, *L'Oeuvre au noir,* refers to that moment in alchemy when the baser substance dissolves and separates into nothingness before achieving its metamorphosis into a higher substance. It is thus a total loss of existence before transformation to a higher plane and can be compared to the Christian idea that one can never truly find oneself until one has lost oneself; then to rise like the phoenix from the ashes of one's former life. The role of alchemy in the novel adds to the local color and sets it firmly in sixteenth-century Flanders. It is also the prime motivation of Zénon whose quest for the philosopher's stone governs all his emotions and actions. In many respects, Zénon represents the anti-Hadrian. If the emperor embodies the moment in history in which truth seems established and irrefutable, the alchemist represents the opposite moment when there are no certainties and the whole world seems in fusion, gestation, and flux.

In *The Abyss* Yourcenar uses solid historical, biographical, and scientific material to provide the background for her fictional character. In a note appended to the text she writes that in order to give a fictional character "that specific reality conditioned by time and place, without which a historical novel is merely a more or less successful costume ball, the author can draw only upon facts and dates of man's past, that is to say, also upon history."[12] Yourcenar explains the way in which history informs her novel. Zénon, supposedly born in 1510, would have been nine years old when Leonardo da Vinci was dying in Amboise; thirty-one at the death of Paracelsus; thirty-three when Copernicus died; thirty-six when the printer Etienne Dolet was executed and forty-three when the Spanish theologian and physician Michael Servetus, who, like Zénon, sought to trace the circulation of the blood, was executed. She presents Zénon of Bruges as almost an exact contemporary of the anatomist Vasalius, the surgeon Ambroise Paré, the botanist Cesalpino, and the philosopher and mathematician Jérôme Cardan. Yourcenar remarks that the philosopher imagined in her story has much in common with those historical characters as well as with certain others who had lived in the same places as he, run similar risks, or pursued the same goals. She notes that the illegitimate birth of Zénon and his education for an ecclesiastical career recall some elements in the life of Erasmus, while certain violent aspects of his youthful character could remind us of Etienne Dolet. His periods of study, his travels also recall the lives of historical characters. In the domain of more private matters, she notes, the suspicion of sodomy (and sometimes the risky practice) played its part in the lives of Leonardo da Vinci, Dolet, Paracelsus, and Campanella. Also, the precautions taken by the alchemist-philosopher in seeking protectors, among both Protestants and Catholics, are typical of those of many atheists and deists of the period, who were often persecuted. She writes: "On a purely intellectual level, the Zénon of this novel, still marked by scholasticism, though reacting against it, stands halfway between the subversive dynamism of the alchemists and the mechanistic philosophy which is to prevail in the immediate future, between hermetic beliefs which postulate a God immanent in all things and an atheism barely avowed, between the somewhat visionary imagination of the student of cabalists and the materialistic empiricism of the physician."[13]

The action of the novel takes place between 1510 and 1569 in Catholic Europe, in large part in the city of Bruges. When the novel begins, Zénon is on the road from that city to Santiago de Compostela to see the world and acquire self-knowledge. He is accompanied by his cousin Henri-Maximilien Ligre, who is in search of military honor and glory. Henri carries with him a manuscript sheaf of sonnets "from which he had hoped for a little glory, or at least for some success among the ladies," and which ends "in the bottom of a ditch, buried with him under a few shovelfuls of earth."[14] In a series of flashbacks, we learn that Zénon is the son of Hilzonde Ligre, seduced and abandoned by a young Italian prelate, and reared in the home of his wealthy merchant uncle, Henry Justus Ligre of Brussels. Hilzonde marries Simon Adriansen, a rich merchant much older than she, with whom she finds peace and love until they are swept into the whirlwind of Anabaptism. They ultimately depart for the City of God founded by Jan Matthyjs and Hans Bockhold, the new king and messiah, where Hilzonde meets her death at the hands of the bishop's troops who invade the city.

Zénon, originally destined for the Church, abandons his studies to search for knowledge. Drawn to the subversive dynamism of medieval alchemy, he studies it first in Ghent and then in Spain. Then he goes to France to study medicine and anatomy in Montpelier. His travels take him through sixteenth-century Europe and the Levant torn by plague, war, and religious and social upheaval. Always suspect for his writings, his knowledge, and his barely hidden atheism, he is attacked by Catholics and Protestants alike. As with Jean-Jacques Rousseau two centuries later, his books are censured and burned both in France and in Switzerland. He returns finally to Bruges under an assumed name and carries on a charitable medical practice. Both as physician and as philosopher, Zénon seeks to understand the components of the body and the soul.

In Bruges, he is compromised by his association with an adamite sect[15] with unconventional erotic practices, but he is condemned in reality for his blasphemous thoughts and writings. Defending his own case, Zénon argues about physiology, astronomy, and physics, always rejecting unscientific theories and conclusions. He could save himself if he would agree to recant and disown his books and ideas, but he refuses, partly through weariness, partly to give reason a chance to triumph one day. To avoid being burned at the stake, and also to have control of his own death, he opens his veins.

Marguerite Yourcenar has always spoken against and refused to be included in the category of "women writers." Her central theme of male homosexuality, with its frequently sadistic treatment of women, has placed her squarely in the misogynistic tradition of "l'esprit gaulois." Accusations against her of misogyny and contempt for women have been countered by critics who cite various female characters with supporting roles in her work. Mention has also been made of women who are "essential to the action of the story and the psychology of the protagonists,"[16] including Marcella *(A Coin in Nine Hands)* and Sophie *(Coup de Grâce)*—both of whom, however, were motivated in their actions by unheroic, homosexual rejection. Arguments such as these are rejected by feminist critics. Marguerite Yourcenar is indeed a "woman" novelist, that is to say she is a woman who writes novels within the great French classical tradition. But her portrayal of women also reflects the negative vision of women conceived and fostered within that tradition.

Chapter Three

Toward a Female Subject: Elsa Triolet and Zoé Oldenbourg

Elsa Triolet and Zoé Oldenbourg were both born in Russia, where they spent their early years. Their works show the dislocation of living in a foreign place and express the loneliness of the exile, one that echoes the essential loneliness of woman, the eternal exile. In their novels we find the woman alone whose consciousness has been shaped by masculine structures, witness not only of her own evolving concept of self but also of woman's situation in general.

Elsa Triolet

Elsa Triolet (1896–1970), born seven years before Marguerite Your-cenar, is her antithesis in almost every way, both in her life and in her work. While Yourcenar shuns autobiographical elements in her novels, Triolet is present in all her works. Every novel, according to Triolet, is autobiographical in one way or another, whether the novelist transposes his or her life so that it passes for fiction, or whether he or she attempts to make fiction pass for autobiography.[1] Triolet stated elsewhere that "life for the novelist is her life plus that of others, plus dreams, plus everything that exists and everything that doesn't: everything that, in the final analysis, becomes a novel."[2] While none of the lives of the women in her novels is traced in its entirety, by juxtaposing them one can produce a complete biography, which stretches almost from birth— that is, from the moment of self-awareness—to the moment of awareness of approaching death, a biography that is traced with lucidity and enriched with the experiences of a lifetime. In the aggregate, Triolet's works constitute a modern female bildungsroman. From these tightly linked novels, a female witness emerges, one who reflects Triolet's evolving self-awareness. Although she did not belong to the women's movement, which came after her, she issues an appeal on behalf of women by showing how the destinies of her female protagonists hinge on the vagaries of their personal lives, politics, and sexual discrimination.

In most cases, despite their courage and determination to struggle against adversity, they succumb, victims of life in general and society in particular.

Witness not only to her own evolving concept of self and of woman's situation, Triolet was also witness to the principal events of her lifetime. Her work is a text on contemporary history from pre–World War I Moscow to revolutionary Russia; from post–World War I Berlin and Paris to the period of Allied appeasement of Germany and the Munich agreement of 1938; from the German invasion of France in 1940 to the Resistance; from the Liberation to post-Liberation disillusionment; from the cold war to the search for international understanding. The social and political events reflected in her novels, whether the threat of the atomic bomb or the abuses of a consumer society, are all presented from the viewpoint of the quadruple exile—from country, language, sex, and religion—an exile infinitely more acute than that of Hélène Cixous, also a woman and a Jew, also exiled from her native Algeria, but who never experienced the supreme alienation, from her native tongue.

Elsa Triolet's first novels, which were written in Russian, provide the keys to her early life. *Fraises-des-bois* (Wild strawberries, 1926) tells of her childhood and youth in Moscow, where she was born in 1896. Her father, Youri Kagan, was a lawyer who specialized in artists' and writers' contracts; her mother, Hélène Kagan, was a pianist and composer. In her novels, Elsa often appears in the guise of a singer or an actress. There, too, she also often expresses her jealousy of her beautiful older sister, Lili Brik, lover of the Russian poet Mayakovsky. It was Mayakovsky who introduced Elsa to Louis Aragon in 1928, a meeting that was to alter the course of both of their lives. In 1918 Elsa married the Frenchman André Triolet, with whom she went to Tahiti. *A Tahiti* of 1925, a novel also in Russian, describes their life there. In 1920 she returned to Paris alone and traveled to Berlin and the Soviet Union. The years from 1924 to 1928, which she spent in Paris, are described in her last Russian-language novel, *Camouflage* (1928), which provides a key to the dominant theme of solitude in her work; the solitude, not only of the exile looked upon with suspicion by the chauvinistic French, but also that of the woman alone.[3] It is by means of her heroines that Triolet expresses her own situation, thoughts, and emotions.

The years of loneliness in Paris ended when she met Aragon in 1928. From that moment until her death, excluding a short period during the so-called phoney war before France's surrender to Germany, they were never apart; she was never again alone. Yet, despite this, she never succeeded in ridding herself of feelings of solitude, for she could never escape the definitive solitude of the one who knows that even in a happy love there is always something in the other that escapes us. It was due to Aragon's influence that she began to write in French, and it is in her first work in French, a collection of short stories entitled *Bonsoir Thérèse* (1938), a series of variations on the theme of solitude, that the woman alone makes her first appearance in French literature. Jean-Paul Sartre wrote that he discovered in *Bonsoir Thérèse* the heretofore unknown world of those solitary women who never seem to be waiting for anyone but who sit on café terraces with their eyes fixed straight ahead.[4] "When you are completely alone," Triolet writes, "you can look at things endlessly, as you would look at fire, at the sea, and at very little children. . . . You see people, streets, and objects. Nothing prevents you from seeing them when you are alone."[5] Although many books had dealt with the lives of women without men, this was the first to speak of a woman completely alone. While Colette's Renée Néré *(The Vagabond)* lives alone, she lives in her own country, among her own friends and associates, and has chosen a profession that satisfies her. She is able to find human warmth and companionship with Max and, if she finally rejects him, it is her choice. But Thérèse is not looking for a man, she is not even looking for a friend, but only for another Thérèse, a mirror image of herself. The subject of the novel, writes Sartre, adapting an expression of Heidegger, is "the being-in-the-world" of the woman alone.[6]

Bonsoir Thérèse is a nontraditional novel that challenges the structure of the traditional novel; the stories it contains are like chapters in a novel, tied together not by a single plot or character but by the theme of chance in a woman's life. The title story shows Elsa, the foreigner, living alone in Paris. To beguile her solitude, she listens to the radio. One evening, she hears a man's voice say, "Good evening, Thérèse," a sentence that is not part of the program but is spoken in an intimate tone of voice to a real woman. Completely confused, she sets out to find this Thérèse and thinks she sees her everywhere, including her own apartment. When she describes Thérèse, she paints her own self-portrait: short, a bit stout, with light hair, pointed teeth, and a beauty mark. Thérèse turns out to be Elsa, who has been searching for her own identity.

"La femme au diamant" (The woman with the diamond) is the most important story of the collection. Thérèse, who is now called Anne, meets Jean on a beach. It is a case of love at first sight. She lives with him without knowing the source of his great wealth. Only later does she learn that he is an arms dealer. In despair at having been so deceived, she shoots him and tries, but fails, to kill herself. After Jean's death, Anne wanders around Paris, an anonymous mad woman in cotton stockings and a luxurious sable coat—the one remnant of her life with Jean—until she finally dies from starvation. Her fate is illustrative of the danger of permitting one's life to depend entirely upon a man and to derive its meaning only from him, a danger Elsa feared for herself and which inspired her to write in order to justify her existence.

Le cheval blanc (The White Horse), 1943, is Triolet's first full-length novel in French. She wrote that it is the most autobiographical of her novels in that it is closest to the way in which she saw and experienced life. She put herself entirely into this novel, she explained, and Michel Vigaud, the protagonist, is she. "I led a life like his . . . I felt the same solitude . . . [and experienced] his foolish purity." With Michel, she continues, "I created a 'child-man' as they say a 'child-woman,' unaware of the destructive nature of his powers of seduction."[7] Versions of Michel reappear throughout Triolet's work. He is a modern picaresque hero, always seeking new and different adventures. But, unlike that of the picaro, his search is an effort to give a meaning to life, to find a reason for living and dying. Triolet explains, "Michel made a mess of his life because he was never given a chance to sacrifice it for something or for someone. Was it his fault if, in our twentieth century, no one needs sacrifice. He was born too late, when no one knows the meaning of sacrifice, heroism, honor, love."[8] Michel always thought that there must be something to justify living and dying but he was never able to discern what it was.[9] He finally finds it, as he dies in a beet field on 31 May 1940, while saving the life of another French soldier.

But if Elsa transposed herself into the character of Michel Vigaud, she also appears in the idealized portrait of Elisabeth Krüger, a woman of mystery, a life force who first appears in *The White Horse* and reappears in *Le rendez-vous des étrangers* (The foreigners' rendez-vous, 1956); and in one of the stories of *Le premier accroc coûte deux cents francs (A Fine of Two Hundred Francs)*, 1945. It is through Elisabeth, who is Swedish, that Elsa expresses the emotions of the exile: "There is no nationality that is innate in me. My misfortune is that I am a person without a country."[10] Michel's love for Elisabeth is the only passion that runs through the novel; it is the only lasting sentiment he ever feels, but it is she who dictates the terms of their relationship and who finally breaks with him because of his disinterest in political and economic affairs.

While the events covered in *The White Horse* end before the German victory, those described in the four stories in *A Fine of Two Hundred Francs* take place during World War II. These stories, for which Triolet was awarded the Prix Goncourt, present an extraordinary panorama of occupied France with its fears, corruptions, humiliations, and acts of sacrifice and heroism. "Les Amants d'Avignon" ("The Lovers of Avignon"), which is partly autobiographical, is one of the best accounts written of the Resistance. Here Triolet wanted to show how extraordinary circumstances can influence the course of a life as banal as that of Juliette Noël, a typist. When her brother is killed in Libya, Juliette joins the Resistance, and takes on dangerous and important missions on which the lives of others depend.

The second story, "La vie privée d'Alexis Slavsky" ("The Private Life of Alexis Slavsky"), centers around an artist, a self-absorbed antihero interested only in his art. He is the prototype of those who choose to remain spectators of the war taking place around them in order to protect their private lives. He finally does become involved through the influence of a journalist, Louise Delfort, who will die before a firing squad for her Resistance activities. Louise is the protagonist of the third story, "Cahiers enterrés sous un pêcher" ("Notebooks Buried beneath a Peach Tree"), which takes place chronologically before the preceding story in which she meets her death. Louise has been hiding from the Germans in a small village. Alone and without occupation, she thinks back over her life and writes her memoirs in a notebook which she eventually buries. Details of Elsa's own life are mixed here with fictional embellishments. The fourth story, "A Fine of Two Hundred Francs," serves as an epilogue to the others and recounts a true incident in which Triolet and Aragon took part, a parachute drop of guns into a small village in the south of France just before the Liberation.

Anne-Marie, published in 1952, combines two novels that initially appeared as *Personne ne m'aime* (No one loves me, 1945) and *Les fantômes armés* (Armed ghosts, 1946). The first volume is divided into two parts, each centered around a different woman. The protagonist of the first part, which takes place during the brief period of peace following the Munich agreement and which ends with the premonitory signs of war, is Jenny Borghese. Her story is told by Anne-Marie, her childhood friend. Even as a young child, Jenny had suffered from her family's lack of understanding and felt unloved, a feeling shared by all

Elsa's heroines, her alter egos. Both left their native village as young women, Jenny to study in Paris and Anne-Marie to become the wife of a doctor and mother of two children. When her husband became bored with France, he took his family to live in Tahiti, separating Anne-Marie from her friend. After several years, the couple decides to return to France, and Anne-Marie goes on ahead to find an apartment.

Jenny, who is now a famous actress, invites Anne-Marie to live with her in Paris until her family arrives. As they resume their former intimacy, Anne-Marie discovers that Jenny supports many left-wing causes, including that of the Spanish Republicans. Yet, her political commitment is not enough to sustain her, and, despite her success, beauty, and wealth, Jenny kills herself. In her suicide note, she explains that solitude and lack of comprehension were at the root of this desperate act. The fact that Jenny's state of mind reflected Elsa's at that time is revealed in the preface to *Anne-Marie* where Elsa writes, "No one loves anyone. Everybody sleeps with everybody, and even when it doesn't seem so, it *is* so."[11]

The second part of the novel centers around Anne-Marie. She has barely recovered from Jenny's suicide when she and her country are engulfed in World War II. Cut off from her family, she lives alone in Paris. Toward the end of 1941, she leaves Paris for Provence where she becomes active in the Resistance. Like Triolet's other heroines, Anne-Marie evolves and changes under the pressure of events—she becomes a capable, dynamic woman very different from the retiring person who previously followed in Jenny's wake. At the Liberation, she is acclaimed a heroine. Little by little, however, life resumes its normal course and the heroism and fraternity of the war years are forgotten. Anne-Marie sees with great sadness the beautiful entente among the French disappear as Communist is pitted against non-Communist.

The action of the second volume, *Les fantômes armés*, takes place between the summer of 1945 and the autumn of 1946 against the background of a postwar France in which collaborators are welcomed back and Communists persecuted. Not only internal conditions in France, but also events in Indochina and Algeria, as well as the Nuremberg trials, form the background of the novel. After an absence of five years, Anne-Marie returns to Tahiti where she finds her husband living with a mistress. Neither her daughter, who is about to be married, nor her son wish to return to France. Anne-Marie realizes that a mediocre husband and self-centered children can never constitute a raison d'être and she returns to France alone to work out her destiny. There she has a love affair with a former Resistance hero, a Communist, who is killed soon after by former comrades in the Resistance. Anne-Marie discovers with horror that his murder and several others were planned even before the end of the war by anti-Communist members of the Resistance who anticipated a struggle for power after the Liberation. She also sees that Liberation has not brought the happiness that was anticipated; that people now suffer from the boredom of their daily lives, from an inactivity that weighs heavily upon them.

The fear of the atomic bomb hangs over *Anne-Marie,* a fear that is realized in the nuclear holocaust that occurs in *Le cheval roux ou les intentions humaines* (The red horse or human intentions, 1953). Triolet wrote that she made Elsa Triolet the protagonist of the novel "because every news item carries greater weight when one knows the victim or victims, even if only by name. . . . *Le cheval roux* is a transposition into the great collectivity of my personal feelings on death and on old age, with which I am now begininng to become acquainted."[12] During this period Triolet was haunted by the thought of aging and loss of sexual attractiveness. Despite her significant achievements as political activist, member of the Resistance, and writer, she was still a victim of the age-old patriarchal imperative to please men. As early as 1941, Triolet had the heroine of the short story "Mille regrets" commit suicide because she fears the reaction of her returning lover to the changes in her brought about by age.

Le cheval roux is a precursor of the contemporary female utopian novel. Unlike previous utopias conceived of by men and for men, Triolet's text expresses a profoundly feminine social dream well before the raising of female consciousness and the creation of feminist literature. *Le cheval roux,* like all utopian texts, takes its point of departure from aspects of society the author considers unacceptable. The choices made here and the values Triolet emphasizes are, as in similar works, indicative of the author's thoughts and experiences. It is for this reason that the utopian text, which is always by nature intensely personal and auto-biographical, easily finds its place in Triolet's oeuvre.

The novel opens after the blast of the atomic bomb. Elsa Triolet, a writer who has been monstruously disfigured by the catastrophe, is one of the survivors. She is found by Henry, an American bomber pilot, who has also been transformed into a grotesque monster by napalm. They are the most hideously marked among the terrified, irradiated, contaminated survivors of the blast. The need for companionship, an insatiable need for communion, attaches her to her former enemy, who has become her companion in misfortune. Since utopian texts are usually tales of voyages, Elsa and Henry travel—they visit five different societies. Each of the trips has the same structure: Elsa arrives, accompanied by Henry in all but one of the journeys; the characters belonging to that society greet them and explain their situation; the travelers become part of that society until evil erupts; they flee to another society, where the process begins again. In the village of Saint-Normienne, the entire village is destroyed by hunger as the inhabitants turn to cannibalism; in Stockholm, the society is ruined by a vile dictator. In the luxury Hotel des Alpes in Switzerland, the servants revolt against the guests and refuse to serve them. The new arrivals join with the servants, leave the hotel, and form their own community, a new society in which one must work in order to eat and in which men and women share equal responsibilities. Yet, even this communist society succumbs, for it has not broken entirely with the past world order created exclusively by men. The radiation poisoning that ultimately destroys it is symbolic of the poison at the heart of all traditional institutions.

Only one group, a small splinter group that meets on the top of a mountain, manages to overcome death by completely restructuring political patterns, establishing a utopia in which solidarity is achieved through the creation of a collective literature. The message here is that humanity can save itself from destruction by articulating and preserving its dreams in writing. The group is led by Elsa, the narrator-author, whose efforts have led to the realization of this new order. It is not a matriarchy, however, that merely substitutes the domination of one sex for the other, but an ideal society in which the central female figure works with, not above, the others. The novel, while less cohesive than Triolet's other works, is significant because it presents a view of utopia in which men and woman are equal and because it postulates female self-realization through achievement rather than physical beauty.

Le rendez-vous des étrangers is built around the suffering of the foreigner in a strange land. This theme of the suffering of the stateless individual had already been treated in several of Triolet's works and here is expanded to include exiles of diverse origins, from Spanish Republicans, to Russians, to Algerians, to Americans fleeing McCarthyism in the United States. The work is more a fictionalized piece of journalism and a sociological study of foreigners in France than a novel. Each foreigner responds differently to the perpetual mistrust and suspicion he or she encounters. The protagonist, Olga Heller, knows almost all the other exiles in the novel. Like Triolet, she was born in Russia of Russian parents and came to Paris after her parents' death and the failure of a bad marriage. Even as a young child, she suffered from solitude and despair. She would have killed herself, but the war came and made her realize that there were things much more important than her personal problems. Although she played an important role in the Resistance, the French police have harassed her since the Liberation, as they once harassed the young Elsa, because she lives alone and is of foreign origin. Another foreigner in this novel is Elisabeth Krüger, who reappears in this novel as the wife of a wealthy Swedish industrialist and the adoptive mother of Agnès whom she had saved from the Nazi mass roundup of Jews in 1942. Agnès is one of several adopted children who appear in Triolet's novels, although the author, like Colette, Beauvoir, and Yourcenar, never has her female protagonists express a desire for children. Agnès, now a young woman, wants to go to Israel in search of her identity, and Elisabeth, with roots nowhere, permits her to leave because she feels that she does not have the right to prevent Agnès from finding a country for herself, even a mythical country. She does, however, insist that Olga accompany her, and the novel ends with their departure.

In the three novels of the cycle *L'Age de nylon*—*Roses à crédit* (Roses on credit, 1959), *Luna-Park* (1959), and *L'Ame* (The soul, 1963)—Elsa Triolet shifts from political to sociological preoccupations, showing the impact of modern scientific discoveries on contemporary civilization and presenting a critical examination of various aspects of twentieth-century consumer society and its effects on women. The protagonist of *Roses à crédit* is Martine Donelle who, after a poverty-stricken childhood, finds that she is able to satisfy all her material longings by buying on credit. She marries a young man, Daniel, whom she loved even as a child but whose upper middle-class background seemed to preclude their union. In a reversal of the traditional objectivization of the female, however, Daniel, the realization of Martine's childhood dreams, becomes for her nothing more than another cherished possession. When he tries to explain the value of money as well as the dangers of buying on credit, she, like the unfortunate Emma Bovary, is unable to resist the temptation to possess all that she lacked when she was young. Martine's insistence on living only for the pleasures of the moment and her inability to think of future consequences finally alienate her husband. When she can no longer meet her payments and her possessions are seized, she has a nervous breakdown. At the end of the novel, she returns to the miserable hut from which she fled originally, where she is devoured by rats. Her tragic life is used by Triolet to demonstrate the ravages of modern society and the snares of credit for those who are too weak to resist temptation.

In *Luna-Park,* Elsa Triolet creates a female Icarus, Blanche Hauteville. Blanche's country home has been acquired by a film director, Justin Merlin, who retreats there to rest after his last film. Among the belongings Blanche Hauteville left behind is a package of letters addressed to her by seven admirers. Merlin (misnamed here because Blanche is really the enchantress) reads the letters and falls in love with this mysterious woman who is loved and desired by so many men. What he really loves, however, is the person he discovers through the consciousnesses of a group of males; he loves not a woman but a composite masculine vision of a woman. As he continues to read, Justin finds that the letter writers merge, for all of them seem terrified of being controlled and emasculated by a strong, independent woman. Their protestations of love cannot hide their fear of a woman whose sexual attraction does not come from playing a stereotypical female role. In Blanche, the men love an equal and fear this emotion for which nothing in their experience has prepared them.

Blanche had always been passionately interested in aviation and wanted to become the first female astronaut. But, in a final letter, which Justin reads, she reveals that she now understands that it is more important to take care of the problems of our planet than to conquer space. The goal she has set for herself is to attain her own personal utopia, or Luna-Park, where she will be able to realize her aspirations. Triolet introduces in *Luna-Park* the theme of the quest, heretofore a masculine prerogative, a theme that will become important in later feminist literature. When Blanche disappears one day on a mission in search of new sources of oil, Justin Merlin, as the novel ends, decides to go to Africa in search of the missing aviatrice to second her in her quest.

Elsa Triolet was forced to interrupt the writing of the third volume of *L'Age de nylon, L'Ame,* when she suffered a heart attack. Because she was unable to do the research necessary for this novel during the period of her recuperation, she wrote *Les manigances* (Chance, 1962), a novel based on personal experiences. The author describes this novel as a continuation of *Bonsoir Thérèse* because she deals once again with the role played by chance in human destiny. The protagonist of *Les manigances,* the singer Clarice Duval, refuses, however, to bow to fate. Clarice represents a stage in the evolution of Triolet's heroines who, like the author herself, become stronger and more certain of themselves with each succeeding novel.

L'Ame, finally completed in 1963, one year after the end of the Algerian war, contains several references to the action of the OAS (the Secret Army Organization, which sought to keep Algeria French). Nevertheless, it is basically an apolitical novel. The female protagonist is Nathalie, a woman who has never recovered from the tortures she received in a German concentration camp. Now she has become too obese to move from her apartment, but she is surrounded by a loving husband, Luigi Petracci, and many devoted friends. Nathalie is the fulfillment of a woman's fantasy, despite her suffering and premature death; she is loved and sought after although she possesses neither youth nor physical beauty. Nathalie and Luigi's marriage is one of only two successful marriages in Triolet's novels—the other is that of Alexis and Henriette Slavsky in the story "Alexis Slavsky." The reason for the success of these marriages, according to the author, is that each of the partners has, in addition to his or her love and concern for the other, an absorbing interest or passion that is independent of the other. Nathalie is a skilled cartoonist and her husband is a genius at creating mechanical toys. Yet Triolet and Aragon's ideal couple was achieved precisely through the interdependence of their work, as illustrated in the thirty-six volumes of their "Oeuvres croisées" (Interrelated works). Triolet underlined the symbiotic nature of their work when she wrote in the preface to the first volume of the series: "When we finally lie dead side by side, the bond between our books will unite us for better or for worse in that future that was our dream and our principal concern, both yours and mine. . . . With the help of death . . . they will perhaps have tried to and succeeded in separating us. . . . Then our interrelated books will come hand and hand, black on white, to resist that which tears us apart."[13]

The failure of the couple is again made evident in *Le grand jamais* (Never, never!, 1965). Régis Lalande, a famous historian, has just killed himself to escape from an agonizing, incurable illness. During his lifetime, he kept his second wife, Madeleine, originally one of his students, in a dependent, childlike position; he never permitted her to grow and achieve a personal identity. But after his death she begins to develop as an individual. She becomes the defender and champion of her husband's ideas, as she seeks to correct the false interpretations of his critics. She rejects their male arrogance and certainty as they presume to impose their opinions. Thus, the conflict between Madeleine and the critics becomes part of the battle of the sexes, which Madeleine is doomed to lose since nothing in her past as a dependent woman dictates her responses. She is unable to replace the male structures and images she wishes to destroy with appropriate female alternatives.

Triolet devotes a second volume to Madeleine Lalande, *Ecoutez-voir* (Look-see, 1968), in which text and pictures are intertwined. Attacked by critics, evicted from her home by legal action, Madeleine gives up the struggle and becomes a tramp. Her action, on the one hand, is symbolic of a refusal of all types of hypocrisy and, on the other, is a real attempt at self-destruction. The forces that oppose her and prevent her from pursuing her chosen goal overcome her will to live in society. In addition, her decision to become a tramp is a complete rejection of the values of a male-created and male-dominated society.

To complete the chronicle of her life, Elsa Triolet wrote her final novel, *Le rossignol se tait à l'aube* (The nightingale stops singing at dawn, 1970), the confession of a woman on the threshold of death. Here Triolet assumes the persona of an actress. She is the only woman among ten men who have gathered in a house in the center of a vast park, perhaps because she is the only woman from their collective past whose achievements have earned her a place among them. They spend the evening after dinner drinking, smoking, and telling stories about their lives and about friends who have died. The song of a nightingale is heard occasionally. The woman, who is suffering from a heart condition, is obliged to take medicine from time to time. The pills induce a sort of trance during which strange images unfold in her mind. She dreams about her past, the men in her life, her failures, and her successes. The dreams, the nightmares, and the reveries induced by the pills are printed in red ink, the events that take place during the night in black ink. As night ends and dawn begins to break, the nightingale sings its last notes. The woman decides to take a walk in the park. But her heart gives out and she dies, her death anticipating by only a few months that of the author from a heart attack. *Le rossignol se tait à l'aube* thus completes the account of a female consciousness from its first awareness of self to the very moment of death; from the initial realization that a woman must create her own essence, to the completion of an oeuvre that justifies her existence.

Zoé Oldenbourg

Zoé Oldenbourg, (b. 1916), like Elsa Triolet, was born in Russia and wrote her first works in Russian. But whereas Triolet wrote her first novel in French at the age of thirty-two, Oldenbourg wrote almost exclusively in French from the age of fourteen on and felt thereafter as if she were translating from the French whenever she wrote in Russian. While she did not feel alienated from her native tongue as did Triolet, her works bear the mark of the doubly exiled, the alienation of the foreigner and of the female. Her experience as an émigrée is manifest both in her historical novels and in those with contemporary settings, which she, like Triolet, situated in France rather than in the country of her birth.

Two autobiographical works furnish the keys to the basic themes around which Oldenbourg's work is centered. In *Visages d'un autoportrait* (Facets of a self-portrait, 1977), Oldenbourg speaks of her childhood. The life she describes in this work is extraordinary. She was born in St. Petersburg in 1916, like Triolet into a family of intellectuals: her mother was a gifted mathematician; her father, a White Russian historian and journalist, was forced to flee his country in 1920; and her paternal grandfather, a loyal Communist, was Permanent Secretary of the prestigious Academy of Science. In 1930 he was obliged to sign a paper denouncing his son and promising to have no further dealings with him.

Zoé Oldenbourg's description of life in Soviet Russia is presented from the viewpoint of a child who was affected by the all-pervasive atmosphere of terror even though her family was able to escape deportation: "We understood very early in life that we were living in a world in which anyone could be shot or tortured. They didn't tell it to us, but children feel and guess things. Our first years were spent under the terror . . . the one about which the West speaks so little for it struck mainly the so-called 'bourgeoisie.' . . . It left me with a life long feeling of humiliation. . . . For the West, we were outcasts of history, members of a rotten society whose disappearance was most desirable."[14]

In 1925 the author, her sister, and her mother were reunited in Paris with an oppressive, domineering, unstable father. A stranger in a foreign land, the author found her life split between two countries, two languages, and two classes—a professional, respected family in Russia, and an impoverished, anonymous one in France—and two diametrically opposed, dramatically incompatible parents. Confronted on one hand by the hostility and distrust of the French, and on the other by the suspicion of the exiled White Russian community, the Oldenbourgs were strangers in every group and milieu. As a perpetual outsider, Oldenbourg felt great sympathy for all those outside the mainstream of society, for all the victims of history, particularly women, children, the poor, the disinherited, and the persecuted. She remarks that she may have become an author because she needed to create her own language to describe the magnificent and tragic incoherence of her life. In an attempt to establish some kind of order, she built her own universe, "and it is above all a universe of flight," in which, she continues, "women were stronger than men—which was less a manifestation of feminine megalomania than an objective observation: in my family and in the families of my friends the men were in fact weaker than the women."[15] According to Oldenbourg, she has always been a feminist, "spontaneously and without thinking about it, from the age when . . . [she] realized that . . . [she] was a girl (different from others who were boys). Now what human being is perverse enough not to think that he is *normal,* and thus in a certain sense superior, he and others who are like him?"[16] she concludes.

Oldenbourg's second autobiographical work, *Le procès du rêve* (Dreams on trial, 1982), continues the story of the exiled Oldenbourg family and tells of Serge Oldenbourg's influence on the future writer. While a common theme in feminist literature is the thwarting of the heroine's quest for self-realization by paternal expectations, Oldenbourg's account of her father's attempts to seize hold of and direct her inner life carries the excesses of patriarchal domination to an extreme. The morbid paternal abuses are reflected in two of her novels based on the Russian émigré experience in France—*Réveillés de la vie (The Awakened),* 1956, and *Les irréductibles (The Chains of Love),* 1958. In *Le procès du rêve* Oldenbourg describes how her father, impotent in his exile and aware that he could not dictate the conduct of his family or prepare their future, attempted instead to dominate them by taking control of their thoughts as they expressed them in their writing. Parental control became tyranny when Serge Oldenbourg, a gifted but unsuccessful writer, created a family literary review, which he read aloud, as he would read aloud everything they wrote. Through these readings, he controlled the family's dreams. While he had other outlets—he collaborated on a Russian émigré newspaper and published two books on Lenin and the Bolsheviks—the father, exasperated by his daughters' growing desire for independence and grief-stricken over his young son's death from meningitis, devised a new means to dominate his family through the collective writing of a novel on a subject imposed and strictly supervised by him. Zoé Oldenbourg wrote that she suffered, not as a novelist who loved her characters, but as a victim of an incubus who was seeking to rob her of her own life and to impose its own.[17] As the future novelist tried unsuccessfully to explain to her father, literature, far from profiting from excessive flights of imagination, must shun them, because the goal of literature is to make use of the imagination to explore reality rather than, as her father demanded, to attempt to exorcize reality by denying it.[18] To rebel against her father, Oldenbourg made sure that everything she wrote, even the stories situated in the most hypothetical Middle Ages, was unrelentingly realistic. Therefore, she had to learn a great deal about that period to enable her to give substance to a vision that, in and of itself, had to do less with that period than with her own experience of life.[19]

The author states that her novels are inspired by her own life and reflect her own experiences, but that she is unable to explain why she chose to center so much of her oeuvre on the Middle Ages. We may, however, explain her work in the domain of the historical novel as a reaction to the isolation and alienation of exile, an attempt to find in the past the sense of life and community that she had lost in the present. Her particular interest in the Middle Ages suggests a search for roots and for refuge from the uncertainties and anguish of modern life. Unlike Yourcenar, whose historical novels deal with exceptional men, set above ordinary humanity by reason of intelligence and position and who have no perceivable relationship to contemporary reality, Oldenbourg writes of the ordinary individual, female as well as male, whose suffering is universal, but who is at times set apart from the mass by isolated acts of heroism and sacrifice. The author even comments on the relationship between her novels and the modern world: "It is true that in my novels an important role is given to cruelty, to agony, in brief to the tragic side of life. I don't know whether the horrors of our world of concentration camps and, in general, the harshness of our times are partly responsible for that. I think they are."[20] Zoé Oldenbourg sees the past she re-creates in her novels as an episode in the continuous adventure of humanity. As part of her exploration of this continuous adventure, Oldenbourg also wrote nonfictional works of history, which cover the events and periods dealt with in her historical novels. A parallel reading of these works confirms that history tells us what happened, while fiction tells us how it felt; that historians find facts and shape theories while novelists find facts and make fiction.

Oldenbourg's first historical novel was published in 1946. Originally entitled *Argile*—later changed to *Argile et cendre* for copyright reasons— it was published in English in 1948 under the title *The World is Not*

Enough. This novel and its sequel, *La pierre angulaire (The Cornerstone),* 1953, tell the story of three generations of the family of Baron Ansiau de Linnières. The baron marries Aalais, sires her many children, leads the life of a feudal lord in Champagne, jousting and hunting, and leaves with two of his sons for the Third Crusade under the banner of his feudal lord. He fights under Richard I, the Lion-Heart, of England to deliver Jerusalem. When he returns home, he conceives a violent passion for his young goddaughter, Milessant, who dies after the birth of their illegitimate daughter, Eglantine. Scenes from the lives of the women alternate with scenes of battle and adventures. Unlike the women in other historical novels who merely await the return of the jousters and crusaders, Oldenbourg's women are well-defined, active individuals who attend to the feudal domain in the absence of the men. Certain of the events described in the novel are traced in *Les croisades (The Crusades),* 1965, a historical study of the first three crusades, which also gives the historical background of the kingdom of Jerusalem up to the time of its conquest by Saladin. *Saint-Bernard,* 1970, a study of the life of Saint Bernard, particularly his influence on his contemporaries and the role he played in the political and social life of the twelfth century, is another historical counterpart to these novels.

The sequel to *The World is Not Enough, The Cornerstone,* received the Prix Fémina. It tells of Ansiau's old age. Now a widower, he sees his influence diminish as the power of his son Herbert grows. When Herbert countermands his orders, Ansiau realizes that he is no longer master and leaves for the Holy Land to redeem his sins. Blind and guided by a child, he lives on charity. On his way to Palestine, he crosses the Languedoc, the land of the Albigensian heresy, which provides the historical background for the author's next two historical novels, *Les brûlés (Destiny of Fire),* 1960, and *Les cités charnelles ou l'histoire de Roger de Montbrun (Cities of the Flesh),* 1961. When Ansiau finally reaches his goal, he is imprisoned by the Arabs and dies in captivity. The scenes of Ansiau's spiritual quest and the great misery of the wandering pilgrims of the time are contrasted with the elegant, luxurious life of the nobility in Champagne.

In a note appended to the historical novel *Destiny of Fire* the author writes that the heroes of this novel are the Cathars, or Albigensians, a heretical sect that flourished in the Midi during the twelfth and thirteenth centuries. The Church preached a holy war against them and, after a long struggle, their religion was stamped out. This war is generally known as the Albigensian (or "fourth") Crusade. Oldenbourg published a parallel historical work, *Le bûcher de Montségur* (*Massacre at Montségur*), 1959, which recounts the thirty-five-year struggle carried on by the Albigensians to live and die in their faith. The final and most dramatic episode of this struggle took place 16 March 1244 when, after the siege of Montségur and the capitulation of the Cathars, two hundred of them were burned at the stake.

While Oldenbourg calls *Destiny of Fire* a work of imagination, since none of the characters portrayed in it—with the exception of Bernard de Simorre, the Catharist bishop of Carcassonne at the beginning of the thirteenth century—actually existed, she did attempt to convey therein the spirit of the Catharist religion. The novel describes the resistance of the Cathars to the persecution they endured during and after the Albigensian Crusade. "It does not treat this resistance as a whole, but concentrates on certain aspects of it: in particular it tells the stories of Ricord and Arsen, Aicart and Renaud, Gentian and Béranger, and of nameless combatants, members of a Church which today is nonexistent, yet which in their eyes was the only true one. They were a people who believed in it with their entire heart and soul, and [almost all of] their priests preferred martyrdom to abjuration."[21]

The protagonists of the novel, Ricord de Monteil and his wife, Arsen, a Cathar couple, renounce their marital life to seek salvation in a life of perfection. While Arsen goes through the countryside preaching the Cathar doctrine, Ricord, enraged at the persecution of his people, takes up arms against the invaders, massacres monks and crusaders, and finally is captured and tortured to death by the crusaders. His four sons also resist; two are killed and two are reduced to the status of mercenaries. His daughter and son-in-law are also martyred by the Inquisition and his wife, after a long and saintly life, is ultimately burned alive. The novel, then, is a "martyrology." "For the would-be faggot-martyr," Oldenbourg observes, "the route is mapped out in advance; he has no choice for he can recognize only one definition of Good and Evil. . . . [The Cathars] were not the champions of a lost cause; they were not fighting for a 'cause' at all, but for something which, as they saw it, could never be defeated. . . . They were the victorious ones."[22]

The story of the others, those who were defeated because they "asked nothing except the chance to live,"[23] is told in *Cities of the Flesh*. In this novel the author returns to twelfth-century France at the time of the Albigensian Crusade to tell the story from the point of view of the crusaders. Roger de Montbrun, a knight caught in the unending conflict of the time, is a soldier and courtier who fights because he can do nothing else. Unlike the Albigensians, Roger is not interested in religious questions: he is a Catholic who is satisfied to respect without question the opinion of others. But he falls in love with a Cathar woman, and finds himself caught up in the toils of the Dominican inquisition. God's minions hunt down heresy, burn suspects at the stake after interminable trials, raze their houses, confiscate their lands, and throw freshly exhumed bodies of Cathars on burning pyres. The terror provoked by atrocious denunciations crushes the entire region of Toulouse. The most extraordinary part of the novel tells of Roger's experiences in the jails of the Inquisition, where we see the slow disintegration of a person through tortures that remind us of the German concentration camps, the Russian gulags, and the prisons in so many South and Central American countries.

Zoé Oldenbourg returns to the First Crusade in the novel *La joie des pauvres (The Heirs of the Kingdom),* 1970, but she does not trace the adventures of the knights and nobles, the companions of Godefroi de Bouillon who figure in the usual narratives. We see them only from afar, as ordinary people might see them, and do not enter into their lives. Instead, the author tells what it was like to be part of the great mass of the poor who joined the long and arduous trek to Jerusalem, the hordes of disinherited who marched toward the Promised Land with pure hearts and empty stomachs—their adventure motivated as much by hunger as by faith—with nothing to lose but their illusions and their lives. The epigraph appended to the novel from James 2:5 explains both the French and English titles: "Hath not God chosen the poor of this world rich in faith, and heirs of the kingdom which he hath promised to them that love him."

The novel opens in northern France, in the region of Arras, the northernmost point of departure for pilgrims of the First Crusade. The author details the economic pressures motivating the departure for the Holy Land of the weavers and other artisans who were constantly threatened by unemployment and famine and for whom the Crusade represented a provisional solution to their economic difficulties. They were also motivated by religious zeal, stimulated by masterful preaching, which appealed both to the imagination—with visions of the Holy City of Jerusalem—and to the heart—with reminders of the love of Jesus Christ. *The Heirs of the Kingdom* is the story of humble people who followed the army in the naive faith that Jerusalem would fulfill their dream of justice and love.

Oldenbourg tells the story of the three years of suffering that ended with the taking of Jerusalem 14 July 1099. A few characters stand out from the mass. The central characters in the original group from Arras are the young couple, Jacques and Marie, who are scarcely more than children, the village priest who brings along his concubine, and Alix of the Thirty Crowns, a young, beautiful prostitute so nicknamed for her largess. Little by little, along the route, they are joined by others, among them a madman who believes himself to be Saint John, the Greek eunuch Philothée, the young Greek slave, Euphémie. They experience cold, hunger, fatigue, love, adultery, jealousy, crime, and murder. The matter of their daily lives is more important in the novel than the battles, exploits, and massacres emphasized in traditional accounts. While the principal events of the crusade are not forgotten— among them the view of the magnificent city of Constantinople, the taking of Nicée, the first battle against the Turks, the siege of Antioch, the discovery of the Holy Sceptre, and the capture of Jerusalem—they are seen only through the eyes of the humble pilgrims. The last pages are devoted to Marie, underlining once again the importance of the role played by this simple, devout young woman, now a slave of the Arabs, and separated from her husband and son who are in Jerusalem. She cries out for the family and the city she has lost, the Holy City "Too dearly loved, too long desired / So well avenged, so well deserved / Washed in blood, in blood reborn / *Regained but lost again too soon!*"; and the author concludes, "Sing, Marie of Arras. Do not forget, Marie of Arras."[24]

That the writer's experiences dictate the choice of subjects is nowhere more apparent than in Oldenbourg's historical study *Catherine de Russie (Catherine the Great)*, 1966. She states in the preface that her object is not to recount the long and brilliant reign of Catherine II in its entirety, with its wars and social unrest, political and economic problems, and its cultural strides. Rather, she seeks to reveal the woman, not the empress, and more particularly the slow shaping and maturing of the future empress. She adds that Catherine provides virtually the only example of a woman who attained supreme power because of her own ability, or at least because of a conjunction of exceptional circumstances that she was able to turn admirably to her own advantage. While Catherine was undoubtedly an adroit politician and a capable woman of action, she merely canalized, encouraged, and followed the political and economic evolution of a country that was already rapidly expanding. She was, in short, a capable rather than a brilliant sovereign. Catherine continued and in some ways completed the work of Peter the Great and was more the docile instrument of a ruling class than a sovereign guided by personal political ideas. *"But she was a woman,"* Oldenbourg stresses, adding that a man placed in the same situation and possessing the same qualities would undoubtedly have attracted less attention, been less admired and less detested, for it is evident that a woman is not judged according to the same criteria as a man. It is also necessary to note that Catherine, despite her virile character, very often used specifically female weapons to further her own position and power.[25]

While the author's biography explains the choice of subject matter in the historical novels and works, it is the novels based on the Russian émigré experience in France that are the most personal and closely related to the author's own life and experiences. *The Awakened* takes place between 1936 and 1940 and tells the story of two uprooted families in Paris, one from Russia and the other from Germany. The Russian family, the Lanskois, consists of a grandfather, a father, a mother, two sons, and a daughter. The mother disappears early in the novel when she leaves her family for her young lover. The father, who was an officer in the czar's army, is now a worker in the Renault automobile factory, and his friends are either workers or taxi drivers. The children, who go to the local elementary and secondary school, speak Russian at home and French outside. Little by little, despite the Russian Orthodox Church, despite the summer camps where they are taught loyalty to a Russia that no longer exists, the children seek to assimilate into French life. The three young people, André, Elie, and Marianne begin to think of their parents as failures, not uncommon among the children of immigrants, and condemn them because they deny reality by living in an impossible dream. The suffering of the exile is exacerbated by financial worries; there is not even enough money for the young people to stay in school. Elie becomes an industrial designer; André, a nightclub singer; and Marianne, a model.

There is another émigré family in the novel, the Lindbergs, refugees from Hitler's Germany. The dominating figure is Léopold Lindberg, a brilliant professor, a Jew who embraced the Catholic faith from deep religious conviction. The older Lindberg daughter has been disowned by her father for marrying a French Jew; the younger daughter, Stéphanie, is filial love incarnate. Her father, like Zoé Oldenbourg's own father, dominates all aspects of her intellectual and emotional life. A seemingly impossible love develops between Stéphanie and Elie, which tears them apart as they try at the same time to remain faithful to the traditions and families of which they are ashamed but which they continue to love and defend. The young lovers are alone in a country that does not really accept them, in which they have no past, and where they can anticipate no future. For they are exiles, foreigners, suspect only because their parents were not born in France. The war continues the process of separation imposed on them by Stéphanie's father, who is ruthlessly opposed to their marriage. Elie is mobilized, captured, and made prisoner of war. Stéphanie escapes to Marseilles, pregnant with Elie's child but determined to honor the dictates of her father that she never marry Elie, her determination bolstered when her father is arrested as a Jew and deported to a concentration camp.

The Chains of Love, set in Paris between the years 1947 and 1951, is a sequel to *The Awakened.* Elie Lanskoi returns from captivity after an absence of seven years, two years later than the other French prisoners of war because he had been held in an American camp. During his second captivity, in which he was surrounded by Communists, he was converted to the political beliefs of his father's enemies. His conversion has left him even more isolated than before: "Foundations. Where can you find them when it is a question of denying the whole of your past? When your life has been nothing but a series of violent breaks, when you have felt since earliest childhood that everything in your life was provisional? . . . The man from nowhere. Why? It is cruel. I'm in my own country, I've never had any other, I'm a child of the Paris suburbs; I've never claimed to be anything else."[26] But, despite his impassioned plea, his new political friends reject him because he will not make the ultimate political gesture and renounce his French citizenship to assume the Soviet citizenship to which his parentage entitles him, thereby separating him from them as effectively as his new political beliefs have separated him from his family and upbringing.

Elie sees Stéphanie again and learns that they have a daughter Lisbeth, whom Stéphanie has raised alone. But the ghost of Stéphanie's father stands between them; she will never be able to overcome her remorse at having betrayed him. Stéphanie's guilt is paradigmatic of the situation of heroines in fiction in which the fates of the women depend on patriarchal norms that forbid sexual passion to women. The tragic denouements result from a flaw that would not be fatal in a male hero, namely the desire for sexual fulfillment.[27] But Stéphanie's guilt is centered on her first passion for Elie, for whom she feels she betrayed her father, and she is now able to fall in love with another man. Her lover, Aron Leibowitz, a painter of genius, is another exile; he is the incarnation of the wandering Jew. A victim of pogroms in his native Poland, he lost his wife and child to the Nazis, and survived the war only because he was hidden in the unoccupied zone by Stéphanie. Now he lives only for his art; incapable of further emotional commitment he cannot return Stéphanie's love, and finally leaves her when her passion threatens to consume him. Stéphanie, however, is a survivor; she becomes the mistress of a wealthy businessman who gives her and her daughter financial security. But Elie cannot compromise. Unable to cope with his solitude and alienation, he kills himself. Oldenbourg here, as in her other novels, gives voice to the observation she made as a child and young woman that women were always stronger than men.

In 1980, in *La joie-souffrance* (Joy-suffering), Zoé Oldenbourg again returns to the experience of Russian émigrés in France who try desperately to adapt to their new country from which they will always feel excluded. Certain themes of *La joie-souffrance* reappear in *Les amours égarées* (Lost loves, 1987), in which, once again, uprooted, exiled individuals seek to escape solitude and alienation through love. These exiles are the present-day incarnation of Oldenbourg's dispossessed suffering "heirs to a kingdom," but one without God or faith.

Chapter Four
Transition: Geneviève Gennari

Geneviève Gennari (b. 1920) belongs to the first wave of feminist writers, those who before 1968 had discussed and analyzed the problems confronting women in French society, but who had not proposed solutions to these problems. In a series of novels, many of which bear the mark of her own conflict between her intellectual aspirations and the need to conform to a traditional, feminine role, Geneviève Gennari documents the situation of French women in a changing society. Her novels deal with the societal imperative to choose between marriage and a career; between self-fulfillment, with its concomitant loneliness and alienation, and the love and companionship of husband and children offered to the woman who accepts the limiting, selfless role of wife and mother. In an autobiographical work of 1978, *La robe rouge* (The red dress), in which she discusses her life from childhood to the completion of her psychoanalysis in 1951, Gennari reveals how her own conflict influenced her fictional world and how her successful therapy eventually permitted her to express herself both as a writer and as a woman. "If I refused my femininity," she writes, "it was because femininity, in the years 1930–50 during which I was formed, prohibited me from developing without guilt the gift which I believed I had received. All this is widely known today, but at the time, I had to discover it alone—and painfully."[1]

Gennari and other women of her generation were unable to verbalize their distress; each believed that her dilemma was unique. It was Simone de Beauvoir's *Second Sex* in 1949 that made them aware of the universality of their problem and shed light for Gennari on the revolt she had voiced unknowingly in her first novel, *Les cousines Muller (The Restless Heart)*, 1949. Gennari's admiration for Beauvoir inspired her critical study *Simone de Beauvoir* (1958), in which she defended Beauvoir's thesis that there is no difference between men and women, and that women's situation can be explained exclusively by historical and sociological causes. However, in *Le dossier de la femme* (Dossier on women, 1965), a historical study of French women and French feminism between 1889 and 1964, Gennari modified her position and stated that there are essential differences between men and women and that there is a basic feminine nature, an idea that has been embraced by the new wave of French feminists.

The Restless Heart is the most autobiographical of Gennari's fictional works; it reflects her own situation as a young adult imprisoned within the rigid confines of an upper bourgeois family. Several themes can be found here that reappear throughout her oeuvre, including the importance of the individual's relationships with family and social class and the problems stemming from patriarchal definitions of women's role in society. The novel can be read as a psychological study of three women, as well as a critique of the family and society that restrict their destinies. It also treats of the universal desire for love and understanding that is constantly thwarted by misunderstanding and imperfect communication.

The themes and problems around which the novel is built are worked out through the destinies of the three granddaughters of Guillaume Muller, Françoise, Ninon, and Eva, whose struggles for self-realization lead only to defeat. Ninon, like all women of her time and class, was educated for nothing but marriage, and eventually settles for the only available candidate, Jean-Pierre Fourqueuilles. But she is not prepared for the loss of freedom and identity that is the price women must pay for marriage. And so she rebels in a very traditional way by a casual act of adultery. With childlike naiveté, she confesses to her husband, but he cannot pardon her infidelity and they separate. She has nothing to substitute for marriage, however, and returns after a year to Jean-Pierre, with no choice but to live in accord with the usual matrimonial arrangement, made even worse by a lack of love and trust. Like Ninon, Françoise also was taught that marriage was the only option available to her. She had been dissuaded by her grandfather from pursuing her relationship with an aristocratic young man because of what he regarded as an insurmountable class barrier between them. Later on, Françoise tires of loneliness and marries a man from a bourgeois family like her own. But marriage does not bring the anticipated escape from solitude, which she then seeks in religion and motherhood.

The third cousin, Eva, is different from the others. She was raised in Switzerland because her father had disassociated himself from his hypercritical, disapproving family. Eva is a talented musician and aspires to a career as a concert pianist. Her achievements set her apart, and she is rejected by the man she loves because she is too intelligent and gifted. She then marries a man who is her intellectual inferior, because she, like her cousins, was brought up to believe that marriage is the only acceptable state for a woman. Ironically, it is marriage, which was supposed to provide access to adult life, that marks for each of the cousins a complete loss of freedom and personal identity. Their humiliation at being relegated to the role of dependent child is exacerbated by the fact that the lives of all three women are controlled by men to whom they are superior.

The problems facing the woman who chooses to realize herself and lead an egocentric life are at the heart of *La fontaine scellée* (The fountain gone dry, 1950). In this novel the love between the protagonists Esther and Romain is destined to fail because Esther is not prepared to sacrifice her identity for the man she loves. She is unlike Romain's mother and sister, who are self-sacrificing, dependent women. Their lives are centered around husband and family, thereby maintaining and justifying their oppression by family and society. The role they play in perpetuating the values of a patriarchal society becomes an important theme in later feminist literature. Romain's mother raised him to accept without question female dependency and devotion. Yet, while he admires his mother and sister for these qualities, he also looks down on them. These conflicting emotions color his relationship with Esther. On the one hand, he dreams of an adoring wife, responsive to all his needs, while, on the other, he intellectually rejects this concept and loves and admires Esther because of her freedom and her commitment to self-realization. Esther, too, is torn by antithetical emotions and desires. She learned from her mother, a successful novelist and survivor of a terrible marriage, that it is necessary to live for one's self, and that marriage is a threat to freedom and self-realization. Still, she cannot stop dreaming of a strong, protective father figure who will provide love and protection and preserve her from both solitude and the existential imperative to assume responsibility for her own destiny. But the concept of the couple based on an equal partnership proves to be unworkable within the context of a society built on a foundation of misogyny, insecurity, and rampant self-interest. The pessimistic conclusion of the novel reveals Gennari's recognition of the impossibility of progress in male/female relationships within the framework of traditional society.

J'éveillerai l'aurore (I will greet the dawn, 1952), provides insight into the needs of a lucid woman in an intimate relationship, needs shaped and molded by familial and societal influences and affected by the trauma of World War II. Gennari is one of the very few women novelists, with the exception of Elsa Triolet and Zoé Oldenbourg, to show the effects of the war on their female protagonists and to depict the efforts of these women to survive it. The problems of Colette's and Simone de Beauvoir's heroines are unrelated to war, and Marguerite Yourcenar's works are completely removed from this temporal frame of reference. Even Marguerite Duras, whose first-person accounts are among the most vivid and compelling of war memoirs, excludes the war from her novels, while Violette Leduc welcomes the war because it makes everyone as disadvantaged as she.[2] And World War II and the Resistance provide a most unconvincing background for Françoise Sagan's eternal sexual triangle in *De guerre lasse (A Reluctant Hero)*, 1985.

J'éveillerai l'aurore, like Gennari's other novels, is a search for self-knowledge. It is a memoir written by Christa Villemer Gross in an attempt to understand herself and come to terms with her decision to leave France at the end of World War II to accompany her Austrian-born husband to his native land. The memoir recounts the major events in her life that led to this decision. Christa was born in Paris, where she lived with her family until they moved to Prévauté, which is still the family home. After their mother's death, Christa's older sister Marguerite assumed her role. Marguerite accepts without question the attitudes of society and the place assigned to women. She is representative of the type of woman found in all Gennari's novels, who supports traditional values and who stands in opposition to the unquiet, lucid heroine. Christa refuses the suitable husband proposed by Marguerite and marries a musician, Franz Gross, son of an Austrian father and French mother. Christa accompanies Franz to Switzerland and then to Italy at the beginning of the war, but returns to France without her husband to avoid giving birth to her child in a fascist country. Her homecoming is also an instinctive urge to return to the womblike atmosphere of the family. However, the child is stillborn, which forces Christa to assume full responsibility for her final decision.

The German occupation permits Franz to return to France. While he does not collaborate with the Germans, his identification with his heritage makes their marital life unbearable. Torn between her love for her husband and her country, Christa leaves Franz in Paris and returns alone to her family home. Ironically, Marguerite, a patriot and ardent anti-Nazi, feels that Christa is wrong to leave her husband, because in her scale of values the woman's duty to her husband supersedes all others. The problem is solved for the moment when Franz is drafted by the German army and then taken prisoner by the English. During his captivity, his hands are frostbitten, which puts an end to his musical career. When he returns after the Liberation, a displaced person without a career, he asks Christa to leave France and go to live with him in the Austrian mountains. In a prefeminist denouement, Christa agrees to sacrifice her own life and aspirations to remain with her husband, striving to escape solitude through the only traditional means offered to women, marriage.

Le plus triste plaisir (The saddest pleasure, 1956) marks a departure from the family units of Gennari's previous novels to a larger, more diversified group, the passengers on a cruise ship in the Mediterranean, all of whom have embarked on the journey in the hope of effecting a change in their lives. This novel was followed a year later by *Le rideau de sable* (The sand curtain) in which the abuses of sexism are paralleled and underlined by those of racism.[3] The condition of outsider prompted Gennari, as it did many female authors, to feel great empathy for all other victims of society. The protagonist of the novel, Alliette Aliscamp, the wife of a professor, has led a seemingly satisfactory bourgeois life. When the novel opens, Alliette has just spent a vacation with her husband in a fictional African country, where she has become aware of her heretofore unrecognized dissatisfaction with her life. She is offered a research assignment and decides to remain in Africa after her husband's return to France, hoping to rediscover the person she was before her marriage. When the museum curator attempts to block Alliette's research, she continues to work on her own. In the course of her inquiries, she meets and becomes emotionally involved with a black doctor, Liber, who is as alienated by his race as she by her sex.

Her friendship with Liber comes to an end when he proposes marriage. Her rejection unveils her latent racism. Deprived of the companionship of her only friend, and without the routine and distraction offered by work, she becomes increasingly isolated and dependent on alcohol. Gennari has stated that Alliette's crisis is existential: "Her confrontation with metaphysical solitude increases the urgency of her struggle to justify her life in secular terms."[4] Alliette's husband, alerted to her condition by an anonymous letter, comes to find her and takes her back to France with him. Her decision to choose an imperfect marriage and assume woman's traditional role is consistent with her background. While the denouement is in keeping with traditional cultural norms, since Alliette is brought back to reality and reintegrated into bourgeois society under the tutelage of her protective husband, Gennari also tells us that her rescue represents a loss of freedom and a defeat in her search for self-realization; she has sacrificed transcendence for immanence and will forever remain the Other.

"The Solitude of Women without Men," the title of an article Gennari wrote in 1967,[5] is also the theme of Gennari's most outstanding novel, *Journal d'une bourgeoise (The Other Woman I Am)*, 1959. The loneliness of Gennari's women, who live in the constant hope of finding a man to give meaning and justification to their lives, is very different from that of Triolet's women, whose solitude provides an opportunity for them to realize their potential. In *The Other Woman I Am*, we find the anguish of the woman alone who has been conditioned by society to believe that life without a man is meaningless. This loneliness disappears only in the utopian female communities and relationships found in the works of later feminist writers including Rochefort, Wittig, and Cixous.

The novel is written in the form of a journal by Sylvestre Costa Fontaine, who has just been widowed. During her married life, she sacrificed her identity to become a model bourgeois wife and mother. She was never committed to anything outside her home and continually used the excuse of her domestic responsibilities to justify her lack of commitment: she did not take part in Resistance activities because of her young, dependent child; she did not pursue a career because her husband would have considered it an insult to his manhood; and she never had, or defended, any ideas other than those of her husband. After her husband's death, she perceives that she has "lost the habit of seeking any justification for . . . [her] existence other than that of being Mme Joseph Fontaine, the mother of Jean-Christophe."[6]

She finds herself alone for the first time in her life, facing a terrible identity crisis. One of her acquaintances, an intellectual whom she has always admired, confesses that behind the impressive facade she presents to the world there is a woman who feels that her life is meaningless because she is without a man. The opposite point of view is presented by Sylvestre's friend Irina who maintains that, if you do not know how to live alone, you do not know how to live. The friendship between Irina and Sylvestre introduces a new theme into Gennari's work, one that develops into the female bonding found in the works of the second wave of feminist writers. The author also portrays for the first time in her work an independent, professional woman with the financial independence that Beauvoir deemed essential for self-realization. It is Irina who gives Sylvestre the courage to reject a comfortable marriage to a friend of her dead husband in order to accept a challenging job in

South America. While Alliette *(Le rideau de sable)* finds solitude in the marriage to which she returns, Sylvestre is saved from the most desperate solitude produced by alienation from self.

In *The Other Woman I Am,* we find the two basic themes of the modern "odd-woman bildungsroman," or novel of widowhood: on the one hand, there is a exclusion from society, which requires that a woman be part of a couple or family; on the other, there is a feeling of release from relationships and obligations that permits the pursuit of individual goals. In these novels women discover that they are reborn after the death of their husbands and find themselves shedding their secondary identities. The goal that they had previously pursued, namely, relationships with other people, now becomes increasingly secondary, giving way to a preoccupation with existential problems rather than with human entanglements. As she escapes from female roles and duties, the widow becomes whole unto herself, in tune with her own instincts, able to give, receive, or withhold sexuality as she sees fit: "The woman heroes who seek and are transformed by solitude have come to terms with the self-hater of women's psyche and have transmuted polar male and female attributes into a new androgynous consciousness."[7]

Les nostalgiques (Nostalgia), 1963, is the story of two women, Nathalie Elikoff, the illegitimate daughter of a French singer and a Russian soldier, who is orphaned at the age of twelve, and Diane de Trabert, the protected, cosseted daughter of a French aristocratic family. Although she is only five years older than Diane, Nathalie becomes a tutor to the Trabert children in 1938. World War II intrudes upon their peaceful existence. Nathalie marries, but her husband dies during the war. Diane's English fiancé also dies in the war and she marries Michel Montague, with whom she has two children. Alone after her husband's death, Nathalie seeks out Diane, who has devoted herself exclusively to her husband and children. Diane discovers, however, when she participates in an amateur theatrical production—directed by her former schoolmaster and friend Jean Le Pornic—that she has sacrificed for her family her great talent as an actress. She then goes on to pursue a highly successful acting career, but, as traditional morality would have it, she is punished for her achievement; her daughter dies when she is away on tour. Her husband then divorces her and obtains custody of their son. Divorced, childless, and homeless, Diane becomes a social pariah, but she is saved by Le Pornic who marries her and encourages her to return to the theater. Diane's success is paralleled by Nathalie's failure. Although she had formerly achieved a certain limited success as a writer, she ultimately abandons her career for the security of a stultifying bourgeois marriage. Simone de Beauvoir's influence is manifest here, as Gennari portrays her protagonists in a struggle for transcendence. Nathalie fails, but Diane succeeds because she has the courage to make the choices necessary to create her own essence. Her success, however, is tempered by the fact that it is achieved with the aid of Le Pornic.

Un mois d'août à Paris (A month of August in Paris, 1977), like all Gennari's novels, chronicles the author's mental and emotional states. During her late twenties and early thirties, after a severe bout of depression, Gennari underwent successful psychoanalysis, which permitted her to break free from paternal influence and reconcile her writing and femininity. Despite this, she had a second nervous breakdown in 1958, a relapse she details in *Un mois d'août à Paris*. The month of August, when life virtually stops in Paris, is chosen by many authors as a temporal device to exacerbate the existential crisis of their protagonists as they are deprived of normal distractions and are left alone, face to face with their anguish. Françoise, the narrator, feels the first stirrings of her crisis of anxiety and depression when she sees her husband off at Orly airport for a month's business trip. Like Sartre's Roquentin in the novel *Nausea,* she experiences her malaise as physical nausea. She is unable to eat, just as she was during past bouts of anorexia. This mental illness, which is mainly a female psychological disorder, reflects a refusal to grow up to assume the responsibilities of an adult in a frightening male-dominated world. It is also a desperate attempt to keep some semblance of control when confronted either with a dominant figure or with one's own shattered psyche. In the past, Françoise was able to turn to her husband to fight against her anxiety, but he is absent, and so she turns to the therapist who had originally helped her.

Gennari provides a complete description of Françoise's therapy, including the protagonist's changing relationship with the therapist as they work their way toward a cure. Françoise looks forward optimistically to a transformation in her relationship with her husband, but his return merely plunges them back into the concerns of daily life, which is filled with conflict and disappointment. While Françoise still experiences waves of worry and nagging fear, she is once again in control of her senses and demonstrates a newly acquired understanding that permits her to resume her former life.

Gennari, like Triolet, presents in her novels a complete account of her intellectual and emotional life from her first awareness of self, in

The Restless Heart, to advanced middle-age, in *La neuvième vague* (The ninth wave, 1980). According to popular belief, the ninth wave referred to in the title presages the death of the drowning victim. Here, it refers to the death that awaits the protagonist, Charlotte Frogier, and her husband, Victor. The novel portrays the beauty of their enduring conjugal love, which with each year is increasingly threatened by the inevitable separation of death. While Charlotte is still an active, sensual woman at the age of sixty-nine, she begins to realize that neither age nor the passage of time can be denied. The novel poses the question, which was posed in Beauvoir's novella "The Age of Discretion,"[8] whether one should continue to struggle until the very end and try to hold on to things, as Charlotte does, or, like Victor, progressively detach oneself from them and give in to old age. Charlotte wonders how one can continue on alone without the companion of a lifetime or, conversely, how one can imagine being the first to die. Although she toys briefly with the idea of a double suicide as an answer to the problem, she chooses life and the task of creating a successful old age. And, as the old couple declines, their granddaughter, whom they raised after their daughter's death, and her husband are slowly building their life. At the end of novel, they await the birth of their child, Charlotte's great-grandchild, whose birth presages her death.

While Geneviève Gennari's novels are based in large part on her own experiences and reflect her psychological and social problems as well as her metaphysical disquiet, they offer a paradigm of the stages of every woman's life. The struggles of women of her generation, particularly those of the intellectual, to realize their potential as independent individuals despite the guilt instilled in them by a patriarchal society, are still relevant today. While they do not possess the lucidity of present-day feminist heroines, Gennari's women know that there is much that is wrong with their role in society and that much is denied them. It is this awareness that Gennari's novels stimulate, for before one can attempt to solve a problem, one must know that it exists. Gennari's novels, as much as Beauvoir's theoretical work, prepare the feminist revolution.

Chapter Five

The Female Bildungsroman: Françoise Sagan, Françoise Mallet-Joris, and Claire Etcherelli

Françoise Sagan (b. 1935) and Françoise Mallet-Joris (b. 1930) insisted on the right of the young woman to break free from the double standard of prevailing bourgeois morality and assert her own values. They were not prey to the guilt arising from the conflicting demands of freedom and crippling traditional values that tortured Geneviève Gennari. Nor were they torn between the obligation to define themselves and the limitations imposed by patriarchal norms. On the contrary, both of them were intent upon scandalizing the bourgeoisie. Their novels of development, the bildungsromans of the young woman of the fifties who was seeking personal fulfillment within a culture that provided no models for women, were the first French novels by and about female adolescents. While many comparisons may be made between their first novels—Sagan's *Bonjour tristesse (Bonjour Tristesse)*, 1954, and Mallet-Joris's *Le rempart des béguines (The Illusionist)*, 1951—their evolution was along quite divergent lines. Sagan became more and more prey to the existential anguish evident in her early novels, while Mallet-Joris's conversion to Catholicism relieved her of this anguish by providing a meaning for and justification of existence.

Although the novels of Claire Etcherelli (b. 1934) take place within the same period as those of Sagan and Mallet-Joris, the stories they tell are very different, for they speak of the development of the working-class rather than the bourgeois woman—victim not only of a patriarchal society, but also of a depressed economy and of capitalism. Etcherelli's protagonists, subject to the double discrimination of sex and class, are diverted from the search for self-fulfillment by the struggle for survival. Yet, although they have been reduced to the status of toiling automatons, they still strive to maintain a certain identity as subjects rather than as objects for sexual and economic exploitation.

Françoise Sagan

Françoise Quoirez—her nom de plume was borrowed from Proust's Princesse de Sagan—was born into a wealthy family in 1935. Her family lived in Paris from 1935 to 1939 and returned there in 1944, after spending the war years in Lyon. Françoise attended two parochial schools in Paris and was expelled from both. Yet, despite her disorganized academic career, she passed her *baccalauréat* exam and studied at the Sorbonne from 1952 to 1953; but she gave up her studies after she failed her first-year examinations. Sagan's first novel was published in 1954 when she was nineteen years old. It has been followed by a steady stream of novels, short stories, and plays. Her private life—two marriages, divorces, a nearly fatal automobile accident, assorted law suits—seemed to echo the lives of her characters, members of the privileged bourgeoisie leading lives of luxury and excess and seeking vainly to palliate their anguish at the meaninglessness and basic absurdity of existence through studied cultivation of sensation. For them, only happiness can justify existence, and happiness, which the author equates with an escape from solitude, can only be found in love. But, and that is the paradox in Sagan's work, love is always fragile and fleeting, both because it is equated solely with sensation and physical pleasure and also because it is always built on error—the one you love loves someone else, who, in turn, loves still another—condemning you inexorably to solitude. Indeed, the theme of solitude may be considered the leitmotiv of Sagan's work, one which constantly reminds us that we are born, live, and die alone.

In *Bonjour Tristesse* Sagan paints a psychological portrait of her generation, which used the lost years of the Occupation as a pretext to transform life into a perpetual vacation. Many of Sagan's contemporaries saw themselves in her heroine Cécile, who was both precociously cynical and sexually liberated. They identified with her and her problems in establishing her own identity. In the first paragraph of the novel, Cécile wonders about a certain malaise she feels as she reminisces about events that took place the preceding summer when she was seventeen years old. She has been living with her forty-year-old father for two years, having spent the preceding ten years in boarding schools. Cécile's mother died when she was very young, depriving her of the maternal image which is essential in the quest for identity of the female adolescent, whose earliest, unmediated attachment to the mother is never entirely relinquished, and which informs all later relationships. It is both Cécile's search for a mother and her desire to be different from her that determine her subsequent actions.

Cécile and her father are spending the summer in a rented villa in the Midi with her father's current mistress, Elsa. When she first left boarding school, Cécile had difficulty in accepting her father's promiscuity, but soon "his charm, [her] new easy life, and [her] own disposition, led [her] to fall in readily with his ways."[1] Her father, a frivolous man who makes her party to his liaisons, treats her as if she is a "marvelous plaything." Despite her love for her father, Cécile's description of him reveals that she recognizes his weakness, superficiality, and unjustified self-satisfaction. Still, Cécile merely drifts along in life as does her father; her lack of direction is one of the causes of the final tragedy. It is in order to cease being dependent on others and to acquire an independent life that she effects irreparable acts.

One day Raymond tells Cécile that Anne, who was her dead mother's best friend, is coming to spend some time with them. Cécile remembers Anne as an intelligent, forceful career woman whose life reflects her high principles, and she is afraid of Anne's influence. Her fears are realized when her father and Anne fall in love and decide to marry. Anne soon attempts to assume the mother's role and instill order and purpose into Cécile's life, encouraged by Raymond who is delighted to have her absolve him of the parental responsibility he had never wanted, or had the maturity, to assume. Cécile sees Anne both as an awe-inspiring role model and as an overwhelming power against which she needs to revolt in order to assert her own individuality; Anne represents authority, which Cécile finds both attractive and frightening. When Anne sees Cécile kissing a young man, she separates them, thereby precipating the love affair she had been attempting to prevent, for Cécile is spurred on not by passion but by her need to avenge herself for Anne's ascendency. Sagan maintains that Cécile's love affair scandalized the readers of the fifties because she did not pay for her sin by becoming pregnant. Thus, although she lost her virginity, she did so with the freedom enjoyed heretofore only by men.

Anne is not only an obstacle to Cécile's self-expression, but she also causes her to lose her self-respect by offering an example of an intelligent, principled life. Cécile decides that she must free herself of Anne, to find again "the freedom to think for myself, even to think wrongly or not at all, the freedom to choose my own life, to choose myself. I cannot say I wanted to 'be myself,' for I knew I was still soft clay. But I refused to be molded."[2] The effort to achieve an integrated identity, in which aspects of youthful freedom and mature responsibility merge, is too great for Cécile and she opts for the former; she refuses to grow up and assume an adult identity based on Anne's definition of what constitutes feminine maturity.

To rid herself of Anne, Cécile contrives to throw her father and Elsa together and to have Anne surprise them. It is only when Anne flees their corrupt milieu that Cécile realizes that she has wounded a living, sensitive being, a wound that turns out to be mortal, for it precipitates Anne's suicide. After Anne's death, life seems to go on as before for father and daughter; they soon resume their lives as if nothing, or almost nothing had happened. But Cécile, who is by nature superior to her father, is definitively touched by sadness, a feeling she is able to mask during the day but which takes hold of her when she is alone in her bed. Then, she says, something rises in her that she greets by name, "Bonjour, tristesse" ("Hello, sadness"). At the end of the novel, Cécile seems to long for a story that might have turned out differently. Indeed, the cultural and spiritual education of Sagan's female protagonists leads to the same defeat as Flaubert's Frédéric Moreau (L'Education sentimentale, 1869), who emerges neither wiser nor happier, and who is left with the realization of the void at the heart of all existence.

In Un certain sourire (A Certain Smile), 1956, Cécile's "tristesse" becomes Dominique's boredom, which is made manifest by Dominique's lack of motivation and an almost paralyzing indifference. There are many similarities between the two young women. While Dominique is not in thrall to Cécile's unconscious Oedipal love for her father, she does fall in love with a married man who is old enough to be her father. Both Cécile and Dominique have been deprived of responsible parental guidance—Dominique's mother has been mired in acute depression since the death of her young son fifteen years before, and her father is exclusively preoccupied with his wife. Dominique is part of the generation deprived of parental guidance to which all of Sagan's heroines belong. Like Cécile, Dominique meets a woman in her forties who could have become the mother she lacked. And Dominique, too, destroys any possibility for a constructive, meaningful relationship when she becomes the lover of this woman's husband.

The differences between the two young women are, however, as significant as the resemblances. Cécile actively schemes and plots, while Dominique is the frightened, consenting victim of what she regards as her destiny. Cécile feels a sensual, youthful joie de vivre, while Dominique is more cerebral. Yet, while Dominique takes courses at the Sorbonne and passes her exams, she is not particularly interested in her studies. She accepts them with the same passivity as she does everything else in her life, never deciding anything for herself, never choosing but always being chosen.[3] And so, she permits herself to be seduced by an older man. Her feelings for Luc brighten her dismal existence for they bring her a taste for life and a feeling of vitality. But Dominique is just another conquest for Luc who uses a trip to the United States as a pretext to break with her. Dominique's sentimental education leads back to her point of departure as she realizes that nothing has changed, that she is alone once again. "Well, what did it matter? I was a woman who had loved a man. It was a simple story; nothing to get excited about."[4] Her experience brings not maturity, but disillusionment. All that she has learned is that "living, after all, meant contriving to be as contented as humanly possible, and that was not easy";[5] that what was essential in life was to avoid discomfort.

The title of Sagan's third novel, *Dans un mois, dans un an* (1957), is ironic. While Racine's tragic heroine, Bérénice, wonders how she and Titus will be able to bear their separation "in a month or in a year,"[6] emphasizing thereby the victory of true love over time, Sagan's round of love affairs here underscores the ephemeral nature of the physical attraction that passes for love in her world and justifies the English title *Those without Shadows*. This is the first of Sagan's novels written in the third person. It also contains several interlocking plots and a larger cast of characters than previously. "I wanted to describe universal human reactions. I wrote about the intellectual, or so-called Parisian 'scribbling' milieu because it's one I know well and I was less apt to make errors there than in any other. . . . I wanted to write five or six different stories which would be linked by the same quest for something that is most often not found or, if found, not recognized as such. Life is like music, you should be able to listen to it twice."[7]

The pursuit of love is the real subject of the book, a vain pursuit because the one who loves is usually not loved in return. Love is also very short-lived because it is based on a momentary physical infatuation that naturally weakens and dies. Nicole loves her husband, Bernard, who is tired of her, and she tries to hold on to him by becoming pregnant despite her doctor's warnings. Nicole is the traditional consenting female victim whose only weapon is maternity. Bernard continues to write, although he realizes that he is a failure as a writer, just as he continues to pursue Josée, who does not return his passion. Josée, another of Sagan's aimless, undirected "orphans," a social parasite, is supported in style by absentee parents who substitute material goods for care and guidance. She, in turn, supports her young lover, Jacques, who finds their situation quite normal. The couple befriends Edouard, a naive young provincial who has come to Paris to become a writer, and Josée helps him to pay his debts. Edouard falls in love with a beautiful actress, Béatrice, with whom he has a brief love affair, causing his fifty-year-old uncle, Alain, who also loves Béatrice, to despair. But Edouard is soon upstaged by the director Jolyet who is more useful to Béatrice's career. And finally, on this merry-go-round of sex that goes by the name of love, there is Fanny, Alain's wife, the only mature character in the novel. Like her middle-aged predecessors, Anne and Françoise, she is intelligent, sensitive, and perceptive; like them she is the maternal figure who should function as a role model, but becomes instead victim of the aimless, bored young woman who so desperately needs her guidance.

When a bildungsroman ends with capitulation or indecision, it usually invites a sequel, and Sagan continues Josée's story in two subsequent novels, *Les merveilleux nuages (The Wonderful Clouds)*, 1961, and *Un profil perdu (Lost Profile)*, 1974. *The Wonderful Clouds* is an excellent demonstration of the single emotional mood of emptiness that governs Sagan's fictional world. The author's pessimistic realism insists that it is only one's deluded narcissism that sees momentousness when there is nothing. In Sagan's flat world, "where the past is broken promises, the present without compulsion, and the future without suspense, actions are hardly worth doing and the characters droop with fatigue and ennui."[8] Josée is now in the United States, married to a rich alcoholic American, Alan, who is fixated on his mother and obsessively jealous of Josée. While she wants to leave her husband, she finds no pressing reason for immediate action and drifts along, in and out of a few affairs, until she finally breaks with Alan. All Josée accomplishes by leaving Alan is to step into the vacuum that has surrounded her all along.

But Sagan does not abandon Josée until her education is complete, and she returns to her once again in *Lost Profile*. She is back in Paris with Alan after a four-year absence and finds that all their old friends have become mature adults. They now have professional or financial preoccupations that set them apart from Josée, who remarks, "They had rounded the bend into maturity without me, and I had returned among them still an adolescent, accompanied by another adolescent, the idle, well-to-do Alan."[9] Josée meets Julius A. Cram, a self-made millionaire, who falls in love with her, but Alan, who is now quite mad, keeps Josée locked up in their apartment. One day, Julius frees her, then finds a job for her on a magazine, as well as an inexpensive apartment. Josée is now content for she believes that her life has changed. She remarks that "one always thinks that one's feelings, because of a change of partner, or life-style, or age group, are different from those of one's adolescence, whereas they are precisely the same. And yet, each time, the desire to be free, the desire to be loved, the instinct to escape, the instinct of the chase all seem, thanks to a providential amnesia or a naive presumptuousness, to be completely new and original."[10]

But Josée has been misled by her desires, and her relationship with Julius has in no way transformed her life. Change does eventually come, however. When she learns that her position, the low rental on her apartment, the clothes that are presumably lent to her as an advertising promotion, are all part of Julius's arrangements and subsidized by him, her pride is wounded and she breaks with him. "Through a mixture of blindness and optimism, I had allowed Julius to make me look contemptible in the eyes of his friends and no doubt in his too," she states. "And this I couldn't forgive him because if he had really loved me, in spite of his contempt, he wouldn't have allowed others to judge me."[11] Josée has emerged from her lethargy, refusing affronts to her pride and asserting herself as an individual. She also marries and has a child, assuming the responsibility of commitment and choice, which Sagan's other heroines refuse. Despite the fact that Josée chooses the traditional role of wife and mother, at least she has made a choice and emerged from the paralyzing apathy of Sagan's other heroines.

In Sagan's works, the author usually creates a pair of women characters, the youthful protagonist and the older woman on whom she would like to pattern herself, but fears a loss of identity should she succeed in doing so. The dyad of Sagan's first three novels, *Bonjour Tristesse, A Certain Smile,* and *Those without Shadows,* disappears in *Aimez-vous Brahms . . . (Aimez-vous Brahms),* 1959, leaving only the older woman. Paule is a successful thirty-nine-year-old interior designer who, like her predecessors Anne, Françoise, and Fanny, embodies a double image of female adulthood; while she is strong, independent, and clearly superior to her male counterpart, she is also fatally vulnerable to him for financial and/or emotional security. Paule has devoted herself exclusively for the last six years to her lover, Roger, who constantly breaks dates with her, knowing that she will neither protest nor stop loving him. This changes when Paule meets Simon, the young son of one of her clients. Despite the difference in age, he falls in love with her. While everything stands in the way of their liaison, a seemingly trivial question brings them together. When Simon asks Paule whether she likes Brahms, she remembers her youth when people asked such questions and were interested in the answer they elicited. Simon's ardor also recalls youthful passion, while his attentiveness contrasts sharply with Roger's neglect. All of this conspires to overcome Paule's resistance and they become lovers. Soon, however, it is those same youthful qualities that cause Paule to break with him and return to her mature love. Roger has missed her terribly; he now realizes that he must modify his behavior. But, the last scene closes the circle—nothing has really happened; it never does—and traces a return to the point of departure. Paule is awaiting Roger's arrival, when the telephone rings. Even before she answers, she knows that it is Roger and that he will excuse himself for being late because he is held up by a business dinner. By accepting Roger's behavior, Paule, the successful career woman, once again justifies the author's culturally induced anxieties about the possibility of female adulthood, which must be based on feelings of self-identity and worth in a culture that destroys such feelings.

The title of the novel *La chamade (La Chamade)*, 1965, announces another failure, for the chamade is a roll on the drums to announce defeat. *La Chamade* is the story of a young woman whose sensitivity and love of life's pleasures are not enough to give her the courage needed to accept life's responsibilities. Lucile, a beautiful woman of thirty, shares the luxurious apartment and life of her wealthy protector Charles. She may occasionally deceive him, but she is fond of him. In the Paris milieu where amoral enjoyment depends on expensive luxuries, Lucile lives only for each day's pleasures, until she meets the poor young editor Antoine. They fall in love and happiness seems within their grasp.

Antoine is the type of man who wants a total, exclusive love, and asks Lucile to break with Charles. She does so reluctantly because she cannot bear to give up the luxuries he offers her. Antoine also believes that a man and woman should share everything, including work, and obtains a job for Lucile on a newspaper. She accepts the job to please him, but she dislikes their monotonous life more and more. Her annoyance becomes acute one day when she has to wait in the rain for a crowded bus. "The only real charm of money, she thought, was that it permitted one to avoid all this: the exasperation, the other people."[12] Unwilling to work or to cope with discomfort, she leaves the newspaper without telling Antoine and spends her days in her old haunts with her old friends, finding comfort in this type of carefree life. When she finds that she's pregnant, she feels hemmed in by life. She knows that a baby will put an end to her freedom and decides to have an abortion. Antoine accepts her decision because all he wants is Lucile, "that half-woman, that half-child, that invalid, that irresponsible, his love. . . ."[13] Lucile asks Charles for money so that she can go to Switzerland for a safe, comfortable operation instead of to some filthy abortionist in Paris. Her relationship with Antoine is never the same after this; she eventually leaves him. "She walked back toward the flat, toward Charles, toward solitude; she knew that she was rejected forever by any life worthy of that name, and she thought that she truly deserved it."[14] Two years later, Lucile and Antoine meet at a party; Lucile has finally married Charles and Antoine has been made the director of a publishing house. Lucile has returned to her point of departure; the bildungsroman has ended not with growth but with stagnation.

The female novel of development takes an interesting turn in *Des bleues à l'âme (Scars on the Soul)*, 1972, with the brother-sister theme that is so important in Christiane Rochefort's utopian novel, *Archaos ou le jardin étincelant*, published in the same year.[15] Instead of settling for being half a person, which is the same as being a self-destructive nonperson, the emerging woman often casts off her defined role and moves towards androgyny. The closely knit, symbiotic union of brother and sister constitutes the perfectly conceived androgynous being, in which one sees reflected neither the other nor a mirror image, but the other half of oneself. It is a union in which all aspects of love, both homosexual and heterosexual, blend to form the whole that provides a cure for the fragmentation of existence. In *Scars on the Soul*, the protagonist is just such a brother-sister entity, Sébastien and Eléonore Van Milhem. Their story alternates with passages from the author's journal in which she takes the measure of her life and work.

Sébastien and Eléonore originally appeared as characters in the play *Château en Suède* (1960). They are ten years older here and are penniless in Paris. We learn that Eléonore's husband, Hugo, is in prison for murder and that their château has been sold. Their good friend Robert Bessy lends them his apartment while he is out of town, and Sébastien takes care of their other wants by becoming the lover of a middle-aged woman, Nora Jedelmann. The brother and sister spend the summer in the Jedelmann's villa on the Côte d'Azur, where Eléonore amuses herself by having an affair with the gardner. When they return to Paris, they must find another means of support since Sébastien has broken off with Mme Jedelmann. Robert gives Sébastien a job in his advertising agency while he is away in New York on business. At the agency, Eléonore meets Bruno Raffet, a young movie star who becomes her lover. When he returns to Paris, Robert finds that the three young people make up a closely knit trio from which he is excluded. In despair, he kills himself. Sébastien and Eléonore break with Bruno, spend a few months in Normandy with the author, and then return to their native Sweden—still self-sufficient and complete unto themselves—after receiving a telegram from Hugo announcing his release from prison.

La femme fardée (The Painted Lady), 1981, marks what might seem to be the successful outcome of the evolution of Sagan's heroine, which started with the "tristesse," or awakening conscience of the nineteen-year-old Cécile. In truth, it marks an overwhelming defeat. There are twelve people on board the "ship of fools," the S.S. *Narcissus*, for a ten-day "music cruise" of the Mediterranean. These include the protagonist, "the heavily made up woman," of the title, Clarisse, heiress to the Dureau steelworks. The grotesque makeup worn by Clarisse represents the mask placed on her by her husband, the negative vision of herself that he has forced on her. Clarisse is accompanied by her intellectual husband, Eric Lethuillier, editor of *Forum*, a left-wing journal. The cast of characters also includes Edma Bautet-Lebreche, a society hostess and her husband, Armand, a wealthy financier; Captain Elledocq and his homosexual purser, Charley Bollinger; the pianist Hans-Helmut Kreuze and his vicious dog; the diva Doriacci and her shipboard lover, Andreas Fayard, a handsome young gigolo from Nevers; Julien Peyrat, an Australian confidence man posing as an art appraiser; the producer Simon Béjard and a young starlet, Olga Lamouroux.

Clarisse falls in love with Julien Peyrat, who returns her love. Unlike her husband, he does not attempt to humiliate and degrade her, but tries to make her aware of her worth. While Eric's treatment has driven Clarisse to become an alcoholic, he cannot destroy an inner quality that she acquired at birth and that strangely resembles virtue. Eric has dispossessed her of everything—friends, lovers, family, self-respect—but she now seems to be slipping away from him, and he cannot see who on the ship would have awakened the woman within "the somnolent and terrorized creature she had become."[16] He does not realize that someone has given her what he has denied her, the assurance of being accepted and loved as an equal. And so Clarisse leaves her handsome, successful, disdainful husband for Julien. She does even more, she saves Julien from being arrested for having sold Eric a fraudulent painting. It really does not matter that Julien is dishonest, for his financial dishonesty is negligible in comparison with Eric's moral dishonesty. Besides, Clarice remarks that Julien will no longer have to be dishonest because she has all the money he will ever need. In exchange for her fortune, he offers her happiness, giving her the better half of the bargain, according to the author.

While Clarisse has emerged from behind the disfiguring mask imposed by a dominant male, she has not done so through her own efforts. She is still sleeping beauty, awakened by the kiss of a rather unconventional prince. Sagan has moved from her first probing, psychological novel, which was written with classical restraint, to the romantic fairy tale, with its stock-in-trade cast divided between good and evil characters. Cécile, at least, initiated her own actions, however misguided they ultimately turned out to be. She sought to assume the masculine prerogative of influencing her own destiny. She is not "lovable" according to gender role norms, but she is an authentic being. Clarisse, more than twenty years her senior, conforms in every way to traditional feminine role requirements. Thus, Sagan's novels in the aggregate do not constitute a bildungsroman but merely reflect a physical passage from youth to middle age without comparable psychological growth.

Françoise Mallet-Joris

Françoise Mallet-Joris, like Françoise Sagan, began her literary career with a novel that explores the problems the female adolescent encounters as she attempts to establish an individual identity in a culture that provides no models for women. Unlike Sagan's oeuvre, however, Mallet-Joris's evolved from an expression of individual revolt to a more sweeping indictment of the condition of women in general, expressing an ever-increasing feminist bias.

Françoise Mallet-Joris, the nom de plume of Françoise Lilar, was born in 1930 in Antwerp. Her father, Albert, was a lawyer, professor of maritime law, and statesman; her mother, Suzanne, was a writer and a member of the Belgian Academy. Both belonged to the French-speaking upper middle class of Antwerp, a closed circle that was proud of its history and nostalgic for its former splendor and privileges. This class figures prominently in Mallet-Joris's first two novels, *The Illusionist* and *La chambre rouge (The Red Room)*, 1955. The author tells us in her autobiographical *Lettre à moi-même* (*A Letter to Myself*), 1963, that it was the superficiality of the bourgeoisie among whom she grew up that stimulated both the antipathy for hypocrisy and pretentiousness she expressed throughout her work as well as her rebellion against the constraints of her milieu.[17] One of the forms taken by her rebellion was liberation from the sexual taboos of her class as she took a lover at the age of fifteen. The prematurely cynical girl and the older man appear in *The Red Room*, while the revolt against the parental moral code is the framework for *The Illusionist*, a work that has been described as "the most insolent, the most ferocious settling of accounts by a young girl with her father."[18] This novel can also be considered the resolution of the daughter's desire both to emulate her mother and to distance herself from her at the same time. In effect, by writing her novel, Mallet-Joris, even while rejecting her mother's social code, became her mother, the successful author.

The young Mallet-Joris's rebellion against her family and her milieu absorbed her completely and took not only the form of sexual liberation, but also that of a reaction against the religious attitudes of her parents. They were not practicing Catholics, nor did they baptize their daughters, telling them that they could decide about religion later on. Mallet-Joris decided to assert her freedom by making her choice immediately, and so she studied and prepared to be baptized a Roman Catholic. The closer she came to baptism, however, the more she questioned her decision, for she realized that all the priest was offering her was a different set of words, still another series of pat formulae. Even so, her conversion would have taken place had it been prompted solely by a desire to distance herself from her parents' beliefs and practices. It did not occur, however, because it did not satisfy her undefined malaise, a malaise she did not yet recognize as a longing for God, a longing that finally led to her conversion in 1955.[19]

When Mallet-Joris's parents learned of her love affair in 1947, they shipped her off to the United States "like a scandalous and embarrassing package" to study at Bryn Mawr College (*Lettre*, 180). She decided to get married as quickly as possible to free herself of parental authority. Accordingly, she married her professor, Robert Amadou, divorced him, and returned to Paris, "just eighteen years old, pregnant and divorced by one, in love with another, and struck with wonder before a delightful newborn baby" (181). Her lover supported her and her son and sent her to study at the Sorbonne. He continued to support her even after they had grown apart. In 1952 she married and then divorced Alain

Joxe, a historian, and in 1958 she married the artist Jacques Delfau, the father of her second son and two daughters.

Mallet-Joris's first novel, *The Illusionist,* had as great a succès de scandale as Sagan's *Bonjour Tristesse.* The protagonist of this novel, Hélène Noris, an independent, brave, and resolute young woman created in the author's image, is the prototype of all the heroines in Mallet-Joris's subsequent works. She refuses to play the role assigned to her by society and revolts against the hypocrisy of her milieu. Her rebellion is personal and is directed solely against family and society; it is only the heroines of the novels written after the author's conversion in 1955 who join a spiritual to the social disquiet. In all cases, however, the heroine's refusal to conform, as well as her lucid, disabused view of society, condemn her to solitude.

The Illusionist is the story of a girl who becomes a woman. Hélène moves abruptly from the extravagant world of childhood, with its excesses and illusions, into the adult world of compromise and surrender, a world she does not accept. It is Hélène, as it was Cécile, who tells the story, and the reader sees everything through her eyes. While the events are recounted in strict chronological order, with background material supplied in flashbacks, they are events that took place two years previously when the narrator was fifteen years old. Hélène's mother, like Cécile's, died when she was a child, and she had been cared for since then by a well-meaning, but ineffectual cook who was unable to satisfy the girl's need for guidance and affection. Hélène's father, René Noris, like Cécile's, is a benign, uninvolved parent, easily manipulated by both his daughter and his lover. He is too preoccupied with his textile firm, his investments, his political ambitions, and his Russian-born mistress, Tamara, to consider his daughter's emotional needs. Without adult guidance, Hélène has been left to her own devices, her solitude exacerbated by the lack both of organized activity and of family and friends. Alone in her room, she often prays for a miracle that will change her life.

One day, her prayers are answered in the most unexpected way when her father asks her to telephone Tamara to explain that urgent business has caused him to cancel his appointment. To satisfy her curiosity about Tamara, Hélène decides to take advantage of the opportunity offered by her father and deliver his message in person. And so she visits Tamara, who lives in a disreputable neighborhood near the waterfront in an apartment house that was formerly a brothel. As she approaches the building, Hélène is thrilled by its poetry and mystery, but when she meets Tamara her joy is tempered by a nameless fear, which is caused, we later discover, by an unrecognized sexual attraction. In Tamara's apartment Hélène enters into a lesbian relationship with her father's mistress, in which she finds not only physical pleasure, but also a role model and the love of an older woman, both of which had been denied her by her mother's death.

Hélène's joy is threatened when people begin to comment on her frequent appearances in Tamara's disreputable neighborhood. Tamara tells her that she must tell her father that she has been visiting her to explain her presence in the area. When Hélène is unable to summon up sufficient courage to do as Tamara orders, Tamara slaps her and refuses to see her again. When she finally begs Tamara's forgiveness on her knees, their relationship changes; it becomes more passionate, more tempestuous, and also more perverted, with tones of sadomasochism. Tamara delights in proving her strength and power over Hélène, while the young girl acknowledges that she takes pleasure in complete submission. Tamara's former (and part-time current) lover, Max Vilar, tells Hélène that her identity, indeed her very survival, depend on separation from Tamara. Tamara, like Anne in *Bonjour Tristesse,* embodies an idealized mother figure with whom the heroine wants to merge, but from whom she must separate in order to affirm her own individuality and realize the possibilities of adult womanhood.

It is only when Tamara cruelly subjects Hélène to the degrading milieu of a lesbian bar that she realizes that her relationship with Tamara might be considered shameful. She finally breaks with the older woman when Tamara announces that she is marrying Hélène's father because she is thirty-six years old and needs stability and security. Her confession shows Hélène that Tamara is no different from the other women she knows and scorns; like them she has also been playing a role. Tamara was forced by circumstances to be a liberated woman and is not really interested in independence; she has only been waiting for an opportunity to settle down. Hélène remarks sadly: "On that face which I had loved . . . had just been painted that odious humility of beggars and beaten women, that cowardice of irresponsible people, that same weakness I had hated in myself and that she had taught me to hate. . . . I no longer admired her."[20] Hélène is disgusted to learn that the strength and honesty she had admired in Tamara were merely a sham, and that she is really a "weak creature who needs a man . . . who begs for his protection."[21] Her relationship with the older woman had seemed normal to her precisely because of Tamara's virile energy and her independence from the constraints of society. According to Mallet-Joris, however, the lesbian relationship in this story of a fallen idol is less important than the relationship between an adolescent and an adult, between a psychologically immature person and a mature individual.[22] The young girl had fashioned a myth around a person who was, in reality, a weak and unstable individual. *The Illusionist,* then, is a most unusual treatment of the subject of so many first novels—the coming of age of the protagonist. Although Hélène is once again alone in the final scene of the novel, she has grown and now accepts her loneliness, for she has chosen it by refusing to compromise her ideals.

The Red Room, a sequel to *The Illusionist,* is another novel of psychological analysis as well as a continuation of the education of Hélène Noris. The young girl has changed; Tamara's betrayal taught her to steel herself against "vulnerable emotions [and] degrading sub-missiveness."[23] To complete her sexual education, and also to take revenge on her stepmother, Hélène decides to take Tamara's thirty-five-year-old admirer as her lover. What surprises Hélène is that Jean, despite his wealth and success, seems as fearful as she of being duped and as intent as she on dictating the terms of their relationship. Despite her resolve to avoid emotional subservience, Hélène does fall in love with Jean, a love that makes her vulnerable. Jean, too, has fallen in love. To prove to himself that he is still in control, he has a few fleeting love affairs, thereby provoking Hélène to do the same. Because each is intent on remaining dominant, each is unable to accept the fact that one must cultivate trust and compassion to build a true love. The destructive quality of their love stems from the need both have to assume the male role as it is defined by society. Jean leaves, and Hélène is once again alone, but this time her solitude does not mark a moral victory, as it did in *The Illusionist.* It now signals a defeat, for she has sacrificed her true self to her fictive persona. At the end of the first novel, Hélène is freed of false illusions and is ready for new experiences; at the end of *The Red Room,* she sees the vanity of all her actions. Hélène's defeat demonstrates the danger of lying to others and to oneself, a leitmotiv of Mallet-Joris's work.

In 1956 Mallet-Joris published a collection of two novellas and ten short stories, *Cordélia (Cordelia and Other Stories),* that serve as a transition between the author's first two novels and her other works. It is here that the first-person narration with a single point of view becomes the third-person narration with multiple points of view that the author uses in all subsequent works. The basic themes of the first two novels are found in the stories, particularly that of the weak male and the strong female—a theme common to feminist literature—and are repeated with many variations in subsequent novels. While it is the search for truth that motivates the behavior of her heroines, the men in Mallet-Joris's work are, for the most part, inauthentic beings who have directed their efforts toward creating an image of themselves that will free them from the existentialist imperative to create their own essence. There is a sharp contrast between what they pretend to be and what they are. The danger of such behavior is made manifest in *Les mensonges (House of Lies)*, 1956, and *L'Empire céleste (Café Celeste)*, 1958, where the male protagonists find ultimately that the personas they have created have destroyed their true being, leaving nothing in its stead.

House of Lies has been called a Balzacian novel because of its depiction of the closed-in atmosphere of family life and the family conflicts provoked by money. The protagonist, Klaes van Baarnheim, sacrificing all to his need for power, can be compared to Goriot, Grandet, or any of Balzac's monomaniacs driven by a single passion. Klaes is a violent, domineering man who has made a fortune as a brewer and who rules despotically over relatives and employees. Only one person has ever refused to obey Klaes, Elsa, a former mistress and the mother of his illegitimate daughter Alberte, whom he took into his home on his fiftieth birthday. Elsa's flamboyance and her constant complaints about Klaes disturb him, and he tries to make her leave town. But neither his bribes nor his threats can make her leave the only home she has known for most of her life. Klaes feels threatened by her refusal and his determination to rid himself of her becomes an obsession; he decides that if money will not sway Elsa, her daughter will.

Alberte agrees to help Klaes send Elsa away. Strangely, she is not angry with him for having abandoned her and her mother. Instead, she admires the cleanliness and order of his life as well as his imperious, domineering nature. It is against Elsa that Alberte's anger is directed; Elsa's alcoholism and mythomania have always humiliated her daughter. Klaes tricks Alberte into signing a paper to put Elsa into a psychiatric hospital. When she goes there to visit her mother, she is shocked by the change that has taken place in her. Instead of a drunken, extravagantly neurotic woman, she finds an empty shell, a pathetic creature emptied of illusions and overcome with shame. She understands that her constant refusal to permit Elsa to see reflected in her daughter's eyes the complaisant image she has created of herself is as hostile an act as Elsa's refusal to be a flattering mirror for Klaes. For Mallet-Joris, as for Sartre, the one who refuses to reflect a desired image becomes the enemy.

Although Klaes has succeeded in freeing himself of Elsa, he knows that Alberte still escapes his domination. When he has a stroke and realizes that he is dying, he determines to be master of his own death, something his entourage had tried to deny him by hiding the truth about his condition. He insists that "if he must die at least let his death belong to him."[24] For this to happen, he must finally control Alberte, the only one who has ever escaped him. He will transform her into a grasping, acquisitive bourgeoise in his own image. He, therefore, sends for his notary and draws up papers recognizing her as his sole heir. But Alberte refuses his inheritance; like her mother she will not be bought. Like Hélène, too, she must determine her own destiny and not be trapped in the lies of others. Without understanding why—for Alberte is not a lucid, introspective person—she feels instinctively that accepting the inheritance would also entail accepting the lies that oppressed her in Klaes's home where everything was false. Furthermore, she feels a certain remorse at having permitted her mother to be locked up and deprived of the illusions that had enabled her to survive. Alberte's choice of freedom over social position and wealth affirms that there are values in life, such as human dignity and integrity, that justify existence.

Café Celeste, like *House of Lies,* centers on the divorce between reality and illusions as well as on the concomitant theme of the destructive power of self-delusion. Here, however, Mallet-Joris leaves the smaller family unit of the previous work for a larger, more diversified group, co-owners of a cooperative apartment house on the Rue d'Odessa in Paris. The unifying element within the apartment house, which is designed to function in the manner of a grand hotel or a "ship of fools," is a Greek restaurant, named l'Empire céleste, on the ground floor of the building. The co-proprietors meet in the restaurant on Monday evenings, ostensibly to discuss matters pertaining to the management of the building. In truth, the meetings are social gatherings that bring the tenants together to escape their loneliness.

The protagonist of the novel, Stéphane Morani, is a weak, forty-five-year-old tubercular, third-rate musician who plays the piano in a rundown saloon. There he is admired uncritically by the middle-aged ladies who come to hear him and who still find him handsome. Stéphane has made Martine, another tenant in the building, his platonic confidante. He confides in her with a desperate need that he never dared to satisfy before because he was secretly afraid of being judged. Martine's ugliness and her lack of charm are for him a guarantee; she, herself, has too much to fear from his judgment to become dangerous. But an even more reliable confidante than Martine is his diary, in which he transforms himself daily from a middle-aged failure into a gifted artist who has sacrificed his life through altruism. The diary has become his salvation; it wraps him in a protective cover and provides an image that flatters and deceives. It is a means for him to create a persona that he finds more admirable than his real self. It has even enabled him to convince himself that he married his wife, Louise, a former prostitute, to save an unfortunate creature. In truth, he married her because he felt that her background provided assurance that she would never presume to judge him. But she does judge him; she sees behind his mask and deprives him of his comforting illusions. She also refuses to play the role of repentant whore, grateful to Stéphane for having taken her out of the gutter. Louise's honesty and her indifference to outside opinion have alienated her from the other apartment owners, and they are relieved that she does not attend their Monday night meetings. For her part, Louise cannot understand why they, like Stéphane, complicate their lives unnecessarily by worrying about the proper pose to adopt, instead of giving themselves over to the simple business of living.

Martine discovers that Louise is having an affair. Spurred on by Martine, the tenants force Stéphane to conform to his noble image by leaving his adulterous wife. He is too weak to resist their pressure. Were he to repudiate his noble persona by admitting that he depends on Louise and is indifferent to her infidelity provided that she care for him, he would force the others to look within themselves and question their own behavior. His departure will permit them to continue to wear their masks and believe in the roles they play. And so Stéphane goes off alone wondering how he will be able to go on living without the words and attitudes that had ruled his life. He discovers, like Dostoevski's double, that his creation has destroyed the real Stéphane, that without his fictive persona he simply does not exist. Stéphane's destruction is Martine's liberation; she has learned that she must not try to be Stéphane's Antigone but must seek her own identity.

Mallet-Joris abandons the weak male, and returns to her strong prototypical heroine in two historical fictional works, *Les personnages (The Favorite)*, 1961, and *Trois âges de la nuit (The Witches)*, 1968, and two biographical works, *Marie Mancini, le premier amour de Louis XIV (The Uncompromising Heart),* 1964, and *Jeanne Guyon* (1978). The author calls these women *personnes* (authentic beings), because they remain true to their inner selves, and contrasts them with those she refers to as *personnages* (personae), those who hide behind masks and play prescribed roles. Each of the heroines revolts against the hypocrisy and constraints of society and is conspired against and attacked on all sides by hostile forces. Three of the heroines are incarcerated, in either a prison or a convent, one is made prisoner of a tortured psyche, and two are burned at the stake. In three of the works, the author's denunciation of the plight of the heroine becomes a sweeping indictment of the condition of women in general, expressing a feminist bias that continues to grow in importance in her novels. Of particular note in these works is the historical lesson they provide of misogyny and persecution of women.

The plot line of *The Favorite* corresponds for the most part with historical events. Cardinal Richelieu, concerned with the influence of the mistress of Louis XIII, Louise de La Fayette, enlisted the aid of a Dominican priest to persuade Louise to become a nun. Louise did eventually enter a convent where the king continued to visit her regularly. It is within this historical context that Mallet-Joris sets the psychological and spiritual drama of a woman who is led little by little, almost without her realizing it, to God. The spiritual journey of the protagonist parallels in many ways the one taken by the author toward her own religious conversion. Mallet-Joris expresses through Louise de La Fayette her own conviction that God does not represent a refuge or a flight from life, but a constant effort and a constant choice.

The Witches is a collection of tales of sorcery. The "trois âges," or three ages, of the French title refer to crucial periods in the lives of three women: a young adolescent, Anne de Chantraine, and a mature woman, Jeanne Harvilliers, who are burned at the stake, and a wealthy young widow, Elizabeth de Ranfaing, who is exorcized and freed of her demons. Elizabeth then goes on to found a religious order for the rehabilitation of prostitutes, choosing thereby but another outlet permitted to woman. For the woman of Elizabeth's time, piety liberated as much as witchcraft; after the witch and the possessed woman came the devout woman.

The tales are fictionalized treatments of three case histories Mallet-Joris chose from among the accounts of witchcraft she studied. It is significant that the great epidemic of witchcraft took place during the

Renaissance as well as during the seventeenth century, the Age of
Reason. This contradicts the widely held view that witchcraft was a
phenomenon of the Middle Ages, which the learning of the Renaissance
gradually undermined. On the contrary, it was during this period of
enlightenment, when the Church was less secure, that persecution was
widespread. Witchcraft was considered by the Church to be one of a
number of heresies, which also included Protestantism. Yet the case
against witches was not prompted solely by the Church's struggle against
heresy; it also had its roots in the misery and ignorance of the people.
Witches were believed to harm people, animals, and crops, afflicting
them with sickness, sterility, and storms. All of these acts, called *maleficia,*
were at the root of the villagers' hostility to the witch, who served to
deflect rural discontent during times of poverty, sickness, or natural
calamity. The epidemics of so-called witchcraft corresponded in general
to the geographical areas where there had been epidemics, famines, or
other forms of public misfortune. But, and this is emphasized by Mallet-
Joris, the main stimulus for the persecution of witches was the pervasive
misogyny that existed both in village life and in the Church. The
definitive work on witchcraft, *Malleus Maleficarum (The Hammer of the
Witches),* produced by the Church in 1486, asked: "Why is it that
women are chiefly addicted to evil superstitions? Their feebler capacity
is adduced, as well as their debased history . . . and lower nature."[25]

While the witch was most often poor and socially oppressed, the
woman possessed by the devil was generally either a nun without a
calling or a woman from a bourgeois, or even a noble, family who
was stifled emotionally. The possessed woman was a transitional figure
between the witch and her subsequent incarnation as the mentally ill
or hysterical woman; although she harbored the devil, she did so against
her will. But both the witch and the woman possessed were embodiments
of two contradictory misogynistic themes. On the one hand, it was held
that witches illustrated the maleficence and power of women, despite
the fact that the wretched creatures invariably wound up burned at the
stake. On the other hand, the possessed woman was supposed to
demonstrate the weakness of her sex by her inability to rid herself of
the demons who forced her to do their bidding.

Like her historical novels, Mallet-Joris's biography of the seventeenth-
century mystic and writer Jeanne Guyon was motivated by a feminist
idée fixe. She was determined to tell the true story about Jeanne Guyon
and the "horrible" Bishop Bossuet, and to show how a virtuous woman,
full of good intentions, albeit a bit eccentric and headstrong, was vilified

and ridiculed because she would not conform to what the Church and the society of her time considered her role as a woman.[26] While Jeanne Guyon did go beyond some of the bounds set for women by writing theological works and voicing her own opinions, she also embodied the traditional feminine qualities of passivity, self-sacrifice, anti-intellectualism, submissiveness, total obedience, and childlike innocence. She never questioned the social position of women but accepted it as natural and normal. She committed no heresy, nor was she ever convicted of heresy, although during the period in which she lived the hunt for heretics had replaced the witch hunt of the preceding era. According to Mallet-Joris, the reasons for her persecution lay elsewhere. Her first mistake was her refusal to identify with or seek the support of any group. Also, her belief that everything that took place on earth was insignificant, absurd, and unimportant called into question the whole gamut of worldly values, while her espousal of inner liberty was of great concern to theologians. But, Mallet-Joris affirms, the decisive weapon in her enemy's hands was always the fact that she was a woman; misogyny was at the root of her persecution.

Mallet-Joris first establishes the climate for the pervasive misogyny of the period. The traditional image of and attitude toward women had remained unchanged in the seventeenth century. Trials for witchcraft and exorcisms were common in France until the second half of the century, when an ordinance was passed moderating the excessive zeal of certain magistrates. It was then that the concept of witchcraft gave way, little by little, to the idea of mental illness—the hysterical woman supplanting the witch with the debatable advantage of incurring scorn rather than hatred. No one, in truth, envisaged changing the status of women. Montaigne's literary heir, Mademoiselle de Gournay, wrote a work in 1622, *L'Egalité des hommes et des femmes (Equality of Men and Women),* which was considered pure and simple folly by some and a witty paradox by others. "How fortunate you are, reader," she said, "if you are not a member of that sex to which all good things are forbidden . . . to which ignorance, playing the fool, and serving are proposed as sovereign virtues and as the sole source of happiness."[27]

Women who were educated were those who had a certain independence, either aristocrats or wealthy bourgeoises, with time, proper connections, a tolerant husband or family, sometimes unmarried, but most often enjoying the privileged status of widowhood. Even these women had to cope with the prejudiced notion that an educated woman was one who was seeking to evade her responsibilities. Two women of the

seventeenth century—Madeleine de Scudéry and Ninon de Lenclos—
did manage to live independent lives without incurring the disapproval
of society; but they did so by frankly adopting socially acceptable
personas: the old maid and the courtesan. Unlike these women, Jeanne
Guyon did not conform to an accepted type, but broke with all
conventional stereotypes. This led to her persecution. She began to write
in order to convey her mystical experiences to others. Despite departures
from orthodoxy, it was not what she wrote, according to Mallet-Joris,
but the fact that she, a woman, had the temerity to write on religious
matters, that led to Jeanne's persecution. By writing, Madame Guyon
"acted with a scorn for public opinion and for her own interests that
bordered on provocation."[28] It was her insistence on living in accordance
with her beliefs, no matter what the consequences, that makes Jeanne
Guyon spiritually akin to the author's other heroines.

Françoise Mallet-Joris found in Jeanne Guyon's quest for divine grace
echoes of her own search for that which gives a meaning and value to
life. It was the author's own search for an absolute that motivates most
of her protagonists. She explained that "it is only in the novel that
this double plane of truth—the truth of my characters and the struggle
that they carry on for and against it, and this rapport between them
and me, this rapport between their truth and mine—can be embodied
without difficulty" (*Lettre*, 158). It is for this reason that Mallet-Joris
centered a series of novels around metaphysical disquiet and the search
for an absolute.

Les signes et les prodiges (Signs and Wonders), 1966, is the story of
an aborted spiritual quest. The protagonist, Nicolas Leclusier, thirsts for
God but is unable to reconcile an omnipotent God with the evil he
sees everywhere in the world. Unlike Mallet-Joris, who counsels "consent
without renunciation" (*Lettre*, 136)—a consent that sets her apart from
the other novelists discussed in this work—and who has opted for the
struggle of life, he chooses the escape offered by death. The Catholic
critic Louis Barjon finds quite logical Mallet-Joris's treatment of a
spiritual journey that ends so differently from her own. He maintains
that her denunciation of the illusions of a faith that depends entirely
on external proofs invites the reader to reflect on the nature of true
faith. He also points out that Nicolas's search for proof of God's
existence in signs, and then proof of his nonexistence in the falsity of
signs, is motivated only by a desire to appease an unbearable inner
anguish. In so doing, he is seeking not truth, but only himself.[29] Barjon's
contention is borne out by the author's assertion that she does not like

suicides. "It seems to me that there is more grandeur in looking at oneself as one is, than in running away from oneself by jumping out of a window. More grandeur in assuming one's suffering, the sterility of one's creative genius, than in fleeing it" (*Lettre,* 121–22).

Nicolas Leclusier kills himself because he is unable to bear the burden of true faith, which requires acceptance of the existence of evil in the world. Yet, despite his failure, Mallet-Joris sympathizes with him because she admires the spiritual malaise that motivated his quest for the absolute. A person who has failed, she writes, "is a person who has attempted something, and has not been able to find a place in society. Inner wealth, courage, none of that is taken into consideration in our society which pretends to be cultured, idealistic, and Christian. And that is why it is not surprising that saris, gurus, and Yoga meditation hold such fascination for an ardent generation of young people, disgusted with our society."[30]

Dickie-Roi (1979) is the story of the efforts of two groups of young people who dream of beauty, love, and communion to transcend the imperfections and finitude of life. Each group is centered around a charismatic leader: Dickie-Roi (né Frédéric Roy), a pop singer, is idolized by his fans, while "Father" Paul, an enigmatic, rather sinister guru, holds in thrall the members of his religious sect, Végétation. Their search for an absolute makes both the fans and the disciples the spiritual counterparts of Mallet-Joris's other characters. Despite this spiritual affinity, *Dickie-Roi* represents a substantial departure from the author's other works because it is rooted in contemporary mass culture and language.

The novel is also the bildungsroman of Pauline, one of the rock star's fans, who follows his tour through southern France. The theme of her passage from childhood to maturity parallels the novel's principal themes of existential anguish and of the search for an absolute. Like Hélène in *The Illusionist* and *The Red Room,* despite the differences between them of class and education, Pauline goes abruptly from the childhood world of excess and illusions to the adult world of compromise and surrender of principles, a world she refuses to accept.[31] Despite the fact that the novel ends with Pauline on her way to join a religious sect to continue her journey toward self-discovery, this conclusion, according to the author, is not pessimistic. For Mallet-Joris, it is the search that is important, not the way in which it is conducted, for it implies an optimistic belief in the value of striving to go beyond everyday reality.

While the metaphysical disquiet and search for an absolute of Mallet-Joris's later works reappear in *Allegra* (1976) they are accompanied by the search for identity that was characteristic of the heroine of her early novels. In this novel, however, it is not only the heroine but all women who are victims, forced to play assigned roles in a male-dominated society. The author proposes here that, whether women accept or refuse their role, they are destined to lose, because they have been trained to lose, and because they are torn by "an inner duality . . . the shame of being a woman and the need both to disguise it and flaunt it at the same time."[32] In this novel, Mallet-Joris returns to the emancipatory, amoral theme of her early novels, but she goes beyond the revolt of the heroine to show the debasement of all women.

Despite the fact that he is one of the peripheral characters in this novel about women, Dr. Hjalmar Svenson concentrates in his person the anguish that precipitated Nicolas's suicide in *Signs and Wonders*. Dr. Svenson's character and his sublimated angst explain the nature of his third daughter, Allegra. She is as different as he from the other members of the Corsican clan into which he married, which is, in a certain sense, a clan of women. It is a family in which the women predominate, where they have more influence and personality than the husbands, uncles, and fathers. And yet, it is a traditional, conservative family, an unusual matriarchy in which the women are completely devoted to the men—to whom they are generally superior—but in which they are reduced to an inferior status. They themselves are responsible, however, because they have humbled themselves voluntarily and proudly.

The clan is headed by a robust, octogenarian grandmother who believes that women are born to toil, suffer, and serve men. Her daughter Vanina is an elegant brunette, "endowed with that false southern warmth and effusiveness which often hide a complete absence of imagination" (8). Vanina's older daughter, Paule, who is both beautiful and intelligent, has escaped the stifling influence of the family by becoming a career woman. What she does not realize is that the health and beauty institute she has created closely resembles her family; it is also a "community of women functioning for women which, just like the world of the bourgeois housewife, excludes from morning until evening sons, husbands, lovers, all of whom remain 'outside'" (16). While the institute may be a feminine refuge, it is in truth an obligation forced upon women who are made to feel guilty if they ignore the fact that "beauty is a weapon and a duty" (25). According to contemporary mythology, disseminated by women's magazines and romantic novels, the responsibility for the loss of a husband or a lover devolves upon the woman who has neglected her body.

The Svenson's middle daughter, Josée, plays to perfection the role of wife and mother with the intelligence and discretion that are necessary to hide the fact that she knows she is superior to her husband, a doctor of Corsican origin. Like Josée, Allegra, the youngest daughter, has never given anyone cause for concern. With her "unalterable smile" (13) she is almost annoyingly banal, so banal that her family has never felt it necessary to pay attention to her. She always conformed easily to what was asked of her and even permitted her family to select her husband, plan their honeymoon trip to Corsica and Italy, and choose their studio apartment. Allegra is as dutiful a wife as she was a daughter, always acting "as a woman should act, diligently, full of good will, not unhappy . . . knowing admirably, knowing hereditarily . . . how to act with a man, silent when he is drunk or in a bad mood, ready to serve warm meals, understanding smiles, open-eyed admiration, even sighs during mealtimes at the times designated for smiles, a timetable set up for all eternity" (202). Finally, her learned responses lead her husband Jean-Philippe to recognize the source of a certain malaise he has felt underlying his contentment; his relationship with Allegra is governed by a code, subject to a certain law. She seems to move with ease within these convenient conventions, which permit her, while seeming to be totally present, to be totally absent. He realizes that Allegra only loves him as she would have loved anyone else she married, because "one loves one's husband when one has been raised as Allegra was raised" (180).

When Jean-Philippe sees her so detached, he feels that she is living a life different from his, and, indeed, he is not mistaken. Allegra has been withholding a part of herself. She is having an adventure that will turn into a marvelous passion; Jean-Philippe is sharing her love with a mute four-year-old Arab boy. The child plays alone in the courtyard of their building and, each day, he waits for Allegra to return from work while, each day, she becomes more and more attached to him. He is so different from the others, who want her to act in certain ways. She finds him restful because all he asks is a loving presence. The relief she feels only when she is with the child, for whom she need only be herself, explains the secret behind Allegra's immutable smile and docility; they had hidden a revolt of which even she had been unaware. Her love for and understanding of the child lead her to self-knowledge; she realizes that by hiding behind the most conventional female stereotype, she had perpetrated for years the most audacious fraud in the world. No one had noticed it, she no more than the others—except for a slight malaise—until the child came along. Observing him, she discovered her own revolt, "she felt guilty about it; she became a woman" (212–13).

Ironically, it is Paule, the rebel, who conforms completely to archetypical female roles, the first of which is that of the woman who has chosen between a career and marriage and children, and whose loneliness is the price she must pay for her choice. Then, she becomes the lover of Jean-Philippe, who is desperate because he is unable to penetrate behind Allegra's smiling, loving facade. Again, Paule plays a prescribed role, that of the lonely career woman who must content herself with the husband of another. By following the script carefully, Paule does not have to ask herself any questions or feel any responsibility for her actions.

It is not long before Vanina finds out about the affair and tells them it must end. She also tells Jean-Philippe that he must bind Allegra to him by giving her the child that will transform her into a woman. Even as she says this, Vanina knows that she is betraying her daughter, but she rationalizes her action by the thought that Allegra had been the first to betray the clan by loving a child who was not hers. Her own child, Vanina hopes, will make Allegra forget the outsider and play her prescribed role of wife and mother. When Allegra discovers that she is pregnant, for Jean-Philippe has heeded his mother-in-law's advice, she decides to abort the child. Just as Alberte (*House of Lies*) refuses the inheritance she has not chosen, so does Allegra refuse a pregnancy she has not chosen. She knows now that she must make all decisions concerning her life, including whether to have her own child and whether to love someone else's. Creating herself according to her own image, indifferent to everything but the counsel of her heart, Allegra visits a quack doctor. When she returns from the botched operation, she slowly bleeds to death.

In the epilogue, we learn that Allegra's memory has been obliterated by the clan, horrified by the disgrace of her death, and that Paule has married Jean-Philippe and given up her business, which her husband now heads, to care for their own children. She conforms perfectly to the rules of a society in which men can combine love and work as two facets of "normal" lives, but women must subordinate their love and work to male priorities.

Françoise Mallet-Joris's portrayal of male and female characters is reminiscent of Colette's. Her females are strong, lucid individuals in search of authenticity, while the males are weak, inauthentic beings who abdicate all responsibility for their lives (Stéphane in *Café Celeste*), commit suicide (Nicolas in *Signs and Wonders*), retreat into alcoholism (Dr. Svenson in *Allegra*), or fit into the mold of dynamic, young businessman/adulterous husband (Jean-Philippe in *Allegra*). In her work, the author has given the historical and cultural background for the mistreatment of women in a society that relegated them to the role of witch, then of woman possessed, and finally to that of the hysterical woman—reinforced later in Freudian myth—all of which served to justify existing discrimination and persecution.

It is thus surprising that Mallet-Joris's work is excluded from all considerations of feminist literature. This may be due to her religious beliefs, which postulate an acceptance of misery and suffering as part of the order of the world, even while one struggles against it. But it is not only her belief in God and in an ordered universe that set her apart. It may also be because her novels remain within the framework of the traditional French novel with its notions of normative human behavior, causality, and coherent chronology. Because Mallet-Joris believes that the most important element in any novel is the story, her plots are well constructed. She tells her stories as a sequence of events in a linear construction that proceeds from well-explained causes to well-determined results, satisfying in this manner a need for understanding and reflecting what has been traditionally a masculine need for a rational organization of the world.

Claire Etcherelli

Claire Etcherelli was born in 1934 within just a few years of both Françoise Mallet-Joris and Françoise Sagan but under very different circumstances. She was born in Bordeaux to a working-class family. Her father was killed by the Germans during World War II and as a result she received a scholarship that permitted her to continue her studies for a short time. She then went to Paris and worked on an automobile assembly line for two years, an experience that was to be the source of her first novel *Elise ou la vraie vie* (Elise and real life), which won the Prix Fémina in 1967. This novel is the prototype of her other two novels, which Etcherelli describes as stories of women who are enriched and strengthened by painful experience.[33]

When the novel opens, Elise, the narrator, is about to leave Paris where for nine months she has experienced "real life": dehumanizing work on an automobile assembly line; love and the loss of love to racism; sexism and its link with racism; and, finally, desperate loss, the death of her beloved brother, Lucien. The "real life" Elise found in Paris was the antithesis of the one she and her brother had imagined during their youth of provincial privation and isolation when they promised one another: "One day, we will experience real life. . . . We'll do everything we want to do . . . we'll realize our dreams . . . we will join those who feel as we do. Our minds have already awakened and moved ahead, our bodies will soon follow."[34] During the nine months in Paris, a new Elise is born in suffering and in anger, one who finally understands the true nature of "real life."

As Elise awaits the arrival of her dead brother's former lover Anna, who will now occupy the room she is leaving, she thinks back on her political, social, and sentimental education. When they were children, the orphaned Elise and her younger brother, Lucien, were taken in by their grandmother who supported the three of them by working as a domestic. Dreaming of sacrificing herself for her brother so that he would lack for nothing, Elise left school to work at the age of sixteen. She neither questioned her life nor understood that there could be anything different, until she saw her brother skating one day, floating free on the ice. "I could almost feel his happiness, this freedom in the fog, the sweetness of solitude, without responsibilities, the sensation of liberty, the drunken joy of going straight ahead, without impediment, with eyes wet with cold, with frozen hands and burning feet" (13). But this is not the only lesson she learns from Lucien, whom she will follow as he initiates all the changes that take place in her life.

Unlike Elise, who has found a certain compensation in her self-effacing maternal role, Lucien remains dissatisfied, always seeking something different from the life he is leading, the "real life" of his imagination. Yet each of his activities in search of this "real life" is doomed to failure because each represents flight, not positive action. When Lucien decides that perhaps he will experience "real life" in marriage, he marries Marie-Louise, a young neighbor. The couple moves into the overcrowded apartment and, despite the fact that Elise sees Marie-Louise as the eternal female victim, she is unable to overcome her jealous dislike of this intruder. Marie-Louise continues to work in a factory—both after her marriage and after the birth of her daughter— to support her husband, who is a student, and their child. In the evening, Marie-Louise and Lucien sit together in their room while Lucien attempts to educate his wife who, unlike Lucien and Elise, has had virtually no education. But, just as Marie-Louise has glimpses of a universe beyond her world of ignorance and drudgery, Lucien loses interest in her. He had never really wanted to play Pygmalion to his wife's Galatea, but had only used her as a sounding board. When he resumes his relationship with a former school friend, Henri, a bourgeois intellectual, Lucien finds someone with whom to exchange ideas. As a result, Marie-Louise is left more alone than ever; she is no longer sufficiently ignorant to be oblivious to everything outside her limited sphere, but she is also not able to continue on alone. When Lucien stops trying to communicate with her, Marie-Louise often remains seated on the bed, useless, seeming to reflect without understanding. In an effort to regain his attention, she tries to ask "intelligent" questions, but Lucien ignores her. While he continues to enlarge his horizons by reading and by talking with Henri, and while Elise reads avidly, Marie-Louise is completely abandoned by them. She is also set apart from the other women in the factory who resent her having married a student. Marie-Louise, who belongs nowhere, is the incarnation of the woman who has no separate identity, but who exists only by virtue of, and for, the man she loves. She never revolts, she is never impatient or angry with the husband who neglects her. Instead, she tries to become what she thinks Lucien wants her to be, while, in truth, Lucien wants only to be free of her. When she sees that she is more and more abandoned, she gives up trying to bridge the intellectual gap between them and attempts instead to correspond to the ideal "feminine" image she sees reflected in women's magazines. She spends what little money she has on makeup and junk jewelry. Marie-Louise is the quintessential woman exploited from every point of view. She is nothing more than a beast of burden and, as long as she is able to work, her husband lets her support him, even after he becomes involved with another woman. When Marie-Louise can no longer work, he abandons her. When Lucien leaves, he even steals their baby's monthly subsidy. Lucien's abominable behavior is prompted by his desire to escape from despair and to survive at any price.

When Lucien's lover, Anna, and his friend, Henri, leave for Paris, Lucien follows them, again looking for something else, for a way to escape and find the "real life" marriage has not offered. But the real life he finds in Paris is work on an automobile assembly line. He invites Elise to share this life which he romanticizes in his letters: "I have been obliged for financial reasons to accept a difficult, but extremely exciting job. I am going to join real fighters to share the inhuman life of factory workers. In the midst of Bretons, Algerians, exiled Poles, I am going to establish contact with the only reality that is on the move. And when I've finished the day's work in the factory, I will take up my papers, my notebooks, for, Elise, old girl, I will bear witness for those who cannot do so themselves" (58–59). But he is too dehumanized by this work to do anything but seek oblivion in sleep whenever he is not working. It is only the bourgeois, here represented by Henri, who has the leisure to testify about something never directly experienced. Ironically, Lucien, although he shares their struggle, is alienated from the other members of the proletariat because he is privileged by reason of his race, sex, and education.

Elise responds to Lucien's call, as always, and joins him in Paris. She, too, finds work on an automobile assembly line, where she experiences all of the horrors of real life—exploitation, racism, and sexism—and discovers that they are inextricably bound together. When she first appears at work, she is taken in hand with paternalistic concern by a French inspector whose dislike of the Algerian workers even outweighs his prejudice against women. He makes sure to inform Elise of the separation between the two national groups. "We have to stick together" (86), he informs her. Elise understands that these divisions are carefully nurtured to divide the workers and preclude a united protest against the degrading, dehumanizing conditions of their lives.

The women who work in the factory make superhuman efforts to remain "presentable," paying attention to their hair and makeup despite their exhausting ten hours on the assembly line. Like Marie-Louise, they are trying to conform to the female images in the popular magazines. "There was something there that went beyond coquetry: a display, an instinctive defense against work that finally divested you of all human qualities" (134–35). In order not to succumb completely, not to abdicate totally all human dignity, they need to be considered sexually desirable by men. Sexual desire is essential for their self-image; I am desirable, therefore I exist. They are thus in a traditional double bind, for they must arouse desire to prove that they are alive, but they must never satisfy it, or else run the risk of being categorized as whores. Thus, a woman who goes out with an Arab or any other foreign worker immediately forfeits the validation she has derived from her sex appeal. That is why Elise fears that her liaison with an Algerian coworker Arezki will be discovered and cause her to be excluded from the group.

Her fear, the fears of her coworkers, and of the other women she encounters all reveal the same thing: the most impoverished and miserable person can only assert his or her "humanity" by conforming to a ready-made model. This need to conform is an absolute requirement which does not bring any human warmth, but only a vague existence on the social level, one in which the struggle for human survival never leads to solidarity or personal happiness and in which women are the most alienated. They are always perceived as objects (at best erotic, in general reproductive). Since they are most subject to constant tension, they are also the most apt to grasp at any opportunity for childish pleasure.[35]

Just as the women take pains with their appearance so that they will receive the attention that proves that they exist, so too do the Algerian workers construct their own defenses. They refuse to wear overalls and shout and whistle when women pass in order to show that they are men, and that, despite the hatred they encounter and their dehumanizing work, they have remained capable of appreciating women. Their appreciation, however, like that of their French counterparts, is limited to the female as a sexual object. Etcherelli tells us here that no matter how far down on the social and economic scale the male may find himself, there is always someone whom he objectifies and to whom he feels superior—the female.

Elise loses the two men she loves—one to racism, the other to its inevitable counterpart, sexism. Arezki is caught up in a racist roundup and disappears, probably deported to Algeria. Elise cannot learn his whereabouts and will never see him again. And she loses her brother to sexism, for Lucien dies in an attempt to measure up to society's image of what a "real man" should be. His last gesture is as meaningless as all the others in his life—he takes the motorbike of one of the employees at the tuberculosis sanatorium, to which he has been sent, in order to attend a workers' demonstration. He rides too quickly on a slick road at night without lights, because he feels that his presence is necessary "to bear witness for those who cannot do so themselves." This misconception conforms to the deceptive image he has of himself, the image of the dynamic male fostered by society. Instead of a champion of the workers, he becomes just another accident victim.

The men disappear, but Elise survives. Her bildungsroman tells of her discovery of the degradation of human beings by poverty, sexism, and racism. At the end of the novel, she leaves Paris to return home where she will wait, with the patience that has always been necessary for female survival, to convalesce from the sickness born of real life.

Underneath the sadness and suffering "inevitable hope will stand fast. I do not know from where the wind will come that will stir it up. I do not know in what direction it will drive me. I feel it. . . . Indistinct, shapeless, impalpable, but present. I am now closed up within myself, but I will not die of it" (276). Elise will wait until she, unlike Lucien, will be strong enough to bear witness for those who suffer, even for Marie-Louise whose grief, she exclaims, "unjustly fills me with horror. She is a victim and I detest her [for it]" (274).

In *A propos de Clémence* (Concerning Clémence, 1971) we are once again in the world of poverty seen in Etcherelli's first novel. While the setting here is different, the misery is not; it is not the world of the Renault automobile assembly line, but that of "la Campa," a shantytown on the outskirts of civilization, "surrounded by a sort of trench, combination sewer and dumping ground . . . [made up of] shacks and sheds, planks and sheet metal, trucks without wheels, broken down buses. Without roads. Bumps and holes, bushes strangled by cut barbed wire, only one mutilated tree [with] its lower branches cut off. A pathetically bare wayside cross."[36] In this novel, as in *Elise ou la vraie vie,* a love affair takes place against a background of dehumanizing poverty. The male protagonist is an exiled Spanish Republican, Villaderda, "a man on his guard who places little faith in love and even less in friendship. In exile for twenty-three years. Who goes from city to country, but never his own; right up to the border and never crosses it; who lugs about in his suitcase souvenirs and papers, dossiers and socks" (53). Villaderda is loved by Gabrielle Fardoux, a patient, self-effacing, gentle, and lucid woman who functions as a witness. She, like Elise, becomes Etcherelli's alter ego, who brings to the reader a woman's perspective and insight into the lives of the victims of society.

Gabrielle is the author of "Clémence," an autobiographical novel about her love affair, which she has written in an attempt to understand why and how it ended. Passages of this novel alternate with sections describing events that take place in the present, principally meetings and conversations between Gabrielle and Simon, an actor, who has adapted her novel for the stage, and who wants to star in it. Simon seeks out Gabrielle to question her about Villaderda, in order to gain insight into the character he is going to play. He also wants to uncover the real nature of Gabrielle, whom he was prepared to love even before he met her. But his attempt to gain insight into Gabrielle's thoughts through her fictional alter ego Clémence are unsuccessful, for she hides herself from him, as she did from Villaderda, in an effort to remain separate and autonomous: "Hidden behind external appearances, I remain invisible to all. Who knows me?" (230), she writes. Simon is equally unsuccessful in his attempt to stage the play because its plot—like that of the novel—presents an exiled Spanish Republican in an ambiguous light and the city council deems it inappropriate to cast discredit on Spanish Republicans in this way. They do not want to have the truth shown; they act "as if life on the fringes of a materialistic society did not undermine a man. [As if] there were only pure, strong men who went forward with heads held high, their hair blowing in the winds of history, and smiling the dazzling smile of supermen" (225).

While Villaderda's past was heroic, his present life is pathetic: the hero of the Spanish Civil War is disillusioned, uprooted, and exhausted. Gabrielle (Clémence) loves him and tries to understand his shifts in mood, drunken binges, morbid suspicion, and brief moments of tenderness. He finds her presence both beneficial and, at the same time, unbearable, because she is witness to his impotence and failure. Because he cannot bear his present life, he can only continue to exist by denying it and living in his glorious past. Villaderda, the man who loves Gabrielle, exists only as a projection of his former heroic self. For this reason, he suddenly becomes tired of seeing Gabrielle at his side because she reminds him of the contrast between what he was and what he is, and he severs their relationship. Like Lucien, Villaderda is unable to reconcile his present existence with his dreams; like Arezki, he is unable to reconcile the revolution with a personal life that he feels betrays the revolution. All of Etcherelli's males leave behind women whose sex-defined role, which emphasizes patience and nurturing, enables them to survive.

The woman's nurturing role is underlined by the title and subject of Etcherelli's third novel, *Un arbre voyageur* (A traveling tree, 1978). The protagonist of the novel, Milie, is the "traveling tree," who moves from place to place, unable to put down roots, but sheltering and protecting all who have been cruelly forgotten by society, giving them sufficient strength to take their own lives in hand before she moves on. She herself learns in the process to achieve selfhood and take charge of her own life. Her story thus constitutes, like Elise's, an authentic working-class female bildungsroman.

The novel is divided into two parts. In the first, a woman named Anna tells of her life in Paris and her relationship with Milie, in a narrative that conveys her own self-sufficiency and Milie's passivity and dependence. Here, as in Etcherelli's other novels, there is a character named Anna who acts as a foil for the heroine. At first, it seems as though each Anna is able to take charge of her own life, but, as the novel progresses, it is the protagonist, whether Elise, Gabrielle (Clémence), or Milie who proves stronger, while Anna retreats into dependency and adopts the traditional female role, eventually able to live only through and for a man. In *Elise ou la vraie vie,* after Lucien's death, Elise understands Anna's desperate need for a man. "Her successive lovers will have been nothing more than bandages on a wound, the wound of her badly built, congenitally lame life. But, after each man, the wound gapes even more" (275).

The second part of the novel centers around Milie and her three illegitimate children in a small village where they have taken shelter after leaving Paris. A major digression in this part deals with Milie's background, against which she must struggle in order to finally achieve selfhood. The author here underlines the traditional acquiescence of the mother in transmitting the values and standards of the patriarchy. When Milie was fourteen years old, her mother,

repository of a truth transmitted by the women from whom she came, now had to pass this knowledge on to Milie. Prepare her for her destiny. Man is made to roam, woman to suffer, to come to marriage *intact,* to hold on to a man, to be wife or mother, interminable litany which marks out the painful path that must be followed without deviating. But Milie found the antidote to this at school where the revelation of love that redeems ran through expurgated texts, providing the only hope of escaping from the promised fate . . . [explaining that] the alternative to the misfortune of being born a woman, is flight through passion. Then let the beloved come. This hope compensates for the boredom of everyday life.[37]

When Milie does finally become pregnant, and when she tells her mother about it, her mother lets forth the great cry of suffering of a devastated life. "A thousand women in a long procession rising up toward her breathe these words that Milie, torn with anguish, hears. She is taking her place this evening in the chain and she finds herself in the center of a whirlwind of misfortune which has seized her and will never release her" (148). But Milie does eventually succeed in securing her own release. The story of her social and political education, which includes her exploitation as a worker in the temporary jobs she is able to find, takes place against a background of the major political events of the day, from the Algerian war to the mass student and worker strikes of May 1968. It is the revolution of 1968 that finally makes her liberation possible as she lucidly accepts the necessity for taking charge of her own destiny, rejecting "what all women know instinctively, which is that in the subconscious mind of the world in which they live, the woman without a male protector is cursed" (181). Milie, like Etcherelli's other protagonists, recognizes the inequities of the system under which she lives and refuses to be crushed by it as she struggles to assume her identity.

Chapter Six

Toward a New Language and a New Vision: Nathalie Sarraute and Marguerite Duras

Nathalie Sarraute and Marguerite Duras have redefined and extended the novel; both have been preoccupied with the problem of breaking free from the confines of traditional structured language in order to center their fictional exploration around previously unexplored mental and emotional states. Their work manifests the alienation from normal concepts of time and space that is often found in contemporary women's fiction. This alienation stems from their situation in society, since the concept of time of persons outside the mainstream inevitably deviates from ordinary chronology. Their plots, as a result, take on cyclical, rather than linear form; they do not move through time in a straight line, but seem rather to float inside an infinite sphere. The reader of their novels "has seen time cease to be that rapid current which pushes forward the action, in order to become still waters in whose depths are being evolved subtle decompositions."[1]

Nathalie Sarraute

Nathalie Sarraute (b. 1900) maintains that there is no connection between a writer's life and his or her work. She stresses particularly that the writer's sex is of no importance, because she believes that the writer must be androgynous. She has also presented most unflattering portraits of women in her works, depicting them as disagreeable, empty-headed, superficial beings, interested only in clothes, money, and marriage. When accused of a somewhat misogynistic portrayal of women, she responded, as did Simone de Beauvoir when similarly criticized, that she showed women not as they should be but as they are, playing the roles imposed upon them by society, roles they have both accepted and adopted. She adds, however, that what really interests her is not how people appear on the surface, but how they are in the depths of their being, where all people are alike and respond in a similar fashion; she is not interested in external actions, but in all that lies behind the protective shield of gestures and words.

And yet, although she has divorced all social and political preoccupations from her work and although her female characters are usually weak, superficial, and vain, Sarraute has been hailed by many contemporary female authors as a precursor because she has challenged the rational, linear construction of the traditional novel, and has rejected its conventional masculine language in an effort to *"make audible* that which agitates within us, suffers silently in the *holes of discourse,* in the unsaid, or in the non-sense."[2] Sarraute's constant goal has in fact been to express what cannot be expressed in traditional forms, to find words and images that give the reader the impression of simultaneously experiencing the same feelings as the characters. The new women novelists, in Sarraute's wake, "emphasize the aspect of feminine writing which is the most difficult to verbalize because it becomes compromised, rationalized, masculinized as it explains itself."[3] They also reflect Sarraute's changed attitude toward time and its influence on the notion of action.

Sarraute's enduring interest in "tropisms" as well as in the reader's experience of them has remained constant since her earliest work *Tropismes (Tropisms),* 1939. The concept demonstrates the new territories she charted for writing, particularly women's writing. The best definition of tropisms, the driving force in Sarraute's work, was given by the novelist herself: "I thought they might be called 'tropisms,' after the biological term, because they are purely instinctive and are caused in us by other people or by the outer world and resemble the movements called tropisms by which living organisms expand or contract under certain influences, such as light, heat, and so on. These movements glide quickly round the border of our consciousness, they compose the small, rapid, and sometimes very complex dramas concealed beneath our actions, our gestures, the words we speak, our avowed and clear feelings."[4] Sarraute felt the need to extend and change the novel so that it would convey this unexplored dimension of human psychic reality, these tropisms, or complex inner movements that underlie the most ordinary human interchanges. She wanted to convey what is barely felt, never verbalized, fleeting, never arrested, impersonal, common to all, and developing at different levels of awareness. Since these tropisms encompass experiences that can neither be formulated in thought nor captured in words, tropisms defy expression. They can no more be expressed in traditional forms than the new feminist perceptions because, Sarraute explains, "Scarcely does this formless thing, all timid and trembling, try to show its face than all powerful language, always ready to intervene so as to re-establish order—its own order—jumps on it and crushes it."[5]

While Colette, notably in *Duo,* had been able to catch at thoughts and words that hung in the air without being spoken and crushed by "all powerful language," she was still basically concerned with narrative in a way Sarraute would regard as old-fashioned. Sarraute's rejection of traditional narrative, which characterizes all her works, is first manifested in *Tropisms,* which is made up of twenty-four brief, disconnected texts— prose poems, microdramas, vignettes—their only link being the unifying concept of tropisms. They are "fugitive glimpses of people and relationships, momentarily transfixed as if by the camera's eye. Each reveals a minuscule situation, an arrested moment of time, an indistinct place inhabited by nameless people who are caught up in the web of their interdependence."[6] Each one shows some foible of human behavior as the characters move in a dull, monotonous circle of boredom and resignation.

All particularities of time and place are similarly dispensed with; Sarraute's characters exist in a chronological vacuum. The basic emotions underlying their relationships are fear and misunderstanding. To make existence bearable and to avoid the anguish of contemplating the horror of the human condition, Sarraute's characters think and speak in clichés. They are depersonalized entities from whom the writer extracts words, thoughts, and responses; they are deprived of separate identities in order to emphasize their shared humanity. Yet, Sarraute's anonymous women are very different from the anonymous "elles" in Monique Wittig's *Les guérillères,*[7] who are shown changing the world in which Sarraute's virtually interchangeable women barely function.

While *Tropisms* is a collection of separate texts unified only by the concept of tropisms, Sarraute's next three works retain the appearance of novels because they contain a rudimentary plot and a few recognizable characters. But they still lack the well-made plot, fully rounded characters, and psychological analysis of the traditional novel. Sarraute explains, in a series of essays on the novel entitled *L'Ere du soupçon (The Age of Suspicion),* 1956, why plot, setting, and character are reduced to a minimum in her novels. "The reader, indeed even the most sophisticated one, as soon as he is left to his own devices, tends to create types, he simply cannot help it."[8] Not only do readers create types, corresponding to people or characters they think they know, they also create situations, plots, or themes in order to mold the text into the stereotyped forms provided by culture and education. For this reason—just as characters and relationships are not explained to the reader by Sarraute—external events are never explicitly narrated but are divulged almost accidentally through conversation or other indirect means. The situation in question holds no particular interest for Sarraute; it is only the tropisms that it calls forth that are important.

In *Portrait d'un inconnu (Portrait of a Man Unknown)*, 1948, Sarraute undertook to uncover the many tropisms that lurk beneath the surface of a relationship instead of isolating separate tropisms as she had done before. Here an unnamed first-person narrator, motivated by psychological curiosity, observes and tries to approach an old man and his daughter to understand their nature and their complicated relationship, but the constantly changing figures refuse to be converted into consistent characters, and the narrator refuses to give them names arbitrarily. He finally realizes, as he attempts to uncover the complex inner movements that exist beneath the surface of casual, everyday exchange, that it is impossible to really know another person. One day, the narrator sees an unsigned portrait of an unknown man in a Dutch museum. His comments about the half-finished painting announce what have become the aspirations of much contemporary fiction, particularly women's fiction: "I believe that rather than the most perfectly finished works, I prefer those in which complete mastery has not been attained . . . in which one still feels, just beneath the surface, a sort of anxious groping [. . .] before the immensity . . . the elusiveness of the material world . . . that escapes us just when we think we have got hold of it . . . the goal that's never attained . . . the insufficiency of the means at our disposal."[9] The narrator's visit to the museum has revealed to him that there are no certainties about people, and he now prepares to make a new attempt at characterization, as he moves from the role of observer to that of creator. He decides to depend on his imagination to create his own characters, a more satisfactory method than first-hand observation and reliance on hearsay, and he devises more and more complicated, intricate scenarios. One day, however, he again catches sight of the father and daughter. They are in the presence of her fiancé, who is provided with a complete biographical description, including his name, profession, and physical attributes. His mere presence puts an end to the narrator's flights of imagination and he finds himself back within the context of concrete everyday life. For a brief moment, the narrator had become a creator of character, but he failed. At the end, he is ready to return to the world of external appearances, the world of the traditional novel.

Martereau (Martereau), 1953, also narrated in the first person by a character within the novel, takes up where the preceding novel left off. While *Portrait of a Man Unknown* ended with the destruction of tropisms by the introduction of a conventional character, *Martereau* starts with the seemingly well-defined and solid character of Martereau. It then subjects him to scrutiny and speculation until he is nothing more than a confusing mass of possibilities. Again, like *Portrait of a Man Unknown,* the novel contains the semblance of a plot. The narrator lives with an aunt and uncle who decide to buy a country home. In order to avoid tax complications, the uncle asks the narrator's friend Martereau to lend his name for the purchase of the house. Because Martereau fails to furnish a receipt, and because he installs himself in the house while repairs are being carried out, he is suspected of fraud and they fear that he will not consent to relinquish it when the repairs are completed. At the end of the book, they receive a letter from Martereau that sets their fears to rest, but they find it difficult to view him in the same light as before. This "plot," however, is irrelevant; it serves simply to provoke the tropisms that constitute the essence of the novel.

In *Le planétarium (The Planetarium),* 1959, the author has eliminated the first-person narrator. Now, there are many voices—none of which is readily identifiable—that relate domestic conflicts and the clashes of bourgeois and intellectual attitudes. The disappearance of a central narrator, which permits the author to enter into the consciousness of a larger number of characters, leads to the complete disintegration of characters in Sarraute's later novels. *The Planetarium* is centered around two incidents in the life of Alain Guimier: his attempt to deprive his spinster aunt Berthe of a spacious apartment so that he and his wife may move into it, and his endeavor to ingratiate himself with the writer Germaine Lemaire, who represents the traditional approach to literature. When she ridicules the trivia that provoke the tropisms on which Alain's stories (and, by extension, Sarraute's novels) are based, Alain becomes disillusioned with her and realizes that he has mistaken the false sky of a planetarium for the true sky overhead.[10] But underlying the events, which are of minor importance, are the significant, secret, hidden tropistic responses they elicit.

The ostensible plot of *Les fruits d'or (The Golden Fruits),* 1963, involves the rise and fall of a novel's reputation. Tropisms among an indeterminate number of people, which are presented from many points of view, arise in reaction to an imaginary novel called "The Golden Fruits." The novel becomes popular in Parisian literary circles. As critics and opinion makers praise the novel, these tropisms multiply, only to disappear as the novelty wears off. The novel is ultimately discredited and a new fad takes its place, leaving only a handful of discriminating readers who still read and remember the novel. In this satire, Sarraute traces the making and unmaking of a novel's image as contrasted with its intrinsic merit. She demonstrates that the genuine response to art is of an immediate and personal nature, and is thus a form of tropism. It is essentially a wordless conversation between the author and the reader and depends on the cooperation of the reader and his or her willingness to assume the same responsibilities and prerogatives as the author.

In *Entre la vie et la mort (Between Life and Death)*, 1968, Sarraute again eliminates both plot and characters, leaving only disembodied voices that are indistinguishable from one another. The novel takes the reader into the consciousness of the writer in the act of writing, examining the creative process itself rather than the critical reception of a literary work. The circular movement of the novel begins with a writer who is already successful and famous and then goes back to trace his beginnings, his career, and finally returns full circle to the successful writer of the opening scene. The writer, whose book has made him famous, explains how he works. Then a series of flashbacks show his early sensitivity to language, his mother's encouragement, the acceptance of a manuscript by a publisher, and his literary success. Yet, even as she has the writer speak about himself and the way he writes, Sarraute is not attempting to convey the technique of writing, but rather the creative impulse itself, which for her is the most interesting side of writing and which, in its incipient stage, is like a tropism.[11] The writer must be able to express this wordless event by means of words, which are the basic components of literary creation.

In *Vous les entendez? (Do You Hear Them?)*, 1972, Sarraute is still concerned with the ultimate fate of the work of art. Here, however, the novel is centered around not the creative artist but the art lover, as it examines the series of tropisms set in motion in an older man's relations with his children by a shared encounter with an art object. A father and an old friend are seated in front of a coffee table examining a pre-Columbian sculpture. The children have retired upstairs to their bedrooms. Soon, however, their laughter filters down to the men below who are discussing art. Each of their outbursts of laughter provokes tropistic responses in the father, who feels that they are making fun of his cherished piece of sculpture. The father's "reactions to his children's ambiguous laughter become the focus for a forum on aesthetic values . . . [especially as reflected in the generation gap] . . . the subjective experience of art, the dynamics of family intercourse, the creative needs of the artist, the forces of conservatism versus modernity, the struggle between submissiveness and freedom, guile and innocence, age and youth."[12]

The title of *"disent les imbéciles"* *("fools say"),* 1976, refers to the universal tendency to call people "fools" whose ideas differ from yours. In this novel, one or perhaps several narrative voices merge with and stand apart from the other anonymous voices and succession of "I's" that function as a central consciousness in ten of its thirteen chapters. The work dispenses more completely than any of the preceding novels with characterizations and a semblance of a story line; it is made up solely of dialogue spoken by characters who are disembodied voices without discernible relationships or social function. Unlike the early *Tropisms,* however, it contains a unifying theme, a concern with the free flow of ideas. Sarraute demonstrates here even more clearly than in her preceding works the danger of applying labels to people, for words are powerful enough to deprive individuals of freedom of thought or even of their sense of self; words create a cast of characters set up at a distance. The opening scene illustrates this thesis; it shows a grandmother and her grandchildren, who characterize her as a lovable old woman. One of the grandchildren refuses to go along with the others and cast his grandmother into a mold by saying, "How cute she is . . . couldn't you just eat her up?" His refusal to pin a label on her and thereby relegate her to the status of object distresses the others who feel threatened that the image they have created of their grandmother may disappear. From this opening scene to the conclusion of the novel, the author calls for freedom from the tyranny of stereotyped images and labels, a demand at the heart of the women's movement.

L'Usage de la parole (The use of words, 1980) continues to explore the use of language as a form of noncommunication. The work is composed of separate pieces, like *Tropisms,* but they are even more abstract than in the first work. Sarraute concentrates here on exploring the resonances and reverberations of certain words. What really fascinates her is the power of the word, the waves it stirs up, once pronounced, in the other person's unconscious, the impulses it sets in motion, and the behavior it determines. But in this work the tropisms are no longer triggered by catalytic objects, as in works like *The Planetarium* and *Do You Hear Them?*; for the most part, they derive solely from the speakers' language. In one chapter, however, "Et pourquoi pas" (And why not?), they reveal that Sarraute has perfected her art to the point of recording an exchange of tropisms without words.

Sarraute, however, is not interested in denouncing the banality and inauthenticity of the verbal exchanges that constitute the subject matter of *L'Usage de la parole*. In a 1969 interview, she explained the interaction between commonplace expressions and tropisms. "In my work commonplaces . . . are simply the places where people meet. Tropisms appear on the outside—since they cannot manifest themselves any other way—by means of these commonplaces which make up the conversations and dialogues. They stand out and camouflage themselves beneath the apparent banality of the dialogue. But this dialogue is never there to show banality. On the contrary, it is there to display the tropism, to reveal the tropism which it is more or less trying to camouflage."[13]

The chapter headings in this work demonstrate that Sarraute's concern is with the use of language to communicate acceptance, judgment, or nonrecognition of another. For example, it can be used negatively to withhold affection, as in the chapter entitled "Ton père. Ta soeur" ("Your father. Your sister"), based on the key phrase "If you keep it up Armand, your father will like your sister better."[14] It can be used to assert superiority, as in "Esthétique," when, stimulated by the word *aesthetic,* the proper old lady's "closed and rigid look repulses, puts him [the gentleman] . . . back in his place."[15] In the chapter, "Mon petit," the expression is used as a put-down, immediately establishing a hierarchy, a perceptible distance and difference between two people. "Eh bien quoi, c'est un dingue" (well, he's nuts) is used as a weapon that is even more devastating and derogatory than "mon petit." "Ne me parlez pas de ça" (don't speak to me about that) establishes an unbridgeable gap between the speaker and the listener, while the expression "Je ne comprends pas" (I don't understand) can be used to deny validity to the speaker's words, or even to deny his or her very existence. Sarraute demonstrates in *L'Usage de la parole* the constant interaction between such commonplace expressions and tropisms, between the spoken and unspoken meanings in the words we use.

From the early *Tropisms* to *L'Usage de la parole,* Sarraute's work has become more and more abstract and hermetic, characterized by the absence of characters with definable personalities and proper names, as well as of description, plot or psychological analysis. All that has concerned her has been the uncovering of something that existed prior to language, the secret, hidden subconscious reactions to external stimuli that are at the core of our existence and which she calls tropisms. It is for these reasons that her work *Enfance (Childhood)*, 1983, surprised her readers, for here the author not only presents well-defined characters, distinct individuals from specific backgrounds who are products of their class, education, and psychological makeup, but she also places at the center of the novel the young girl Natasha, who is Nathalie Sarraute herself. What the author has done in this work is to write her bildungsroman at the age of eighty-three, reversing the typical order of literary creativity. The first novel of most writers is often a novel of development that traces the author's early years and education and gives the genesis of his or her literary creativity. Or, at the very least, the story connects at various points with the life of the author. It is only as they mature and develop that authors move away from themselves and continue on in the direction of greater objectivity and abstraction.

But *Childhood* differs from typical bildungsromans in a more significant way, for it blends autobiography with tropistic response, still using language as the catalyst for these tropisms. Sarraute continues here what she has always done; she is still intent on capturing the intense life below the surface of events and language, to bring to the fore the subliminal quiverings of hidden emotions, the mental matter that constitutes what she calls "pre-dialogue." "For fifty years I've been taking the pulse of the mini-dramas which constitute all human encounters. A little trifle may acquire huge proportions, blow up, explode. Under the clichés of daily conversation violence is lying in wait, ready to erupt. You do not need a complicated plot, a calculated climax to have dramatic action in the novel or on the stage. The drama of the commonplace is ever present and fraught with danger. Often it is not even what you say, but how you say it. It is not in the words but in the tone."[16]

A great many of the seventy-one vignettes that make up *Childhood* hinge upon a seemingly innocuous remark or expression that generates tropistic responses in the young girl Natasha, for it is not the agonies of domestic conflict that shape the work, but the terror of language. "If you touch one of those poles, you'll die," her mother says, referring to the telephone poles they pass as they walk along a country road. One of her mother's friends looks at a novel the child has been writing in her notebook and says, "Anyone who sets out to write a novel should first learn to spell." When a maid tells Natasha that a baby stepsister born to her father and his second wife will take over her bedroom, the maid exclaims, "What a tragedy to have no mother." From then on, the word *tragedy* remains engraved within the child's imagination.

The work is made up of the bits and pieces that comprise the childhood of Natasha Tcherniak between the ages of five and eleven. Everything is seen through the eyes of the little girl, who, like Elsa Triolet and Zoé Oldenbourg, was born in Russia to middle-class intellectual parents. Her earliest memories were of being shuttled between the homes of her parents, divorced soon after her birth, and both remarried. Her father, a young revolutionary opposed to the czarist regime, had to flee Russia. He settled in France where Nathalie eventually joined him. Her mother remained in Russia until the Revolution, when she also had to flee with her second husband, who was a conservative intellectual. Nathalie grew up with a moody but well-meaning stepmother, who could not help favoring her own daughter, and a shy, uncommunicative father. Her own mother had lost interest in her. The only loving care the child received was from a step-grandmother who came for an extended visit from Russia.

But, more important than the sorrows and loneliness of the young girl, torn between two homes and two cultures, exacerbated by her realization of the difference between her Russian-Jewish heritage and that of her French-Catholic schoolmates, is the fascination with language and something that antecedes language, something in search of its language, which cannot exist without language. It was this fascination that led Sarraute to chart a new path for the novel—redefining it and extending it as an instrument of exploration—one that preceded and influenced the feminist novel in its search for a new means of expression for women's literature.

Marguerite Duras

Marguerite Duras (b. 1914) has called her work "feminine literature," describing it as "organic, translated writing . . . translated from blackness, from darkness." Because, she continues, "women have been in darkness for centuries. They don't know themselves. Or only poorly. And when women write, they translate this darkness. . . . Men don't translate. They begin from a theoretical platform that is already in place, already elaborated. The writing of women is really translated from the unknown, like a new way of communicating rather than an already formed language. . . . I think that feminine literature is a violent, direct literature and that, to judge it, we must not—and this is the main point I want to make—start all over again, take off from a theoretical platform."[17] Duras refuses to imitate masculine literature by "taking off from a theoretical platform." Instead, what is found in her work is a descent into the darkness of the unconscious, the liberation of the imaginary, the freeing of words from their voluntary, conscious associations, and the disengaging of language from its ordinary uses. Unlike many of her contemporaries, however, Duras has never permitted language in and of itself to become the dominant concern of her texts. Instead, she has structured it to reflect her protagonists' psychological and metaphysical anguish.

Duras's first three novels—*Les impudents* (1943), *La vie tranquille* (Peaceful life, 1944), *Un barrage contre le Pacifique (The Sea Wall)*, 1950—are autobiographical. Together with *L'Amant (The Lover)*, 1984, they tell the story of a young woman in search of a man to give meaning to her existence. Duras's heroines, like those of Beauvoir and Gennari, are passive because they live at a time when women are cut off from one another by society. Unable to join forces and take a common stand, they feel impotent, unable to establish their identity as human beings without the aid of men. For Duras, the apparent passivity of her female protagonists is an "organic, feminine intelligence" to be contrasted with the intelligence of logic and rationality. Through centuries of oppression and silence imposed on them by a male-dominated society oriented toward abstraction and reason, women have turned in on themselves. It is this inwardness, according to Duras, that is at the basis of feminine discourse and that constitutes a paradoxically "passive" force: the power to refuse to comply with male-oriented society.[18] But passivity is also justified by Duras on the grounds that reacting against male society would be to give it validity as something against which to react. To challenge society, Duras states, is to acknowledge it.[19]

It is not only their sex, however, that condemns Duras's heroines to the condition of "otherness"; it is also the transposition of the author's experiences in a desperately poor white family in colonial Indochina, isolated by poverty from the other colonizers and by race from the colonized. Marguerite Duras was born in Phnom Penh in 1914, the youngest child of Emile and Marie Donadieu, two French school teachers on assignment in Indochina. She adopted a pen name because she refused to use the inherited patronymic,[20] which she considers to be an insurmountable barrier to woman's creativity. After her father died from amoebic dysentery when she was four years old, Marguerite moved with her mother and two brothers to a house outside Saigon. Her childhood was shadowed by the family's difficult financial problems and by the resentment she felt toward her older brother, who received the major share of their mother's love. Duras speaks of him as a murderous devil and accuses him of indirectly causing the death of her other brother, whom she worshipped. "My only relative: this little nimble brother, so slender, with slanting eyes, wild, quiet, who at the age of ten climbs the giant mango trees and at the age of fourteen kills the black panthers of the rivers of the Chaîne de l'Eléphant, how much love. How much love for you, little dead brother."[21] Some recent criticism has postulated that the madness and alienation of Duras's heroines in the major portion of her work results from her incestuous passion for this brother and her growing awareness of the nature of this forbidden passion after his death.[22]

In Duras's first novel, *Les impudents,* we find an equally unbearable family situation from which the heroine cannot escape on her own. Caught between an assertive mother and a dissipated brother, Maud, the protagonist, retreats into lethargy and helplessness, imprisoned by feelings of inferiority and worthlessness. Her passivity makes her the prototype of many of Duras's other heroines. To escape from the stifling family atmosphere, Maud has a love affair. Her liaison is also a deliberate attempt to break the rules of traditional morality that relegate women to the status of eternal child, bound economically and sexually. Maud's "impudence" thus also becomes a feminist protest. But when she becomes pregnant, she feels compelled to return to the family cell. Only when she seizes the initiative and asserts herself by denouncing her older brother as a criminal to the police, does her mother reject her, a rejection that is, in effect, a liberation.

In *La vie tranquille,* again, we have the story of a young girl who through scandal and violence wrenches free from an oppressive family atmosphere by means of the intervention of a stranger. It is, however, *The Sea Wall* that is the most autobiographical of these early novels, for it presents the same mother-brother-sister triad, but moves it from France to situate it within the context of Duras's early, poverty-stricken life in Indochina. Like Duras's mother, the fictional Ma left France with her husband to teach in Indochina. While their colonial adventure started out well with both parents teaching, after the death of the father Ma was left virtually penniless with two children to support. Duras's younger brother, who appears in *The Lover,* is absent from this novel as well as from the two preceding works. The mother gave French lessons and piano lessons and played the piano at the Eden cinema for ten years. By rigid economizing, she was able to set aside money to buy a land grant from the French colonial government. Unfortunately, she was unaware of the corruption in the awarding of land grants and found herself with an uncultivable tract of land that was inundated by the Pacific Ocean every year. In a fruitless effort to hold back the flood waters, she borrowed money to build a series of dikes, which were undermined by hordes of sea crabs that ate away at the sea wall.

When the novel opens, Ma and her two children, Suzanne and Joseph, have been living in poverty, having waged their foredoomed fight against the Pacific Ocean for six years. Ma has finally realized the hopelessness of their situation and has retreated into pills and sleep. Joseph devotes himself to women, tinkering with a dilapidated old car, and listening to phonograph records, while Suzanne, playing the typically passive role of Duras's heroines, waits patiently on the road from Ram to Kam for something to happen. Perhaps a man will pass by, notice her, and save her. Finally, her waiting brings the desired result; a wealthy man, Mr. Jo, falls in love with her and gives her many gifts in an effort to seduce her. But despite her family's encouragement, Suzanne is repelled by his ugliness and consents only to appear naked before him. For many reasons, the arrangement does not last, and Suzanne's suitor disappears. When Joseph sells the diamond Mr. Jo gave to Suzanne, Ma uses the money to pay off a fraction of her debts, and the family soon finds itself in the same financial straits as before.

While the economic misery caused by the corrupt French colonial administration would seem to be at the center of the novel, the oppressive family situation bears down even more heavily on the female protagonist, whose suffering is caused principally by her deeply troubled relationship with her mother. Suzanne's pain results from her mother's preference for her brother and from her rejection of Suzanne as an extension of her own persona. Like Emma Bovary, Ma sees a daughter as a continuation of herself, an eternal victim, while a son has the potential as a male to become the redresser of the wrongs she has suffered. Suzanne's battle to conceive herself as separate from her mother's image of her, to resist her mother's fate, and to assume her own identity is at the heart of the novel. Underlying *The Sea Wall,* as it does all of Duras's life and work, is the daughter's effort to rise above crippling maternal rejection through understanding. It is finally her mother's death, as well as her realization that she owes her own strength of character to her mother's defiant attitude toward life, that frees her. Yet, while she learns to identify her mother's strengths as her own, she still carries through life the scars of the mother's rejection. Suzanne's problem of freeing herself from familial influences and establishing an individual identity is a variation on the basic theme of every female bildungsroman in which the protagonist struggles for authenticity against the limitations of familial enclosures.

Suzanne finally loses her virginity to a young neighbor whom she hardly knows and for whom she has no particular feelings. This sacrifice of her virginity to a man to whom she is indifferent is a deliberate act of rebellion. By giving away for nothing what traditional morality considers her most precious possession, she ceases to be merely an object for barter. Her rebellion is a refusal to accept the subordinate social status accorded women and a rejection of the prohibitions of traditional morality that prevent a woman from freely disposing of her own body. It offers, finally, the best way "for a girl to learn how to leave her mother."[23]

While the empathy Duras feels for her mother can be seen in the portrait of the mother and in the devotion of her children to her, her despair is also evident in the portrayal of the emotional havoc a woman, who has been destroyed by her environment, wreaks on her children, particularly her daughter. Duras spells out this despair in 1984 in the preface to *The Lover:* "In the books I've written about my childhood, I can't remember, suddenly, what I left out, what I said. I think I wrote about our love for our mother, but I don't know if I wrote about how we hated her too, or about our love for one another, and our terrible hatred too, in that common family history of ruin and death which was ours whatever happened, in love or in hate, and which I still can't understand however hard I try, which is still beyond my reach, hidden in the very depths of my flesh, blind as a newborn child."[24] While Duras wrote about the members of her family in her first three novels, they were then still alive and, therefore, she states, she did not deal with them in depth, and spoke only of "clear periods, those on which the light fell" (7–8). In *The Lover,* however, she talks about certain facts, feelings, and events that she buried, revealing without reticence the part of her life that she had kept hidden for almost fifty years (7–8).

The story of *The Lover* is told by a narrator, now in her sixties, who is looking back on an episode of her adolescence and its emotional consequences on her life. Here Duras's younger brother finally appears and the author reveals, in addition to her love for him, the full extent of her hatred for and jealousy of her older brother:

I wanted to kill—my elder brother, I wanted to kill him, to get the better of him for once, just once, and see him die. I wanted to do it to remove from my mother's sight the object of her love, that son of hers, to punish her for loving him so much, so badly, and above all—as I told myself, too—to save my younger brother . . . my child, save him from the living life of that elder brother superimposed on his own, from that black veil over the light, from the law which was decreed and represented by the elder brother, a human being, and yet which was an animal law, filling every moment of every day of the younger brother's life with fear, a fear that one day reached his heart and killed him. (7)

Duras also reveals in *The Lover* that her hatred for her brother was not founded exclusively on her mother's preference for him; she also detested him because he was a thief and a gambler. He stole from the poor native boys to buy opium. He even stole from their mother who sold everything in order to pay his gambling debts. When he was young, he tried to prostitute his sister. He would even have sold his mother. Also, nothing was ever enough for him. Yet, despite all this, it was only for him that the mother wanted to live. When she died, he forged her will in his favor. After the Liberation the brother was pursued for collaboration and sought refuge in Duras's apartment where he stole everything she owned, including food she had been saving in the hope that her husband had survived his imprisonment in a German concentration camp.

In *The Lover,* Duras makes explicit the fact that the stifling atmosphere of her early novels, as well as the protagonists' desperate desire to escape from unbearable poverty, an unstable mother, and a despicable older brother were based on her own experience. She reveals, too, that she first made her escape from her family at the age of fifteen and a half when she became the mistress of a Chinese multimillionaire whom she met on a ferryboat crossing the Mekong River. It is this crossing of the river that constitutes the leitmotiv of the novel; it symbolizes not only the passage from childhood to adulthood, but also the crossing of the barrier that separated the colonizers from the colonized. Duras considers this crossing to be the decisive event in her life. While it led her eccentric family to be ostracized by other members of the French community, it also provided the money to secure her liberation.

The lover and the girl singlemindedly indulge their passion. As in many of Duras's other works, the female protagonist is a slave of love, driven by her passion, but also passive. "I used to watch what he did with me, how he used me, and I'd never thought anyone could act like that, he acted beyond my hope and in accordance with my body's destiny" (100). While the protagonist experiences strong sexual desire, she, like so many of Duras's females, is portrayed particularly as an object of sexual desire. The male lovers, on the other hand, are not defined in terms of their bodies, but of their desire, and thus play the role of subject.

The affair described in *The Lover* ended when the author was seventeen years old and went away to school in France. After her departure, the lover was lost in the past "like water in sand" (114). But, "years after the war, after marriages, children, divorces, books, he came to Paris with his wife. He phoned her. . . . And then he told her. Told her that it was as before, that he still loved her, he could never stop loving her, that he'd love her until death" (116–17).

In *Le marin de Gibraltar (The Sailor from Gibraltar)*, 1952, Duras's fourth novel, it is no longer a question of heroines who look forward to a future perfect love, as in the first three novels, but rather, as in *The Lover*, to a past idealized love. Here Duras introduces the theme of the search for love remembered. The narrator of the novel is a civil service employee who is vacationing in Italy with his mistress. Tired of both his job and the woman, he abandons both and seeks employment on the yacht of a wealthy widow named Anna, who has spent the preceding three years seeking a sailor from Gibraltar with whom she had once fallen in love, with whom she had lived for a while, and by whom she had been abandoned one day in Shanghai. She has been searching for him for years in all of the ports of the world, and she now enlists the aid of the narrator, who embarks with her on an endless voyage in search of her irretrievable past. In the course of their voyage, it is little by little the quest itself that emerges as more important than its object, illustrating Duras's central theme that the power of our obsessions takes precedence over our fidelity to the remembered object of our obsessions.

Anna is Duras's characteristic heroine who is driven to neurosis by her obsessive memory of a lost love (usually a feckless, inconsequential man) who might return to offer her some form of liberation, and for whom she is willing to wait indefinitely. . . . [Duras's] women identify so totally with the male object of their obsessions that their loyalty is ultimately a form of fidelity to the self. Their fixations far transcend any erotic longing, are almost mystical in their irrationality and fervor. And their hallucinatory, faithful waiting embodies the author's ambiguous feminist vision—woman as both passive victim and active redeemer, woman as sanctuary of mythic memory and principal interpreter of human suffering.[25]

While Duras's novel of 1953, *Les petits chevaux de Tarquinia (The Little Horses of Tarquinia)* retells the story of a woman's fruitless search for a perfect, idealized love, the title novella of *Des journées entières dans les arbres*[26] *(Days in the Trees),* 1954,[27] continues the confessional tale of the familial trio of Duras's three early novels and *The Lover.* Duras remarks that this story is so autobiographical, so close to events she experienced with her mother and brother, that it scarcely seems as if she wrote it.[28] While we still have the privileged relationship in the mother-son dyad, the daughter's role of outsider to their relationship is played in this work by the son's mistress Marcelle. Here, too, the author expresses her bitterness and jealousy at the mother's unjustified but overwhelming preference for the brother. Were it not for the fact that the mother dies at the end of the *The Sea Wall,* this could almost be a sequel to that early novel. The story, which obeys the classical unity of time, unfolds during the twenty-four-hour visit paid by a mother to her son. Unlike the mother of the first novel, this one has made a fortune in the colonies. She has come to Paris from French Indochina to see her favorite child, her middle-aged son Jacques, the youngest of her six children. Duras's confidences about her older brother in *The Lover* reveal the intimate ties between her older brother and his fictional counterpart, a gambler, drunkard, and occasional thief.

Jacques has never matured beyond the young boy who would spend days climbing trees and playing hooky from school, encouraged by his mother to remain a dependent child forever. We learn in the course of the narrative that the mother's visit is also motivated by her desire to have her son return with her to Indochina to take charge of her business, trying in this way to regain her former hold on him. But Jacques, who has spent his life trying to free himself from her, refuses. When Jacques steals his mother's jewels, it is his attempt to affirm his independence and to attain by that act the status of adult that had been denied him. The mother now realizes the futility of her endeavor, and cuts short her visit after twenty-four hours to return to Indochina alone.

Jacques's mistress Marcelle, like Jacques, holds down a job in a cheap Montmartre nightclub. She has no family and is dependent on Jacques, vying with the mother for his love. She clings to Jacques, who wants above all to be free of all ties. Because she is motivated entirely by a desperate desire for security, she does not look to the future, but holds on tenaciously to what she has, fearing any change in the status quo. For Marcelle, as for all Duras's women, the world is unlivable because they are dispossessed within a patriarchal structure that makes them dependent. Duras's women have no power to choose or control their lives, and they are forced to find sufficient strength to endure the hardships they encounter.

The only way a Duras heroine can temporarily maintain a hold on life is by making herself indispensable to a man. This is evident in *Le square (The Square)*, 1955, a novel that has essentially only two characters, a traveling salesman and a young nursemaid who meet by chance on a park bench. A remark by the child in the woman's care sets off a conversation between them, interrupted three times by the arrival of the child who wanders back and then goes off again. As they talk with each other, the clichés they utter form a bond between them. The maid reveals that she is waiting for some man to find her and to marry her, and dreams of finding her liberator at the ball she attends every Saturday night. Only if she is chosen will she acquire an identity. "You must understand: you must try to understand," she tells him, "that I have never been wanted by anyone, ever, except of course for my capacity for housework; and that is not choosing me as a person but simply wanting something impersonal which makes me as anonymous as possible. And so I must be wanted by someone, just once, and even if only once. Otherwise I shall exist so little even to myself that I would be incapable of knowing how to want to choose anything, that is why, you see, I attach so much importance to marriage."[29]

The maid is imprisoned not only by her situation but also by her belief that she is powerless to change it through her own efforts. Her expectations, which prevent her from thinking of anything but her possible savior, make her refuse anything that could make her life more tolerable. While the maid's thoughts are oriented only toward the future, those of the traveling salesman go back to a happy moment in the past when, uncharacteristically, he decided to visit an exotic foreign country. He has no faith in the possibility of future happiness and is concerned only with basic necessities. His refusal to believe in himself or in the future imprisons him in a quest for simple survival. The novel ends when the maid finally leaves the park. The man, watching her, understands that they will meet the following Saturday at the dance hall.

Marguerite Duras states that while *The Sea Wall* is the most autobiographical of her works in terms of events and facts, *Moderato cantabile (Moderato Cantabile)*, 1958, is the most autobiographical from the psychological point of view, for it reflects the crisis she went through after a very violent sexual experience. "The story I tell in *Moderato cantabile*, that woman who wants to be killed, I lived it."[30] But, according to Duras, not only this woman but all her heroines are torn apart by desire.[31] Indeed, with each succeeding novel, this desire becomes more violent.

The protagonist of *Moderato Cantabile*, Anne Desbaresdes, the wife of the wealthy director of a smelting works, accompanies her ten-year-old son every Friday to his piano lesson on the other side of the city in the port area.[32] On the Friday on which the novel opens, the lesson is interrupted by a scream which comes from a nearby café. After the lesson, Anne goes to the café where she finds a man embracing the body of the woman he has just killed. The event has a profound effect on her and she returns to the café the next day with her son. While the child plays outside, Anne goes into the café, orders a glass of wine and starts to speak to a man who is reading his newspaper at the counter. The man, whose name is Chauvin and who, coincidentally, once worked for her husband, shows as great an interest in the crime as Anne and tells her that the man killed the woman out of love. Anne and Chauvin meet five times in the course of the next nine days to reconstruct the crime and attempt to understand the psychological motivation for this love-death, for they do not doubt that the woman asked the man to kill her as the ultimate proof of his love. Their verbal reenactment of the events is merely a pretext for Anne to seek vicarious satisfaction by acting out her fantasies of passionate love through the lives of others. As she discusses the murdered woman, Anne reenacts the crime of passion in a ritualistic ceremony with Chauvin and becomes aware of her own sexuality and her general dissatisfaction with her life. She starts to identify completely with the murdered woman and succeeds for a limited period in escaping from her real existence by having an affair in which desire is both created and satisfied with words. Anne is but another incarnation of the Duras heroine who is incapable of the effort required for positive, dynamic action and who must, therefore, live through another. Duras suggests in *Moderato*

Cantabile a theory of love in which Eros and Thanatos are inextricably linked in an overpowering love-death.

Violent death is again presented as the logical conclusion to consuming passion in *Dix heures et demie du soir en été (Ten-Thirty on a Summer Night)*, 1960. The events in the novel take place during twenty-four hours in the lives of a married couple, Maria and Pierre, who are on vacation in Spain with their daughter Judith and Maria's friend Claire. They stop at a hotel in a town where a man named Rodrigo Paestra has just killed his young wife and her lover. Maria sees the hunted criminal on a nearby rooftop at the same time as she observes her husband embracing her friend Claire on a nearby balcony. The juxtaposition of the two events, the fact that Maria sees herself as a spectator unable to kill, is, according to Duras, the moment that interests her, the point of departure of the entire novel.[33]

Maria yearns to be with the criminal, who represents revolt and escape while she is condemned to passivity. Although Rodrigo, like Maria, has been deceived in love, unlike her he has reacted to this betrayal violently. Because she identifies with Rodrigo, Maria decides to save him from capture by the police. She hides him in her car and takes him outside of town with instructions to wait for her to return the next day to smuggle him across the border. But her rescue proves to have been in vain, for Rodrigo commits suicide during her absence. The novel ends as Maria passively observes the end of her marriage and the beginning of the new love affair between Pierre and Claire that will take its place. To the casual reader, Maria's failure to make any attempt to save her marriage is surprising. She merely adopts a purely passive attitude of morose, desperate contemplation; instead of reacting, instead of struggling to preserve her marriage, she takes refuge in alcohol. The explanation for this would seem to lie in the author's philosophy of love, which is shared by her heroine, one that conceives of love as an absolute, irresistible fatality.

Maria, condemned to passivity, is interested in Rodrigo not only because he is able to act out her own fantasies of revenge, but also because he, like she, is a victim of society. Duras's female characters have no money or power of their own and seek out men who are as dispossessed by society as they. Her heroines either search for or identify with the most dispossessed, the most fallen of men; the one who knows as much about abandonment and deprivation as they. The sailor from Gibraltar, like Rodrigo Paestra, is a hunted murderer; the traveling salesman in *The Square* is totally isolated from society; and Chauvin

(Moderato Cantabile) has no place either in the community of workmen or in Anne's milieu. In *L'Amante anglaise (L'Amante Anglaise)*, 1967, Claire Lannes fantasizes about a love affair with a menial worker, while Anne-Marie Stretter in *India Song*, 1973, is attracted to the disgraced and deranged former vice-consul of Lahore.

In 1974 Marguerite Duras remarked that she loved Lol V. Stein and could not stop writing about her.[34] Not only is she the protagonist of *Le ravissement de Lol V. Stein (The Ravishing of Lol V. Stein)*, 1964, but she is also present in *L'Amour* (1971) and the film scenario of that novel, *La femme du Gange* (The woman of the Ganges, 1973). Resonances of the novel can be found in the novel *Le vice-consul (The Vice-Consul)*, 1965, as well as in *India Song*, classified as "texte-théâtre-film." It is thus possible to speak of a Lol V. Stein cycle in which *The Ravishing of Lol V. Stein* is the point of departure for succeeding texts and films. This novel marks a turning point in the work of Duras, for it demonstrates her growing feminist awareness as she portrays a totally alienated consciousness, driven mad by frustrated desires. Such desires, thwarted by the imperatives of a patriarchal society, are at the root of the madness that pervades Duras's work.

Lola Valérie Stein is engaged to Michael Richardson, but on the night of the ball at the Municipal Casino on T. Beach in S. Thala she is jilted by her fiancé who leaves the dance with an older woman, the elegant and mysterious Anne-Marie Stretter. While Anne-Marie here serves merely as a catalyst for Lol's mental illness, she is the protagonist of *The Vice-Consul* and *India Song*. Richardson's abandonment causes Lol to withdraw into an imaginary world of madness. Her madness explains the term "ravishing" in the title, which here does not denote either physical or spiritual ecstasy, but rather the state of alienation in which the heroine lives—her detachment from life and the strange distraction that accompanies her behavior. A few years later, Lol marries Jean Bedford and leads a seemingly normal life of bourgeois wife and mother. But her alienation and her excessive need for order demonstrate an underlying disorder, one that stems from suppressed desires and that is ubiquitous among Duras's heroines. Ten years later, Lol returns to S. Thala with her family, where she begins to spy on the lovers, Jacques Hold, who is later revealed to be the narrator, and Tatiana Karl, the friend who was present at the fatal ball at which Lol was abandoned. Hiding in a field, Lol regularly watches the two in a hotel room, finding vicarious pleasure in the role of voyeuse. Duras explains this flaw in Lol's personality. "A progressive loss of identity is the most enviable experience one can have. It is in fact my only preoccupation: the possibility of being able to lose the notion of one's identity. It is for this reason that the question of madness tempts me so in my books. Today we are all suffering from that loss of identity, from that split in the personality. It is the most widespread sickness—you must appreciate its positive aspect. [Lol V. Stein's] sickness is symbolic of a type of happiness. Lol has the ability to be able to live through others."[35]

Finally, Lol decides to become more closely involved with Jacques and Tatiana in order to relive the triangle that precipitated her original trauma; she goes to the same hotel room with Jacques and spends the night there with him. But this experience does not cure her madness and she returns at the end of the novel to the field of rye from which she had originally spied on the two lovers. But, Duras remarks that she is a *voyeuse* looking into the void, for she cannot see what is happening in the hotel room where by rights she herself should be.[36]

The author explains the denouement in which Lol gives in completely to madness. "Lol goes to a hotel room with the man she loves and experiences the same happiness as other women. For the first time, she does not live through someone else. She lives directly. The shock of that experience is so violent that she completely loses her head. Let us say that the world she knew . . . was shattered. It is as if she had just been born at the age of thirty-five."[37] Lol's wish to completely absent her body from the sexual act in order to experience a voluptuous state of nothingness, although representing an extreme, is the logical extension of the passive behavior exhibited by other female characters in Duras's novels. Lol's subsequent appearances in *L'Amour* and *La femme du Gange* show her as completely mad and in the constant care of an attendant.

While Anne-Marie Stretter plays only a peripheral role in *The Ravishing of Lol V. Stein,* she reappears as a central figure in *The Vice-Consul,* and her affair with Michael Richardson (his surname abbreviated here to Richard) is alluded to as a passionate love of the past. Anne-Marie is based on a woman Duras met in Vinh-Long when she was an adolescent who represented for her a certain type of women. Here Anne-Marie appears as the wife of the French ambassador to Calcutta. She is a charming hostess, an accomplished musician, and an exemplary mother to her two daughters. But, despite these external signs of good fortune, she, like Lol and Duras's other heroines, is prey to aimless longings. Occasionally, she leaves Calcutta for the comfort of the Delta Isles, where she is surrounded by a coterie of lovers, including Michael

Richard. Among her admirers is the French vice-consul from Lahore, who appears in Calcutta where he has been summoned to explain his apparently mad action of shooting into a pack of dogs and lepers in the Shalimar Gardens beneath his windows. Duras explains his action by stating that he fired on pain and suffering. "The lepers who live in this garden are, in fact, a reflection of life . . . he did not fire on anyone in particular. He fired on an idea."[38] Anne-Marie is the only member of the diplomatic community who understands the inner misery that prompted his action. But when the vice-consul tries to approach her, recognizing in her his own alienation, his own passionate quest for absolute love, she refuses to confront this mirror image and returns to the protective cocoon of her lovers.

The denouement of *India Song,* which has essentially the same plot, is quite different. In this last version of the story, the vice-consul appears on the island, and comes into the elegant Prince of Wales hotel where Anne-Marie and her friends are dining. Later on, Anne-Marie sees him in the park and dismisses her guests. That night, a young attaché, who is one of her lovers, comes back and sees them seated near one another on the grass, immobile and silent. The next day, Anne-Marie disappears and they subsequently find her robe on the beach at the water's edge, leading to a verdict of suicide. As for the vice-consul, he resigns from the diplomatic corps and disappears without a trace.

There is a third alienated character in *The Vice-Consul* and *India Song,* a poor beggar woman who haunts Calcutta and who forms part of the native background of misery. Her role would seem to be accessory were it not for the fact that, according to the author, she is at the center of the novel. Like Anne-Marie Stretter, Duras remarks, this beggar woman has her origins in Duras's childhood experiences in French Indochina. "The blind beggar woman who abandons her child came to our house in Cochin-China and she returns in almost all of my books. She came with her baby, a little two-year-old girl who looked as if she were six months old, and who was full of worms. I adopted her, my mother gave her to me. She died, we could not save her. That was extremely traumatic for me, I was twelve years old."[39]

Peter Morgan, an Englishman, who frequents the French diplomatic community, is fascinated by the mad beggar woman who is constantly foraging for food in the embassy garbage pails and endlessly singing an incomprehensible song. According to legend, she walked to Calcutta all the way from far-off Savannahket in Indochina. The wandering of the beggar woman constitutes an exemplary myth in the story of women who have always been absent from history.[40] Morgan is writing a novel in which he imagines her past and attempts to explain her remarkable journey. In his story, the beggar woman was abandoned by her mother and chased from their home when she became pregnant, because there was not enough food to feed another mouth. She is shunned and mocked by those she encounters all along the way. Finally, in Vinh-Long, her child is taken away from her by a white woman and she continues on her ten-year walk toward Calcutta, and madness. The beggar woman is a symbol of the alienation and despair of Duras's female protagonists.

Madness, a traditional form of escape for women, in Duras's work is a form of freedom which is attained by the refusal to live within accepted structures or boundaries, or even to allow these boundaries to exist. Claire Lannes, the protagonist of *L'Amante Anglaise,* embodies this refusal. The novel is the second of three versions Duras wrote of a crime reported in the newspaper about portions of a dismembered woman's body found on trains in various parts of France. All the trains had passed under one viaduct in the department of Seine-et-Oise, the common denominator that permitted the police to find the murderers, an elderly retired couple. They killed their deaf-mute cousin, who had been their servant for twenty-seven years, dismembered the body, and threw the various pieces onto trains passing beneath the viaduct near their home. While in the play *Les viaducs de la Seine-et-Oise,* the first version of the story, it is both the man and wife who commit the murder, their action motivated mainly by boredom, in the novel, the crime is committed by the woman, Claire Lannes, alone.

The novel begins after Claire's arrest and conviction, and consists of three interrogations by an anonymous interrogator who wants to write a story of her crime. He first questions Robert Lamy, the owner of the town café, then Pierre, Claire's husband, and finally Claire herself. The reader learns that Claire—like Lol V. Stein—had a youthful passionate love affair with a man who abandoned her. After an unsuccessful suicide attempt, she, again like Lol, left the scene of her abandonment (in her case Cahors), moved to another town, married, and led an ordinary, uneventful life. Claire, who was excessively sensitive, was oppressed by the overpowering presence in her home of her cousin Marie-Thérèse, who, she said, was too well adapted to life. "When she ate and walked about, sometimes I could hardly bear it . . . I'm the sort of person who can't bear other people eating and sleeping well. She was very fat and the rooms are very small. I found she was too fat for the house."[41]

To escape from Marie-Thérèse's overpowering presence and to counteract the effects of her heavy cooking, Claire would sit on a bench in her garden next to her English mint plant—in French, la menthe anglaise, which she spelled phonetically as *l'amante anglaise*—which supposedly had digestive properties.

Marie-Thérèse had a lover, Alfonso, an Italian migrant worker, the object of Claire's erotic fantasies. Because Claire had thought that she might be able to relive with him the youthful passion of Cahors, it would seem as if the murder was motivated by jealousy of her cousin. But Claire's action was prompted less by jealousy than by a desire to kill the animal within herself, which had always filled her with revulsion. Claire kills Marie-Thérèse because, in her madness, she considers her cousin to be the embodiment of petit bourgeois comfort, the guardian of the oppressive order of society. The ultimate paradox of *L'Amante Anglaise,* however, is that Claire does not really dispose of her cousin and all she represents, but instead takes on her characteristics. Like her cousin, she becomes mute, refusing to answer her interrogator to reveal the location of the victim's head, a revelation that would cause him to lose interest in her and return her to her former anonymity.

In all of Duras's work, there is repeated the story of the passion and violence of love, the madness of love and its fatal entanglement with violence and destruction. Destruction is necessary to make a tabula rasa of everything in order to begin again. Destruction is also necessary to overturn the barriers that imprison the intuitive, libidinal forces within the individual and to make possible the establishment of new modes of behavior, such as the new vision of love seen in *Detruire, dit-elle (Destroy, she said),* 1969. For the characters in this novel, love is an ideal sharing or communion with others brought on by the loss of identity and of self in madness. Both madness and destruction are for Duras unexpected forms of freedom, attained by the refusal to live within old structures or boundaries, or even to allow these structures to exist.

Max Thor, his wife, Alissa, and the writer Stein are patients in a sanatorium, who form a new kind of love triangle in which each person may partake of the emotions and experiences of the other. It is a perfect triangle in which jealousy does not exist; there is only appreciation and love for the other. When a young woman, Elizabeth Alione, comes to the sanatorium to recover from a miscarriage, she is invited by the others to join their mad world. Although she is tempted by their offer, she is finally won back to the world of rational—read patriarchal—

society by her boorish husband, Bernard, with whom she leaves at the end of the novel, rejecting the internal world of imagination and desire. But it is Alissa, not Elizabeth, who plays the capital role in the novel; it is she who initiates the dissolution of the tightly knit, monogamous couple, which contradicts what Duras conceives of as the profound logic of desire and passion. The destruction of this small unit aims at much wider social and political destruction. By upsetting the established code of the couple with her sexual adventures, Alissa becomes the initiator of a broad revolutionary project.

That the goal of all of Duras's literary production is such a broad, revolutionary project is made manifest by the author. She notes that in *Destroy, she said,* it is Alissa who passes from one world to another, it is a woman who joins Stein's world because "now it is only women who are capable of effecting great organic and political transgressions. I don't believe," she continues, "that men are capable of it. . . . I think that a young man would not have been capable of Alissa's disobedience. I believe that man is profoundly alienated. The struggle of women for their emancipation is the most difficult of all. . . . Man when confronted with woman is still man confronted with the animal. When you speak of women's liberation to a man, even one who is enlightened, he will in ninety-eight percent of the cases set forward the argument of, what? *Nature!* He claims that woman's nature inclines her to servility. That is precisely what can be called recourse to the fascist argument. . . . Are knowledge and interpretation of nature thus masculine? Of course, they are convinced of it."[42]

Chapter Seven

Rebellion, Alternate Life-Styles, and Visions of Utopia: Christiane Rochefort, Violette Leduc, Monique Wittig, and Hélène Cixous

The novels of Christiane Rochefort, Violette Leduc, Monique Wittig, and Hélène Cixous, with their feminist visions of liberated sexuality and female transcendence, are the culmination of the movement by twentieth-century French women writers to disrupt traditional patterns of thought and expression. Their works attack the abuses of patriarchal society and advocate its overthrow by revolution; they propose new concepts and modes of sexuality; and, with the exception of Leduc, even set forth blueprints for the creation of utopian societies. They seek independence not only from oppressive relationships, but also liberation from internalized cultural prescriptions for female behavior and thought. Basic to their revolution is a subversion of the oppressive mechanisms of language itself, because they feel that use of the same language will perpetuate the same ideas. The challenge facing women today is to "reinvent language, to re-learn how to speak; to speak not only against, but outside the specular phallogocentric structure, to establish a discourse the status of which would no longer be defined by the phallacy of masculine meaning."[1]

Christiane Rochefort

Christiane Rochefort, (b. 1917) carries on the tradition of those who refuse to accept the world as it is: those who question established morality and denounce the evils and injustices of a society that crushes the weak and denies their legitimate aspirations; and those who seek, at the same time, to establish a free and equitable society. Rochefort refuses to accept society's male-enforced myths and instead explodes these myths to arrive at the truth. One of her most effective tools is humor, and this sets her apart from the other novelists considered in this study. While she has always fought against oppression, she has, with her increasing understanding of patriarchal society, become more militant in her espousal of moral, political, and social revolution. Thus, while her first novels present the problems inherent in society, her later novels propose alternative societies, utopias conceived from the feminist point of view. Yet, despite the differences among them, all her novels can be classified under the heading of philosophical tales in which the author uses her characters and plots to set forth a vision of the world and a code of ethics. All Rochefort's novels express her political and social message and all stress the divorce between the conflicting needs and demands of the individual and society.

Christiane Rochefort's first novel, *Le repos du guerrier (The Warrior's Rest)*, 1958,[2] had a great succès de scandale because its apparent theme, the humiliating submission of a bourgeois woman to the erotic demands of a bohemian male, seemed to conform to preconceived, masculine ideas—or adolescent fantasies—of a perfect sadomasochistic sexual relationship. Because the novel was perceived from this point of view, the author's intent was overlooked. In truth, Rochefort questions here the basic fabric of bourgeois society; she attacks the roles for men and women sanctioned by that society and shows the mutually alienating effects of society on both sexes. Indeed, according to the author, "there is one thing missing in *The Warrior's Rest* and that's sex. Sex is absent. Sex, that is to say the desire, longing, feelings, and emotions that are really connected with sexual energy, with the body itself in its purely sexual manifestation. Sex is an organ of communication. But when you take a look at what actually happens, that's not at all what you see."[3]

The story is narrated retrospectively by the female protagonist Geneviève Le Thiel, a young woman with a respectable bourgeois upbringing. While in a small town to settle details of the inheritance left to her by an aunt, Geneviève inadvertently enters the wrong hotel room and finds Renaud Sarti, who has just tried to kill himself. She saves his life, and with this gesture she initiates their stormy liaison. Sarti returns to Paris with Geneviève, moves in with her, and spends his days in bed, drinking and reading murder mysteries. In return for his keep, including large quantities of alcohol, he gives Geneviève the sexual pleasure she had never dreamed possible. At the same time, he uses his sexual prowess to assert his power over her. He even humiliates her in public, making her desire for him a source of ridicule. Renaud wants Geneviève to recognize the true nature of what she feels for him; it is not love, which is based on an exchange between two subjects, but lust for a sexual object. In fact, Geneviève has reversed the traditional male-subject / female-object pattern; she supports Renaud in exchange for sexual gratification.

But Geneviève is torn between her desires and her deep-rooted fear of female sexuality, which stems from the historical interdiction laid on expression or even recognition of female sexual desires. She is a victim of a cultural heritage that does not acknowledge women's desire and as a result she is frightened of her behavior. When she attempts to analyze her responses lucidly, she finds herself reduced to the only two possibilities provided by conventional language: either she is "mad" or she is "in love."[4] "The blood rushed to my face. I wanted those hands to touch me. I was mad. My body underwent an intense metamorphosis, I was going to wake up as a caterpillar or a white whale, I was going to scream, weep, yelp, or bray I loved him. I loved that man. And I had from the start."[5]

Because she cannot reconcile her sexuality with her culturally ingrained values, Geneviève falls ill, transforming her obsession—which she equates with madness—into the socially acceptable form of physical illness. Renaud, as defeated as she by this illness, which is symbolic of the sickness of society, agrees to enter a hospital for detoxification and to marry Geneviève, who is now pregnant. Geneviève's conditioning prevents her from understanding why she is not elated by what society would deem the happy outcome of her story, nor does she know why "such a total victory, won at such great cost, has suddenly left [her] . . . uncertain. It frightens . . . [her]."[6] Only the defeated existentialist Renaud, who speaks for Rochefort, understands that they have accepted prefabricated identities because they have not been equal to the task of creating meaning for themselves.

Rochefort's second novel, *Les petits enfants du siècle (Children of Heaven)*, 1961,[7] like *The Warrior's Rest*, ends in defeat. In both novels, the female protagonists accept their prescribed roles, both are imprisoned by thoughts, language, and institutions that are imposed on them by society. *Children of Heaven*, like Etcherelli's *Elise ou la vraie vie*, is a female working-class bildungsroman, but here the narrator moves in an opposite direction from Etcherelli's protagonist; she goes from lucidity to incognizance and from refusal to acceptance. To the double disadvantage of class and sex suffered by Etcherelli's protagonist is added that of age, for Josyanne also suffers from the widespread discrimination against children. She is living in the police state of childhood and, like children and prisoners everywhere, she dreams of escape. Josyanne begins her account with information about her own conception, which she describes as the creation of another product in a consumer oriented society. "I was born of the Family Subsidies[8] and a holiday morning stretching comfortably to the tune of 'I love you and you love me' played on a sweet horn. It was early winter, the bed felt good, there was no hurry."[9] She then details her life—starting at the age of eleven— in a low-income housing project, a life devoted to taking care of an ever increasing brood of younger brothers and sisters. The monotony of this existence is broken by a sexual encounter with Guido, an Italian construction worker whom she comes to love for the pleasure he gives her. But when Josyanne returns from a vacation with her family, Guido has gone to another construction site, and she spends much of the rest of the novel looking for him.

Girls in this novel, as is the case in the society it depicts, are more victimized than boys, just as women, whose sole purpose in life is the production and raising of children, are more exploited than men. Both sexes, however, are locked into place by their class and their sex roles. Like the workers in Etcherelli's novels, they have neither the time nor the energy to relate to one another. They also lack the education that would permit them to understand the socioeconomic causes of their oppressed condition. At first, Josyanne realizes that something is missing from her life and that she is unfulfilled in her role of "little mother." She tries to obtain the education that would permit her to escape the life of drudgery and pettiness society has prepared for her, as well as for all the women around her. But, since society has decreed that there is nothing else for her in life than motherhood, she finally becomes pregnant, decides that she "wants" the child, and gets married. At the end of the novel, she and her husband are counting on the material advantages this pregnancy and subsequent pregnancies will bring. Rochefort finds that Josyanne's fate is a tragedy; she will continue the cycle of her mother and all the other women around her who see each child as another object for exchange.

In *Children of Heaven,* Rochefort attacks the French system of social planning, which provides family subsidies and thereby fosters a life-style degraded by consumerism. Women are more degraded by it than men, since they have been restricted to the role of consumer, and they find that, as each child brings with it certain material goods, it also creates the need for others. Rochefort maintains that the emphasis on material goods has transformed the institution of marriage into a legalized form of prostitution, which provides consumer goods in exchange for each baby produced. Josyanne remarks that the working-class family produces children to fight in France's colonial wars (here the Algerian conflict) and to consume the products of French industry:[10]

Paulette plowed a path for her own through the others and walked out full of dignity belly first with her refrigerator inside and behind that the washing machine pawing the ground waiting to be fertilized.

She had a boy. She made nothing but boys, and she was proud of it. She would provide the nation with a firing squad at least, all by herself; it's true the nation had paid for them in advance, it had the right to them. I hoped there would be a war in time to put all this material to use, they wouldn't be much good otherwise, seeing they were all a bunch of dimwits. I imagined the day someone would tell all the sons Mauvin Forward March! and boom, there they are all flat on the battlefield, and they put a cross over them: here fell TV Mauvin, Jalopy Mauvin, Refrigerator Mauvin, Electric-Mixer Mauvin, Washing-machine Mauvin, Carpet Mauvin, Pressure-cooker Mauvin, and with the pension they could still buy themselves a vacuum cleaner and a family vault.[11]

But marriage as a form of legalized prostitution is not limited to the working class, as Rochefort shows in her novel on bourgeois marriage, *Stances à Sophie (Cats Don't Care for Money)*, 1963. The French title of the novel is that of a song that medical students sing in which they reveal the male attitude toward prostitutes and, by extension, toward women in general, whom they consider to be nothing more than paid sexual objects. A married woman, according to Rochefort, is merely a prostitute who exchanges sex for room and board on a permanent, rather than a temporary, basis. The protagonist of this novel, however, unlike Josyanne who ultimately succumbs to the lure of consumer goods and to the expectations of society, finally escapes and assumes her own destiny. Her victory marks a turning point in Rochefort's previous cycle of defeat.

According to Christiane Rochefort, *Cats Don't Care for Money* is the only one of her works that contains autobiographical elements, but altered for literary purposes. She, like her heroine, was married for four years and her marriage was also a mistake. While many of the events in the novel are fictional, the protagonists are modeled on Rochefort herself and a man similar to her husband. Although the circumstances are changed, she also had homosexual affairs at the end of her marriage. The sexual aspect was of secondary importance in these encounters between two oppressed women, encounters based on reciprocal understanding and similar antagonism to their men. They were, according to Rochefort, truly a sort of "sisterhood."[12]

The story in this novel, as in *The Warrior's Rest*, is told retrospectively by a first-person female narrator. But here the narrator, Céline, has escaped from the constraints of a bourgeois marriage and mentality and returned to an independent life, armed with the experiental knowledge she lacked at the age of twenty-seven when she fell in love with and married an ambitious, upwardly mobile technocrat named Philippe Aignan. After her marriage, she became a typical bourgeois wife—a part she played for four years—but she finally left Philippe to live in accordance with her own beliefs. In *Cats Don't Care for Money*, Rochefort again demonstrates, as she did in *The Warrior's Rest*, how alienation from the dominant language and the consequent fear of madness— which results from being unable to express what they experience—keeps women in a subordinate position. She denounces men and their language as she does later in *Une rose pour Morrison* (A rose for Morrison, 1966), where she writes: "They stole our words from us and they killed them. They kill everything they touch. And we are left with what has no words. What is. The unexpressed."[13]

To illustrate the role language plays in maintaining male domination, Rochefort has Céline write a "Neo-Bourgeois Semantic Dictionary" ("Dictionnaire Sémantique Néo-Bourgeois")[14] in which she counters the dominant language with her own definitions. For example, under "love" she writes: "A: for a woman; total dedication to domestic life, with night service. B: for a man; being satisfied with this."[15] She notes also that for Philippe happiness means security and advancement, while for her it means freedom and joy. But even though Philippe, the white bourgeois Western male, imposes his standards on society, he, the so-called "ruler," is also shown to be oppressed by a system he can no longer control and from which he can only escape by forging ahead blindly. For Philippe is not the creator of a special language, he is simply the spokesman for one that is widespread. Philippe has become what he was programmed to be by his mother: a disciplined follower who takes himself for a leader. Faithful to his conditioning, Philippe has transformed Céline into an object for display; her conspicuous consumption bears witness to his financial success.

Céline recognizes Philippe's emphasis on appearances as a refusal to see her as a person; he wants her to be docile and dependent, to play a socially acceptable feminine role. Céline's conflict is what Simone de Beauvoir described as woman's basic problem—she desires to be an autonomous subject, yet she is forced by men and society into the position of the Other, the nonessential in the face of the essential. When Céline functions as the Other, she receives approbation, when she does not, she is criticized by society in the person of Philippe. Her alienation comes from the role structure that pits society's dictates against natural inclinations and spontaneity. Céline discovers that it is impossible to speak to Philippe because people do not speak to one another in his world: "once they've said 'Personally I,' they repeat what they've picked up from someone else word for word—content, syntax, and vocabulary. The only thing that is personal is the combination 'Personally I,' the rest is pure repetition. Any original thought is contained in that 'Personally I,' any human emotion. The rest is not worth listening to."[16] Besides, she muses, why should Philippe speak to her, since sane people don't speak to objects. As a result, Céline no longer attempts to initiate a dialogue; she decides that it is pointless to waste her energy in such a hopeless endeavor.

Cats Don't Care for Money, like so many modern feminist novels, demonstrates the way in which matrimony dulls a woman's initiative and inhibits her maturation. Marriage restricts the freedom to come and go, which involves the right to make decisions about one's own time, work, and other activities, and which is a basic element of authenticity. The discrepancy between premarital dreams of authenticity and marital realities, the transformation of mates into guardians of the enclosure,[17] the limitations on freedom, submission to husbands, diminished eroticism, which Rochefort details in this novel, account for the depiction of matrimony as a negative institution found in so much of woman's fiction.

Céline is saved from bourgeois marital conformism when she becomes friendly with Julia Bigeon, the wife of Philippe's best friend. Julia shares with Céline her utilitarian concept of marriage. "What's to be gained by talking to them?" she asks. "They're from a different world. You have nothing to do with his business. You're his wife, not his colleague. There's only one thing for you to worry about: that he bring home the loot so you can spend it."[18] Julia has learned that a woman is only worth what she costs her husband; she is merely an expensive object that confers status on its owner. In *Une rose pour Morrison,* the official prayer, which is one of the means for institutionalized indoctrination, ends with the following words: "In the name of the Father, who produces, of the Son who consumes, and of the Holy Dough that circulates between them."[19]

Céline and Julia find mutual renewal in their friendship. The entente between the women generates the strength and energy essential for survival in marriage, which is presented here as a microcosm of patriarchal society. Céline and Julia respect one another as individuals, a sentiment that does not exist in their marriages. Their loving friendship grows to include a sexual relationship. Rochefort speaks about this sexual relationship in an interview in *Homosexualities and French Literature* where she notes that the novel takes place in the early sixties when ideas were quite different from those of the eighties. "You take two women who are deadened by marriage, completely repressed, and who meet each other. It's a meeting of the oppressed . . . [which gives them] a sudden consciousness of their condition. It's the first socialization," she explains.

They socialize as much as they can and they end up in a loving relationship. It's love based on sisterhood, a "sisterhood is powerful" where sexuality is an extension of communication, as it has often been in my relationships; and in my books, when it's really authentic, it's like that. So there they are, the two of them, and they have a loving relationship. They're afraid because everywhere they go they run headlong into the label "lesbian," thanks to men. They're not used to it, they're heteros. . . . Julia and Céline tell themselves they're not lesbians. . . . [Céline, however, henceforth] will have a stronger tendency to love women than before. She will not exactly become a lesbian, but will have a much lower threshold of tolerance for men than before. She'll have an anti-male reflex, maybe even a hatred.[20]

Céline gives way to this hatred when Julia is killed in a car crash as the two husbands race in their new cars, testing out their new toys. While Julia dies, and a child in the car Jean-Pierre was passing illegally is paralyzed, he is only wounded. Céline is horrified to think that Jean-Pierre, who has already injured and killed people in eleven accidents, will drive again. When she visits him in the hospital, she does not console him as social convention would dictate, but accuses him of killing his wife. Henceforth Céline, Rochefort's alter ego, "will put up with less and less from men. . . . she will not be intolerant toward women, who are not her oppressors, and she will be intolerant toward men. She can tend toward more openness to women and more intolerance to men. Then she can love only women. Because of this tendency, not because she has become a lesbian. In fact, that has been the case with many women who are called lesbians. It's just that one can no longer tolerate oppression."[21] And so, when Philippe wins elective office on a conservative ticket, Céline leaves him and returns to the freedom of her bohemian life where she will regain her autonomy, individuality, and her true identity.

Céline denounced the "prison" of the language we use, a denunciation which can be considered the leitmotif of *Une rose pour Morrison*. Here Rochefort again insists, as in *Cats Don't Care for Money*, that both a linguistic and a sexual revolution are prerequisites for a political revolution. In *Une rose pour Morrison*, we find the indictment of marriage of the preceding novel developed and expanded to the social and political planes as Rochefort continues her attack on those forces of society that contain and crush the individual. She describes consumer society as a gigantic conspiracy that only functions by virtue of a system of destruction by war. It is on the last page of this novel that Rochefort prophetically announces the mass student and worker strikes of May 1968. While she does not predict the outcome of this rebellion, the very last word of the novel, *beginning*, rather than the usual *end* suggests an opening onto a new world.[22]

Rochefort gives the surname Morrison to her fictional hero, Amok Morrison, in homage to Norman Morrison, a Quaker, the first American to immolate himself on the Pentagon steps in 1965 to protest the United States' so-called "peace action" in Vietnam. While the novel would seem to belong to the genre of science fiction, which predicts the nature of future societies, it is really an allegory of pre-1968 France in which the characters are personifications of abstract qualities. Despite a large cast of characters, the plot is simple. The rigid police state, dominated by the old Sénile and his Council of Vénerables, a group of old men, is opposed by a young woman, Sereine, whose teleology lectures suggest the possibility of a new, free society. Among her converts are Théostat and Triton Sauvage, a central character in the novel who represents the forces of life and of nature that will transform society. Triton Sauvage becomes a rock star and adopts the stage name of Amoking Bird, taking her first name from the fictional Amok Morrison, a young man who became a deserter from the United States army in Vietnam when he saw that he was engaged in an aggressive, oppressive war. He now travels around the world singing antiwar songs, like those of Bob Dylan, to whom the novel is dedicated, and telling people the true meaning of the words they hear and use. Here again Rochefort describes language as a repressive tool of the ruling class. She also ridicules intellectuals who use obscure, confusing language, particularly the structuralists who devote themselves to analyzing form without regard to content.

Although *Une rose pour Morrison,* like *Cats Don't Care for Money,* ends with an act of rebellion that remains unresolved, it is not purely negative; it announces the 1968 student rebellion, which is treated in *Printemps au parking* (Spring in the parking lot, 1969) and the utopian societies of *Archaos ou le jardin étincelant* (Archaos or the glittering garden, 1972) and *Encore heureux qu'on va vers l'été* (Happy as summer approaches, 1975). *Printemps au parking* begins with a rebellious act, and the novel traces the ramifications of this act. The adolescent, working-class protagonist, Christophe Ronin, is an oppressed member of society; the victim of his class and of a blindly authoritarian father. Their relationship is a paradigm of the unequal power relationships that result from the patriarchal structure of Western society, which treats both women and children as inferior. Christophe runs away from home and goes to the Latin Quarter, where he develops a friendship with Thomas Ginsberg, a twenty-six-year-old sociology student, who is an outsider unable to share the beliefs or goals of the men in power. Thomas's social situation, like that of women, is defined by his lack of power. He has also developed personality traits usually considered typically feminine; he is sensitive, intuitive, empathetic, and caring. Like Céline, he is opposed to the excesses of consumerism and its dehumanizing effects on people; like her, he questions society's definition of normal behavior and sees how it is used as a weapon to benefit those in power. For Thomas, normalcy is the absence of repression of any sort.

The friendship of Thomas and Christophe, like that of Céline and Julia, deepens and becomes a sexual love. While it lasts for only four days, it transforms their lives. The truth of their passion inspires Thomas and Christophe to question other dictates of society. After Christophe has crossed the sexual barrier, he discovers that the boundary was completely imaginary and generalizes this lesson to include all other boundaries. He also learns that it is critical for him to redefine language so that it will communicate what he has discovered. Traditional language does not permit Christophe to describe what began with his desire for Thomas and developed into a passion for knowledge and for life. This passion, which destroys prohibitions, the bars of the inner prison, is transcended by something even more important, which is indicated in the last pages of the novel, the Revolution. Christophe returns home, not defeated, but liberated. Unlike Renaud in *The Warrior's Rest,* who had rejected the world and sought escape in an abortive suicide attempt and alcoholism before being tamed by society, Christophe discovers inner freedom and decides to work for human liberation. The book ends with the assertion "it is Spring,"[23] the affirmation of another "beginning" like the one announced at the end of *Une rose pour Morrison.*

While Rochefort's first five novels merely criticize existing abuses, *Archaos ou le jardin étincelant,* according to the author, is the most positive of her works because it also suggests a solution to these abuses.[24] In *Archaos,* she creates a feminist utopia quite different from traditional male utopias, which are predicated on patriarchal foundations and propose as utopian solutions male-determined governments and economies for the greater autonomy of men. Because the myths, the language, and the literature fashioned by the dominant culture reflect and perpetuate it even as they seek to amend it, in most male-created utopias women exist for men as either maid, monogamous wife, mother, or saint. Feminist utopias, on the other hand, posit societies that women have shaped themselves alone or in concert with men. They present visions of new worlds fashioned by feminist thought and action. This desire to speculate about the future and how it might be shaped can be read as a feminist Eros speaking the long-silenced language of women's desires. What makes *Archaos* and other utopias like it specifically feminist is that women are not dismissed as one question among many; their place is everywhere.

Archaos begins with a prelude, a message from historians who have recovered the lost past of the kingdom of Archaos, which existed "between the end of the Barbaric Age and the beginning of the Barbaric Age."[25] Setting utopia in the past permits Rochefort to present an idealized vision of what might be, based on what was. The use of the historical motif to introduce the utopian plan and then undermining the authority of the genre by questioning the very premises on which history is based, is one of the basic devices used in feminist utopian fiction. Here the story begins during the reign of the king Avatar II. In need of a male heir to continue his rule, he rapes his wife, Avanie (French for slur, humiliation). Bruised by the rape, she is ignored by the doctors who are busy finding a remedy to confer immortality on the king. Consequently, she is treated and healed by a bonesetter named Analogue. A daughter is born, "which was of no use" (15), and the king orders that she be abandoned in the forest. The queen then delivers a boy twin whose cry cannot be stilled until he is reunited with his sister. The queen secretly raises her daughter Onagre along with her son Govan; their incestuous sibling relationship symbolizes wholeness, the rejection of stereotypical separation of male and female in favor of a complete androgynous creature. Androgyny is suggested as a solution in *Archaos.*

Later, the king seeks out his daughter, who unbeknown to him has been living secretly in the castle, to marry her to the noble Acadabar de Bilande. But Onagre, who loves her brother's caresses, detests her fiancé. Fortunately, she is saved from this marriage when Acadabar is mortally wounded by a crucifix during the wedding ceremony. One day the king, who delights in raping shepherdesses, meets his daughter in a field and, mistaking her for a shepherdess, rapes her. When he realizes what he has done—in a parody of the oedipal myth which is in keeping with the reversal of masculine myths in feminist literature—he castrates himself.[26] The inhabitants of Archaos demand that this king, "without head [or tail]" (143–44), abdicate, and it is Govan who accedes to the throne.

Govan's first act is to accept an invitation to a brothel, where he is awarded a good conduct certificate. This brothel also doubles as a convent. By the fusion of convent and brothel, Rochefort blurs the artificial distinctions between them, ultimately undermining these traditional institutions. In the brothel, Govan discovers that "nothing teaches like pleasure" (152), and pleasure in all its forms becomes his ruling principle. The brothel is instituted by Govan as a public necessity and the brothel-keeper Désirade is empowered to certify that only those who have given satisfaction and pleasure may serve in the government. Rochefort describes unfettered sensuality/sexuality, particularly female, as abundant and transformative, especially in the fusion of convent and brothel. Soon, Archaos becomes a country where differences of age and sex disappear, for one can frequent bordelets, bordels, bordelles, bordeaux. Then, new laws are proclaimed: everything is free, work is eliminated, and everyone does what he or she wants. The "glittering garden," a marvelous civilization of happiness, exists as a function of the "chaos" of Archaos, a decentralized cooperative anarchy in which everyone has power over his or her own life. In this respect Archaos is typical of feminist utopias, which are generally anarchist in their politics—power is for everyone and over no one.

Rochefort has stated that there is in *Archaos* "a dream land with sorcerers, songs, music and an enchanted forest. This is the country of the irrational and the other way of thinking and feeling. The character who really makes things happen in the first part of the novel is Analogue, who pushes constantly toward a destruction of patriarchy.

He is a provoker, he provokes through the queen." Although he loves
the queen, Rochefort continues,

his way of living is non-coital—he doesn't make love [because the novel] is
against the finality of intercourse—there is no intercourse, but he says that
he is fulfilled. There are caresses, touching, massage; there is contemplation.
These ways of relating break the pattern of being in love, courting, finally
sleeping together, and that's it. These characters criticize and challenge that
pattern; they try to define another kind of relationship. They frequently make
love at a distance. The book is about how to desire without power. The
women and children take the power but don't exert it. It's a truly utopian
and futuristic message. [Furthermore,] there is no traditional couple in *Archaos*.
If a man wants to have one of the young women, the only way is to be
loved by her. So there is love in the book, but people don't live together
as couples. . . . It's a big fantasy, this book. The country I describe is not
ours. . . . There are no factories, no cars, no freeways, no houses made of
concrete. This world does not exist now or even tomorrow. If you ask me
about my ideal social structure, I would say it's *no* structure, except that a
little child has to be with his/her mother or another person who loves him
or her. *Archaos* is a work about groups.[27]

Thus, in *Archaos,* the heterosexually monogamous couple is obsolete,
further subverting the principles on which traditional society rests.

Rochefort also explains that one of the ways to recreate a culture is
to change the symbols and that is what she tried to do in *Archaos* by
changing the symbols of male and female sexuality. While the "poor
penis" has been taken as a symbol of power, she adds, this is a
perversion of the symbolism of the penis. Therefore, in the first part
of this novel—before the deposing of the king—she destroyed the
concept of phallic aggressiveness, and, in the utopian part—after Govan's
accession to the throne—she made the penis symbolic of waiting, of
passivity, and of invitation. These meanings, in her opinion, exist in
many natural symbols like obelisks, steeples, and trees, which stand
waiting to attract people and to gather them together. Unfortunately,
this sense has been subverted and sacrificed to an imperialist, aggressive
meaning.[28]

Encore heureux qu'on va vers l'été, like *Archaos,* is a utopian vision
but it uses the commune as the primary social unit. Here Rochefort
expresses her faith in children as a revolutionary force as she tells the
story of opportunities seized by children to escape from a society that
stifles them. The novel "describes the joyous revolution, the exhilarating

freedom and collective pleasure of children, adolescents, women, animals and nature—a privileged coalition which forms the core of Rochefort's utopian vision of a vital, triumphant feminist universe."[29] The novel begins in a classroom where the children, bored by their teacher, finally get up and go out to the outside world. Régina and Grâce are two of these children. While they are the protagonists of the novel, they are not alone. Everywhere children are fleeing school and family. Régina and Grâce, who suffer the double handicap of sex and age, confide in one another their distaste for parental and school authority and their happiness with their new freedom. As they go toward the sea, they are sheltered by women who identify with the children, for they also stand to gain from the overthrow of a system that treats them as objects. The children enter a commune in which the members believe that logic and authoritarianism should be replaced by intuition and imagination. In the commune, girls are proud of their sex and Régina and Grâce learn to share this pride, particularly after they become lovers. The girls become friendly with a young boy named David who, in a reversal of traditional values, admires them and wants to be like them. But this is not necessary, for he and they are more united by their shared ideas than separated by their different sexes.

In Rochefort's utopian vision, traditional sex roles and attributes are eliminated and unfettered sexuality replaces theology. All of her works, Rochefort states, illustrate her belief that sexuality is a key to moral, social, and political awareness.[30] The arbitrary, stereotypical separation of male and female, of masculine and feminine attributes, is rejected in favor of androgyny or wholeness; women must cast off role definitions and move toward an androgynous being. Androgyny represents a vision of human possibility in which difference would constitute harmony, not opposition. It represents the negation of gender stereotypes and the absorption of positive qualities of "masculinity" and "femininity" into the total personality; it mandates a rejection of destructive gender norms in favor of more authentic selfhood.

Violette Leduc

"My mother never gave me her hand."[31] "My case is not unique: I am afraid of dying and distressed at being in this world."[32] These opening lines of the novel *L'Asphyxie (In the Prison of Her Skin)*, 1946, and the autobiographical work *La bâtarde (La Bâtarde)*, 1964, announce the solitude and despair that characterize all of Violette Leduc's works.

Whether explicitly expressed as autobiographical confession or thinly disguised as fiction, in her work Leduc (1907–72) speaks of her life as one in which "tears and cries have taken up a great time of my time. I am tortured by all that time lost whenever I think about it. I cannot think about things for long, but I can find pleasure in a withered lettuce leaf offering me nothing but regrets to chew over. There is no sustenance in the past. I shall depart as I arrived. Intact, loaded down with the defects that have tormented me. I wish I had been born a statue; I am a slug under my dunghill. Virtues, good qualities, courage, meditation, culture. With arms crossed on my breast I have broken myself against those words" (4). The same desperate account of a broken life, the same violence of cold despair, and the same repetition of words and gestures that speak of love condemned to destruction and ultimate decay are found—repeated over and over again—in each of Violette Leduc's works. Simone de Beauvoir writes in the preface to *La Bâtarde* that Leduc, who described herself as "a desert talking to myself," introduces the reader into "a world full of sound and fury, where love often bears the name of hate, where a passion for life bursts forth in cries of despair; a world laid waste by loneliness" (vi). Leduc's loneliness is the lot of the lesbian in an age of silence and of reprobation. In her work we have a precise sensual, emotional, and psychological record of a woman defined and diminished by her sexuality. Her world of solitude and suffering is that of a female deprived of maternal love, beauty, and socially sanctioned heterosexuality.

Although Leduc suffered from sexual oppression, she never understood clearly the nature of the patriarchal culture that she was opposing, and fought blindly against it. As a result, her novels, like many novels of love and friendship between women, are characterized by battles about dominance and submission, self-punishment, and despair before gender stereotypes. That is why her novels do not create new worlds for the protagonists, since they continue the same battle with gender norms of traditional novels. We can also understand why Leduc's novels end in defeat, for it is only when the rules of a repressive sexual code are suspended and the characters can act without the fear of being abnormal that there exist possibilities for successful denouements. This occurs in the works of Monique Wittig where the strength to be different and to reach out to create a new world without gender stereotypes frees the characters from the crippling effects of guilt.

While Leduc does not go as far as Wittig, whose lesbian fiction is based on the theory that women can be free from gender roles only by separating themselves completely from the patriarchal enclosure, she is still acknowledged by Wittig as her only predecessor because in her works the narrator as lesbian is describing her own experience; she is no longer seen from an outside point of view.[33] This is true of all of Violette Leduc's works, which can be classified as autobiographical fiction. Leduc's protagonists are women and almost all are projections of herself; they are condemned to solitude and seek desperately, but unsuccessfully, to escape from this solitude through love. There is very little to distinguish the autobiographical *La Bâtarde*, an account of the first forty years of the author's life, from her novels. These novels, which include *In the Prison of Her Skin, Ravages (Ravages),* 1955, and *Thérèse et Isabelle (Thérèse and Isabelle)*—a censored text from *Ravages* published separately in 1966—are merely reworkings of some of the most significant episodes of *La Bâtarde.*

La Bâtarde is the most important of Leduc's works, for it provides a key to the author's life and literary production. Leduc starts by describing the circumstances that determined her destiny. She was born in 1907, the illegitimate daughter of a servant, seduced by the son of the wealthy family for whom she worked. Simone de Beauvoir writes that "throughout the years of childhood, her mother inspired her with an irremediable sense of guilt: guilt for having been born, for having delicate health, for costing money, for being a woman and therefore condemned to the miseries of the feminine condition" (vi). In *La Bâtarde,* Leduc writes,

As we sat at breakfast, my mother would talk to me about the unpleasant side of life. Each morning she made me a terrible gift: the gift of suspicion and mistrust. All men were swine, men had no hearts. She stared at me with such intensity as she made this statement that I would wonder whether perhaps I wasn't a man. There wasn't a single one among them to redeem the race as a whole. To take advantage of you, that was their aim. I must get that into my head and never forget it. Swine. All swine. . . . My mother explained everything to me. I had been warned. I had no excuse for making a mistake. Men follow women, I mustn't let them catch me. (25–26)

Her mother's recriminations made Leduc see herself as belonging to a sex that was cursed and constantly threatened by men. The image of the mother is essential in the female's search for identity, and Leduc's image was that of a woman repressed by all of society's institutions and who projected her feelings upon her daughter, thereby depriving her of a sense of self. Berthe Leduc engraved indelibly in her daughter's consciousness the association of guilt with sexuality, and rejected her daughter as the embodiment of her own guilt. It was Leduc's never ending search for her mother's love, despite her awareness of its futility, that explains her unrelenting quest for love. Yet she was saved from complete rejection for a brief period by the love of her grandmother, who represented for Violette the ideal combination of maternal tenderness and paternal protection. This androgynous figure becomes for the narrator "the first homosexual man to whom I became passionately attached."[34] Unfortunately, her grandmother died when the child was only nine years old. The loss of the one person in the world who loved her produced in Leduc a desperate fear of abandonment, a fear that caused her to poison later relationships, anticipating abandonment by initiating it herself.

When Violette was thirteen years old, her mother married, a betrayal that confused and profoundly disturbed Violette, who had taken her mother's admonitions to heart. The mother who had taught her to hate and fear men betrayed her for one. Three years later, her mother gave birth to a legitimate son; he was to share her life while Violette was sent to boarding school. The novel *In the Prison of her Skin* recounts in fictional form these early years of unrequited longing for the love of a cold, self-centered mother, compensated in part by the love and attention of her grandmother, whom she called "my saviour and my comrade."[35] Her mother constantly reproaches the child for her illegitimate birth, but the child does not understand the crime for which she must assume responsibility and guilt. Her feelings of loneliness and abandonment continue at boarding school and, finally, are exacerbated at the end of the novel when the girl is left to spend her vacation alone in the empty school because no one comes to take her home.

La Bâtarde continues with an account of Leduc's first lesbian love affair with Isabelle, a classmate, which led to her expulsion from school. We see here a major thematic development, one that takes place "when women begin to write about women loving women. The experience of loving a woman is, for the narrative voice, *the* experience of awakening, the revelation of an unknown unsuspected world which, once glimpsed, can never be ignored. It is a momentous discovery whose importance within the text and beyond was until recently obscured by the weighty screen of psychological misreadings."[36] But Leduc is unable to take the step taken by Rochefort, Wittig, Cixous and others; she still is filled with shame at her desire. The love affair ends when Isabelle comes to visit Violette during the summer vacation and their discomfort at this reunion brings an end to their relationship.

The short novel *Thérèse and Isabelle* originally was the prologue to *Ravages* but was censored by the publisher and cut from the work. The scenes of lesbian lovemaking were incorporated with modifications into *La Bâtarde,* and ultimately published as a separate work in 1966. *Thérèse and Isabelle* continues where *In the Prison of Her Skin* leaves off, but here the girl does not long for her mother, as in *La Bâtarde,* but fears her overbearing and dictatorial presence. Here, the rupture between the two girls is caused by the mother's withdrawal of Thérèse from boarding school, a fantasy about maternal interest and involvement absent from the autobiographical *La Bâtarde.* The descriptions of lesbian lovemaking, from the point of view of the participant rather than the voyeur, mark a significant breakthrough in women's literature:

The hand was wandering through whispering snow-capped bushes, over the last frosts on the meadows, over the first buds as they swelled to fullness. . . . Isabelle, stretched out upon the darkness, was fastening my feet with ribbons, unwinding the swaddling bands of my alarm. . . . She was kissing what she had caressed and then, light as a feather duster, the hand began to flick, to brush the wrong way all that it had smoothed before. The sea monster in my entrails quivered. Isabelle was drinking at my breast, the right, the left, and I drank with her, sucking the milk of darkness when her lips had gone. The fingers were returning now, encircling and testing the warm weight of my breast. The fingers were pretending to be waifs in a storm; they were taking shelter inside me. A host of slaves, all with the face of Isabelle, fanned my brow, my hands.

She knelt up in the bed.

"Do you love me?"

I led her hand up to the precious tears of joy.

Her cheek took shelter in the hollow of my groin. I shone the flashlight beam on her, and saw her spreading hair, saw my own belly beneath the rain of silk. The flashlight slipped, Isabelle moved suddenly toward me.

As we melted into one another we were dragged up to the surface by the hooks caught in our flesh, by the hairs we were clutching in our fingers; we were rolling together on a bed of nails. We bit each other and bruised the darkness with our hands. (84)

When Leduc's relationship with Isabelle comes to an end, she has a love affair with Hermine, a music teacher at the boarding school. This affair continues on weekends after she is expelled from school when her correspondence with Hermine is discovered. She then joins her family in Paris and resumes her studies. In 1927, when she fails to pass her *baccalauréat,* she takes a job in the publicity department of Plon publishers, but leaves after a few years because of pulmonary illness. At this time, she meets Gabriel Mercier who occupies a peripheral role in her life for several years. Violette's relationship with Hermine, like all her relationships, is doomed to failure, but this time it is because it mirrors the patterns of the straight heterosexual relationship. Leduc recounts her attempts to become a "real woman," by frequenting fashion houses and beauty salons. She disparages her attempts to fulfill patriarchal expectations but at the same time despairs because she cannot measure up to these expectations, haunted always by her perceptions of her own ugliness. Her relationship with Hermine finally ends when Violette, pursued by her demons and humiliated by the traditional female role she is playing in this recreation of a heterosexual couple, decides to retaliate, humiliating Hermine in turn by persuading her to make love in a hotel room before the eyes of a voyeur. The need to destroy this relationship, as well as all her relationships, is a theme that runs through Leduc's work. She fluctuates constantly between self-love and self-destruction, femininity and masculinity, sadism and masochism, aggressiveness and passivity, constantly caught in the trap that pits women against themselves and condemns them to loneliness and alienation. In 1939, Leduc finally marries Gabriel Mercier because, she writes, of "the fear of becoming an old maid, the fear that people might say: she couldn't find anyone, she was too ugly. The need to destroy, to annihilate what I had had, what I still had then" (302). Besides, Leduc felt that because Gabriel was simple and submissive, she could assume the dominant masculine role in their relationship.

The novel *Ravages* is the fictionalized account of Leduc's relationships with Hermine and Gabriel, here named Cécile and Marc. In the first part of the novel, Thérèse (Violette) picks up Marc in a movie theater in Paris, but does not have sexual intercourse with him because she is afraid of losing her virginity. The next part deals with her lesbian relationship with Cécile, a young music teacher. They lead a simple, domestic life, but Cécile is jealous of Thérèse's relationship with Marc. Thérèse feels trapped and flees Cécile but returns to find that Cécile has fallen in love with another woman. She then goes back to Marc and forces him into a disastrous marriage, which she then makes repeated efforts to destroy. She finally succeeds when she ends an unwanted pregnancy, almost dying in the process. After her recovery, she finds herself alone, but she is fortified by a determination to live for herself.

The work ends with the acceptance of solitude and with the relief and liberation brought about by a renunciation of sexuality. The events described in the last part of *La Bâtarde,* which includes the years of the German occupation, do not appear in any novel. Violette leaves Paris and lives in Normandy with the writer Maurice Sachs, whom she had met just before the beginning of the war. While previously she had always staged the ultimate breakup of her sexual relationships, she now chooses a homosexual partner to avoid any physical entanglement because, however painful sexual indifference may be, it frees her from the destructive effects of sexual passion. It is when all possibility of sexual fulfillment is absent that she is able to write and to live in and for herself. Her attraction to homosexual writers may also be because they provided reinforcement for her own rejection of heterosexuality.

Yet, although seeking a respite from sexuality, Leduc cannot help but be jealous of Sach's love affair with a young man. Her lack of occupation gives her too much opportunity to think back on her unhappy life. One day, exasperated by her constant complaining, Sachs tells her to write down all that she has been telling him. She then starts to write the work that will be *In the Prison of Her Skin.* During these years, she also becomes involved in the black market. Her confidences about money and its importance to her are as unusual as her sexual confessions. In *La Bâtarde,* Leduc admits calmly that the Occupation gave her her chance and that she seized it without question. She finds that money brings independence and she takes increasing risks to sell her goods in Paris, admitting frankly that black-marketeering had for the first time provided her with money and self-respect. "My wealth and my beauty in the paths of Normandy lay in the efforts I made. I kept going until I had what I wanted: I was existing at last. I was succeeding, and my courage led me astray" (488). She knew that a return to normalcy would mean a return to her former, unhappy marginal existence and, indeed, *La Bâtarde* ends with the Liberation, which leaves her adrift in Paris:

1944. I am thirty-seven. I am almost forty. It's odd, I don't feel sad. I am getting older, therefore I shall suffer less and less. I have never had anything and I possess nothing now. I was forgetting: I had a child, it was a well-formed boy, so the doctor said. Gone into the abortionist's grape-trampling, my handsome child. Isabelle is in the Louvre. I shall go and see her. Hermine I see quite often. . . . My mother is preparing to leave Paris forever. Our loves will be fire beneath the ashes. As for Fidéline, she is my little apple who keeps eternally. . . . I am thirty-seven, I still have many years in which to weep. . . . I shall draw my tears from the springs, from the streams, I shall bite into the fruit of my desolation. That is the price of your egocentricity, my little one . . . now, in 1944, I am plunging deep into the abyss of onanism . . . the others all are gone. (487)

La folie en tête (Mad in Pursuit), 1971, is the second volume of Leduc's autobiography and it begins where *La Bâtarde* ended, covering the postwar years in Paris. Through a friend, Leduc's manuscript of *In the Prison of Her Skin* is shown to Simone de Beauvoir and, suddenly, a miracle takes place. Beauvoir likes what she reads, counsels and encourages Leduc to continue her writing. Leduc develops a passionate attachment to Beauvoir, and recounts this adoration in the novel *L'Affamée* (Ravenous), 1948, which is the fictionalized account of Leduc's love for the maternal, unapproachable figure of Simone de Beavoir, here called "Madame."

Violette Leduc's other fictional works, while not direct autobiographical transpositions, are linked by the themes of solitude and alienation. In them, woman's loneliness is exaggerated and takes on a symbolic quality. In two of her fictional works, *La vieille fille et le mort (The Old Maid and the Dead Man)*, 1958, and *La femme au petit renard (The Woman with the Little Fox Fur)*, 1965, the women, cut off from or cast out by society, are lonely to the point of utter isolation. For Leduc, human relationships can be summed up in the pathetic relationships found in these novellas.

Clarisse, the protagonist of the first novella, leads a calm, solitary life, until one day she finds a dead tramp in her café. The rest of the work deals with Clarisse's relationship with the corpse as she cleans and cares for him, hiding him from the few customers who come into her café. She speculates about his identity and his past and speaks to him. Gradually, however, she becomes tired of his silence and realizes that he will never respond to her. The corpse grows cold and she sees in the lifeless body a symbol of her wasted, solitary life. The companion of the woman in the second story, who is a precursor of the present-day bag lady, is a threadbare fox furpiece that she had salvaged from a garbage pail. This furpiece is her only treasure, her friend and her lover. One day, when she is on the verge of starvation, she decides to sell the fur to buy food, but is astonished when her offer is rejected with disbelief and disgust. She goes out into the street and holds out her hand to beg. When she receives money, she is overjoyed and returns to her miserable room and to the companionship of her fox fur which she calls her "angel." Her love of the old fur is reminiscent of Flaubert's "simple heart," Félicité, and her love of her one possession, the stuffed parrot, which she identifies with the Holy Ghost.[37]

All of Leduc's works end with further withdrawal into solitude and silence, the logical outcome of the female condition, because her women are victims of a society in which they lack power and any possibility for self-realization. Cut off and isolated from one another, they have been denied a sense of community and the possibility for bonding that has strengthened the male. Her characters bear witness to the fact that liberty and equality are limited to members of the fraternity. While Leduc poses the problem of woman's madness stemming from their powerlessness and lack of community, she proposes no solutions. She did, however, open the door to contemporary feminist writers by articulating the problem they set about to solve. Her work marks a transition between Colette and writers like Monique Wittig; her influence inspired the new feminist writing.

Monique Wittig

Monique Wittig (b. 1935) maintains that it is necessary to radically rethink and reinvent women and has based her work on the theory that women can be free from gender roles only through a total break with masculine culture. She seeks to end the oppression of women by a male-dominated society, replacing it with a more acceptable social order, and emphasizes the right to be different, without concern for male approval. Like other modern feminist writers, most notably Christiane Rochefort and Hélène Cixous, Wittig insists that language is at the heart of any challenge to literary tradition, cultural practices, and dominant ideological forms and that women's writing is essential for change, for it prepares the transformation of social and cultural structures. While she proposes that revolution must first take place in language and writing, she does not seek to take over the standard terminology and language of male discourse, but rather to deconstruct the so-called "phallic" structure of language, and to reconstruct language in the role of namer or creator of meanings. Since the essence of writing is renaming, to do so the writer must "be free to play around with the notion that day might be night, love might be hate, nothing can be too sacred to the imagination to turn into its opposite or to call experimentally by another name."[38]

Not only is Wittig attempting to give voice to women's language, which has been muted by the oppressively loud voice of the male, but she also seeks to explore women's history and traditions in order to bring about a change in the old ways of thinking. Her works provide insight into women's true experience and contradict male cultural myths; they are not limited to traditional women's genres such as the novel, the memoir, or the autobiography, but instead appropriate and rewrite traditional male literary genres, from epic poetry to bildungsroman. *L'Opoponax (The Opoponax)*, 1964, for example, creates a new type of female novel of development in which the female children reject traditional feminine socialization, while *Les guérillères (Les Guérillères)*, 1969, mocks the traditional epic poem, substituting for the male warriors who fight for God and country, armies of women who annihilate so-called male heroes. In *Le corps lesbien (The Lesbian Body)*, 1973, the author rewrites the biblical Song of Songs, but here the lovers are lesbians. The *Brouillon pour un dictionnaire des amantes (Lesbian Peoples Material for a Dictionary)*, 1975, creates a dictionary that defines the new female language,[39] while *Virgile, non* (1985), transforms the masculine pilgrimage to God of the *Divine Comedy* into the lesbian Wittig's journey through the hell, purgatory, and heaven of a mythic San Francisco led, not by Virgil, but by the female guide Manastabal.

Wittig's first novel, *The Opoponax*, seems at the outset to be a typical autobiographical novel of childhood, as perceived by the female protagonist, designated in the text as "on" (one)—a collective, impersonal subject pronoun which alternates with her full name Catherine Legrand. The text opens with her first day in a boys'·and girls' primary school, when a little boy walks in and asks who wants to see his "weewee-er,"[40] to her last year as a boarder in an all-girls' Catholic boarding school. It focuses at the end on her intense relationship with Valerie Borge and her emergence as a subject who finally says "I," instead of "on" after she has discovered her love for the other girl. This occurs in the last scene of the novel, which takes place at the funeral of one of the teachers in a remote mountain cemetery. To Catherine Legrand and Valerie Borge death is still unreal, and Catherine recites poetry to herself as they lower Mlle Caylus into the ground. It is not the teacher, however, but Valerie Borge of whom she is thinking as she recites a verse by the sixteenth-century poet Maurice Scève: "Tant je l'aimais qu'en elle encore je vis" (So much I loved her that I still live in her),[41] using the first-person pronoun *je* for the first and only time in the novel. But *The Opoponax* is in reality an antibildungsroman, for here the protagonist refuses the education that will lead to her gradual integration into society, demonstrating, as Beauvoir affirmed and Wittig corroborates, that "one is not born a woman."[42] In this novel, the female children, particularly Catherine Legrand, reject with impunity both feminine sex role stereotypes and socialization.

While Catherine Legrand has many friends and acquaintances in primary school, in secondary school she becomes interested in only one person, Valerie Borge, for whom she develops a passionate attachment. Valerie writes poetry, tells fabulous stories, and does not seem to notice Catherine. Her fascination with Valerie inspires Catherine to invent a mysterious creature, either bird or animal, who is of a proud and surly disposition, dangerous when crossed. She names him the *opoponax,* a variation on the spelling of the opoponax plant from which both perfume and healing balm are derived. The opoponax writes threatening letters to Valerie to make her pay attention to Catherine, warning her that he can cause fires and tangles in the hair and that he will be seen at dawn sitting on the windowsill of the dormitory. The other students begin to speculate about the identity of the opoponax but Valerie guesses who he is and puts an apologetic answer to his letters behind the study hall piano. She tells Catherine that she loves her too. The opoponax is power and defiance and "he may also be the love that dares not speak its name—a creature found in convent boarding-schools sitting on the window sill at dawn."[43] When Valerie declares that she also loves Catherine, the opoponax is soothed and is no longer heard from. The opoponax, then, symbolizes emerging female sexuality, latent because the girls do not recognize their own feelings.

The love between Valerie Borge and Catherine Legrand grows in the all-female social milieu. Their choice of reading enhances the female bonding that is already present; their interest is centered, not on the exploits of Roland and Olivier in the great epic *Song of Roland,* but rather on the obscure French epic heroine Guiborc, who successfully led an army of women against the pagan invaders.[44] Thus, while Catherine does exhibit some of the classical patterns of adolescence described by Simone de Beauvoir in *The Second Sex,* she does not dream of a prince charming or even notice boys but instead relates to female heroines, to the girls in her class in general, and to Valerie Borge in particular.

While males are peripheral in *The Opoponax,* they are the object of all-out war in *Les Guérillères.* Here, armies of women, who have declared

war on male language and culture, battle, dance and make love together
in a text in which reflections on past female experiences as well as new
experiences and expectations are all formulated in a new language. This
work exposes the flawed thinking of male-dominated societies and creates
visions of how women can break out of that tradition by the linguistic
and narrative overthrow of masculine literary structures, as "THE
WOMEN AFFIRM IN TRIUMPH THAT / ALL ACTION IS OVER-
THROW."[45] The feminine plural *elles* is used throughout the text to
designate the collective female protagonist, thereby establishing the fact
that women constitute a historical and social class and that the question
of sexual differences is, in truth, one of class struggle, of opposition
between socially and politically constituted groups.

Wittig uses a fragmentary structure in *Les Guérillères* to eliminate
the concepts of linearity and continuity that characterize male discourse.
The work thus is composed of a series of seemingly unrelated and
autonomous episodes interspersed with lists of women's names, printed
in capital letters, which occur every six pages. These names are single
forenames that not only parody male genealogy with its lists of fathers
and sons, but also completely eliminate the patronymic, leaving them
only with

> THAT WHICH IDENTIFIES THEM LIKE
> THE EYE OF THE CYCLOPS,
> THEIR SINGLE FORENAME (13)

The sign of the circle, which follows the opening poem and precedes
the start of the narrative, recurs twice more in the text and introduces
each of the three major parts of the work. At the beginning, the O
symbolizes the vulva, "the valorization of the female principle over the
male. . . . [Here] the essence of female power and potential is not
symbolized by the womb which, in heterosexual ideology, receives,
reproduces and nurtures, but by the vulva, active, empowered, an
autonomous locus of desire and energy which imprints itself aggressively
upon both text and context."[46]

In the first section of the work the author describes the way of life
of an unspecified number of female protagonists who lead a peaceful,
rather primitive existence. They work, play, hunt, and harvest; activities
that are interspersed with ritualistic ceremonies. The women exalt their
bodies, in particular the female genitalia. They sing songs, tell stories,
and read or write books, among them collective works called the

"feminaries." These works serve a valuable didactic function for they provide women with information about their own bodies. The feminaries illustrate the importance of having women write and read their own history as a means of creating a shared consciousness of women's experience. Originally, the feminaries were used to record the symbols, myths, and rituals that bonded women to each other during centuries of oppression. Passing down these tangible elements of women's presence in the world not only comforted succeeding generations of women, but, by representing survival and continuity, they validated the significance of women in a male culture. Later on, however, the women decide that the feminaries have exhausted their usefulness and must be burned, because the language of the feminaries and the reality they create are in the final analysis pages of words that belong to the patriarchy. The burning signifies that any words pertaining to the old order are useless and can only encumber women and their efforts to create utopia. At this point the women decide that they have gone beyond the need to use their bodies as symbols: "They say that at the point they have reached they must examine the principle that has guided them. They say it is not for them to exhaust their strength in symbols. They say henceforward what they are is not subject to compromise. They say that they must break the last bond that binds them to a dead culture. They say that any symbol that exalts the fragmented body is transient, must disappear. Thus it was formerly. They, the women, the integrity of the body their first principle, advance marching together into another world" (72).

The descriptions of female tribal life end as the females suddenly change, in the second part of the text, into "les guérillères"—female warriors whose name is a neologism formed by the joining of "guérrières" (female warriors) with "guérilla," (guerrilla fighter). The main preoccupation of these *guérillères* is the preparation of their war, which is carried out in the third part. Thousands of militant women are engaged in battles in which they attack and annihilate the male enemy. The women are in command, they are invincible, and their war ends only after total destruction is achieved. Descriptions of their battles alternate with militant feminist arguments.

The women say, the men have kept you at a distance, they have supported you, they have put you on a pedestal, constructed with an essential difference. They say, men in their way have adored you like a goddess or else burned you at their stakes or else relegated you to their service in their back-yards.

They say, so doing they have always in their speech dragged you in the dirt. They say, in speaking they have possessed violated taken subdued humiliated you to their hearts' content. They say, oddly enough what they have exalted in their words as an essential difference is a biological variation. They say, they have described you as they described the races they called inferior. They say, yes, these are the same domineering oppressors, the same masters who have said that negroes and women do not have a heart spleen liver in the same place as their own, that difference of sex difference of colour signify inferiority, their own right to domination and appropriation. (101–2).

Peace can only be restored with the destruction of this master/slave relationship and Wittig describes a peaceful future in which men have been destroyed and women live together in harmony, together with those men who have joined the feminist cause.

They go to meet the young men, their groups mingle forming long chains. They take them by the hand and question them. They lead them away on to the hills. With them they climb the steps of the high terraces. They make them sit down by their side on the terraces. The men learn their songs during the hot afternoons. They taste their cultivated fruits for the first time. . . . The women choose names with the men for the things round about them. They make them look at the space which everywhere extends to their feet. It is a limitless prairie covered with flowers, daisies in the spring, marguerites in summer, in autumn white and blue meadow saffron. . . . It is a field shorn of every edifice where as far as eye can see the corn grows the rye or the green barley, the orange-coloured rice. The women make them savour the mildness of the climate, identical throughout the seasons, unchanging by day and night. (137–38).

In a final poem, Wittig summarizes the cycle of destruction and creation at the heart of the modern French feminist utopian plan:

ARISE NO / SYMBOLS MASSED
EVIDENT / THE DESIGNATED TEXT
(BY MYRIAD CONSTELLATIONS)
FAULTY
LACUNAE LACUNAE
AGAINST TEXTS
AGAINST MEANING
WHICH IS TO WRITE VIOLENCE
OUTSIDE THE TEXT
IN ANOTHER WRITING

THREATENING MENACING
MARGINS SPACES INTERVALS
WITHOUT PAUSE
ACTION OVERTHROW (143)

The message here is that action—the act of writing, of creating new language—is the overthrow not only of words, but of the reality and the traditions those words have fashioned and perpetuated. Because naming creates reality, the struggle of the *guérillères* focuses on attempts to destroy existing language and the history it has created and continues to create. The goal of the succeeding work, *The Lesbian Body,* is to create a new language and to provide a means of using it, since to reclaim the power of naming is to destroy the cultural restrictions that prevent the unfettered development of women.

The *Lesbian Body* can also be read as an epilogue to *Les Guérillères,* for it is the completion and fulfillment of its plan to have women unite in the defense of the female principle in order to gradually build a collective female state. The men against whom the *guérillères* fought have disappeared and there is now time and space for women to live and love as they want in a world of women occupied entirely with themselves and with each other. "The Amazons . . . live among themselves, by themselves and for themselves at all the generally accepted levels: fictional, symbolic, actual. . . . It is our fiction that validates us."[47] There are a few glimpses of a kind of utopian Lesbos, but the main preoccupation of the book is simply and symbolically with the female body. "In the beginning is the body and at the end; an indestructible body, singular in the text, but signifying the potentiality of all female bodies."[48]

In *The Lesbian Body,* Wittig continues the process of deconstruction—started in *The Opoponax* and *Les Guérillères*—as she takes up concepts, terms, models, and tools that have lost their value as truth in a given culture, and reinscribes them in a new context, which alters their function as well as their meaning. Deconstructive practice thus preserves, at the same time as it transforms, particular cultural artifacts. Here, by appropriating the style and structure of the biblical Song of Songs, Wittig subverts the power of the original and reaffirms the arbitrary nature of myth; by choosing a biblical text, she demonstrates disregard for the inherent mystery and so-called truth of patriarchal religious belief. Indeed, "there is no . . . stronger challenge to the Judeo-Christian tradition, to patriarchy and phallocentrism than the lesbian-feminist . . . [who is] the only true anti-Christ, the willful assassin of Christian love."[49]

The Lesbian Body is made up of two kinds of writing. There are, on the one hand, a series of short narrative passages that are in effect prose poems describing the limitless ways in which female beings interact with each other and unite. These texts present innumerable encounters between two lovers (j/e and tu). In these narrative passages, lesbianism is treated poetically as one of many neglected aspects of feminine truth. Interspersed between these passages are double pages of bold faced type—unpunctuated and capitalized, as are the lists of names Wittig uses in *Les Guérillères*—which list and celebrate all the parts and functions of the female body, beginning with:

> THE LESBIAN BODY THE JUICE THE
> SPITTLE THE SALIVA THE SNOT
> THE SWEAT THE TEARS THE WAX
> THE URINE THE FAECES THE
> EXCREMENTS THE BLOOD THE
> LYMPH[50]

Wittig's reorganization of metaphor around the lesbian body represents a shift from what was previously the central metaphor, the phallus. "The body of the text subsumes all the words of the female body. *The Lesbian Body* attempts to achieve the affirmation of its reality. . . . To recite one's own body, to recite the body of the other, is to recite the words of which the body is made up."[51] The exploration and description of every part of the female body, the refusal to write only about those parts that are sexually desirable, signifies Wittig's rejection of male criteria and the creation of a radically new discourse. The text also refuses conventional poetic metaphorization of the body (i.e., transformation via metaphor of lips into rubies) because implicit in such metaphor is the rejection of the actual woman as inadequately desirable. Wittig's lovers reverse this literary disembodiment. Here all parts of the body are equally invested with erotic power.[52]

All first-person pronouns—*j/e, m/on, m/a, m/es*—are split to emphasize the disintegration of the self that occurs every time women speak male language: "J/e is the symbol of the lived rending experience which is m/y writing, of this cutting in two which throughout literature is the exercise of a language which does not constitute m/e as subject. J/e poses the ideological and historic question of feminine subjects.

. . . If I (J/e) examine m/y specific situation as subject in the language, I (J/e) am physically incapable of writing I (Je), I (J/e) have no desire to do so."[53] Wittig also uses the slash to represent the disruption caused by the insertion of the lesbian body and lesbian subject into traditional language.

In *The Lesbian Body*, Wittig seeks to destroy the accepted male love discourse as well as male literary stereotypes about the female body. Inhabiting the lesbian body is the woman whose body and desire are no longer defined by man. Her body is subject, not object. "She is no longer a *corps féminin* with an imposed biological destiny, but an active participant in an equal *corps-à-corps*. No longer confined to the status of Other in relation to man, as have-not to have, or is-not to is, she is defined instead as lesbian and mirrored in an Other who is also lesbian. Instead of annihilation of the self in a sexual act, there is recuperation of self; and this self is not fetishized, but constructed, equally importantly, of all her organs, secretions, functions and sensations."[54]

In *Lesbian Peoples Material for a Dictionary*, written with Sande Zeig, women have become namers, creating a new dictionary, a source for feminist discourse unconcerned with male discourse, context, or approval. One dimension of the *Dictionary* involves a gathering of material celebrating lesbian culture and history, the other is the writing of history from a lesbian perspective. The *Dictionary*, then, is a vision of language and culture from a feminist perspective, emphasizing the fictional nature of history. It challenges the concept of history as objective and reconstructs the past with a view toward providing a cultural present favorable to lesbian feminism. Wittig and Zeig set forth, in the form of short entries arranged in alphabetical order, the imaginary world of lesbians in which mythological allusions to the Amazons appear side by side with a celebration of the parts of the female body. These entries plunge the reader into an exclusively feminine universe where man is not even scorned, but is simply ignored.

The authors set their narrative in a utopian future when lesbianism is no longer an aberration and when the companion lovers can revel in their mutual sexual fulfillment. The first entry, "Amazons," is an example of the rewriting of history from this perspective. It points back to a remote time when females were not essentially defined as mothers, nor restricted by any sexual division of labor, and tells of the present Golden Age of the narration in which economic and ideological conditions permit women freedom to choose or reject motherhood and its concomitant occupations:

In the beginning, if there ever was such a time, all the companion lovers called themselves amazons. Living together, loving, celebrating one another, playing, in a time when work was still a game, the companion lovers in the terrestrial garden continued to call themselves amazons throughout the entire Golden Age. Then, with the settlement of the first cities, many companion lovers disrupted the original harmony and called themselves mothers. Thereafter, amazon meant, for them, daughter, eternal child, she who does not assume her destiny. Amazons were banished from the cities of the mothers. At that time they became the violent ones and fought to defend harmony. For them the ancient name amazon had retained its full meaning. From now on it signified something more, she who guards the harmony. From then on, there were amazons in every age, on every continent, island, ice bank. To the amazons of all these times, we owe having been able to enter the Glorious Age.[55]

What Wittig has done here, as in all of her texts, is to make the primary relationship that of "companion lovers," not the unequal one of mother and child. Not only are they sexual lovers, they are also partners in the creation of new relationships based on the rediscovery of elements of a previously suppressed female culture.

Wittig's works can be seen as a continuation of the works of Simone de Beauvoir by reason of her contention that women are produced by the conditioning of society and that the relegation of women to the status of Other in a male-dominated society results from political, economic, and sociological causes rather than from biological destiny. In an article entitled "One is Not Born a Woman," Wittig writes, "Lesbianism is the only concept I know of which is beyond the categories of sex (woman and man), because the designated subject (lesbian) is *not* a woman, either economically, or politically, or ideologically. For what makes a woman is a specific social relation to a man, a relation that we have previously called servitude . . . a relation which lesbians escape by refusing to become or to stay heterosexual.[56] But Wittig differs from Beauvoir, who uses traditional language and seeks nothing more than an equal role for women within society. Going much further, Wittig proposes a transformation of language that calls into question the conventional notions of women and their role and postulates a society in which males and their culture have been completely eliminated.

Hélène Cixous

Hélène Cixous (b. 1937), in both her theoretical and fictional works, challenges the oppression of women by a male-dominated culture and attempts to substitute in its place a more equitable social order. She maintains that women's writing is the key to the transformation of traditional social and cultural structures. But, while she shares Monique Wittig's belief that all changes must first take place in language, she does not agree that feminist theory and literature require a society free of masculine language and cultural forms. Unlike Wittig, Cixous believes that there are specifically feminine drives that should not be discounted but rather exploited to effect changes in masculine ideologies, and she seeks to make the most of the very differences Wittig wants to eliminate.

Cixous's 1975 text "Le Rire de la Méduse" ("The Laugh of the Medusa") is a manifesto of the new women's writing, or *écriture féminine*. Like the works of Wittig, it is a rewriting of a male-invented myth, and shows how history and the future might be transformed if women were the subjects, the tellers of such myths. Here Cixous rewrites the classical myth in which Perseus was warned that he must not look into the face, but only at the reflection, of the horrible female monster whose look turned men into stone. We may consider this injunction as illustrative of man's refusal to see woman as anything but a reflection of his dominant masculinity. In her work, Cixous overturns the horror of the Medusa and writes, "You have only to look at the Medusa straight on to see her. And she's not deadly. She's beautiful and she's laughing."[57] Cixous explains the significance of this laughter in an article entitled "Le sexe ou la tête?" (translated as "Castration or Decapitation?"): "Culturally speaking, women have wept a great deal, but once the tears are shed, there will be endless laughter, instead. Laughter that breaks out, overflows, a humor no one would expect to find in women— which is nonetheless surely their greatest strength because it's a humor that sees man much further away than he has ever been seen. Laughter that shakes the last chapter of my text *LA*, 'she who laughs last.' And her first laugh is at herself."[58] What better weapon is there against a repressive "phallocracy" than to laugh at its pretentions? She who laughs asserts her mastery over events and language.

In "The Laugh of the Medusa," Cixous exhorts women to write in order to destroy the dominant masculine text and to replace it with a feminine text. Here, as in all her works, she aims a blow at "phallogocentric" culture—a neologism coined by combining "phallocentrism" (centered around the phallus) with "logocentrism" (the dominance of the word in certain forms of reasoning and conceptualisms of the world). Women, according to Cixous, have always been silenced and made to assume the role of Other in masculine language and reason. Because she has always been denied access to language and writing, Cixous states, "woman must write her self: must write about women and bring women to writing, from which they have been driven away as violently as from their bodies—for the same reasons, by the same law, with the same fatal goal. Woman must put herself into the text—as into the world and into history—by her own movement. . . . When I say 'woman,' " Cixous explains, "I'm speaking of woman in her inevitable struggle against conventional man; and of a universal woman subject who must bring women to their senses and to their meaning in history" (245).

According to Cixous, language for the woman is closely linked to her sexuality. She believes that because women are endowed with a more passive and consequently more receptive sexuality, as well as with a diffuse sexuality not centered on the penis, they are more open than men to create liberated forms of discourse. "By writing her self," Cixous explains, "woman will return to the body which has been more than confiscated from her, which has been turned into the uncanny stranger on display—the ailing or dead figure, which so often turns out to be the nasty companion, the cause and location of inhibitions. Censor the body and you censor breath and speech at the same time. . . . Write your self. Your body must be heard. Only then will the immense resources of the unconscious spring forth" (250). According to the author, "it is by writing, from and toward women, and by taking up the challenge of speech which has been governed by the phallus, that women will confirm women in a place other than that which is reserved in and by the symbolic, that is, in a place other than silence. Women should break out of the snare of silence. They shouldn't be conned into accepting a domain which is the margin or the harem" (251).

Thus *l'écriture féminine* for Cixous is both a celebration of the female body and a product of its drives, one that will change the old order of life. The injunction to "write from the body" is also an attack on "the male erection, the male preoccupation with getting it up, keeping it up, and the ways in which the life and death of the penis are projected into other aspects of culture; in the need for immortality and posterity, in the fear of death, in the centralized organization of political systems, in the impossibility of living in the here and now."[59] It is a rejection of the phallus as the prime signifier, what the Medusa laughingly calls "the little pocket signifier" (261).

For Cixous, female sexual pleasure (*jouissance*) constitutes a potential disturbance to masculine order and a text that writes of this *jouissance* dislocates the repressive structures of "phallogocentrism." If women are to discover and express what masculine history has repressed in them, they must begin with their sexuality and genital and libidinal difference from men. Because "la mère qui jouit," the figure of the mother experiencing sexual pleasure, has been absent from Western literature,[60] the description of woman's pleasure is one of the essential subjects of French feminist writers, particularly Cixous. She maintains that resistance to male culture takes place initially in the form of sexual pleasure, which has been repressed by that culture. Women, historically limited to being sexual objects for men, have been prevented from expressing their sexuality. If they challenge this interdiction and can recognize and speak about their sexuality in the new language it calls for, they will then be able to challenge all phallogocentric concepts and controls.

In "The Laugh of the Medusa," Cixous writes, "Almost everything is yet to be written by women about femininity: about their sexuality, that is, its infinite and mobile complexity, about their eroticization, sudden turn-ons of a certain miniscule-immense area of their bodies. . . . We've been turned away from our bodies, shamefully taught to ignore them, to strike them with that stupid sexual modesty" (256). Therefore, it is essential that "anything to do with the body should be explored, from the functional to the libidinal, to the imaginary, and then how all of this is articulated at the symbolic level. It is beyond doubt that femininity derives from the body, from the anatomical, the biological difference, from a whole system of drives which are radically different for women than for men."[61]

La jeune née (The Newly Born Woman), 1975, is a joint work by Cixous and Catherine Clément that combines essay, autobiography, and poetic prose. Working through history, myth, and psychoanalysis, it reveals past abuses of patriarchal culture and posits a new "feminine future." The first part of the work is an essay by Clément entitled "La Coupable" ("The Guilty One") in which she draws on Freud's studies of hysteria to analyze images of woman, specifically those of the witch and the hysteric, which she sees as exemplary figures of the female condition.[62] She maintains, as does Cixous, that it is only through a radical bisexuality, the presence within oneself of both sexes, that women can break the bonds of masculine oppression.

Cixous's part of *The Newly Born Woman* is called "Sorties" (Exits or departure), a key word in her work that stresses movement away from traditional language toward a new feminist discourse. In "Sorties," the injunction to "write the body" expands to include the idea of bisexual writing: not one of two halves, but one in which the other sexual component is not repressed. According to Cixous, "female sexuality is always at some point bisexual. Bisexual doesn't mean, as many people think, that she can make love with both a man and a woman, it doesn't mean she has two partners, even if it can at times mean this. Bisexuality on an unconscious level is the possibility of extending into the other, of being in such a relation with the other that *I* move into the other without destroying the other: that I will look for the other where s/he is without trying to bring everything back to myself."[63]

In *The Newly Born Woman,* Cixous explains how sexual difference is to be put into writing and seeks to destroy the premise of Western thought that relegates women to passivity, silence, and "otherness." Thought, she writes, "has always worked by opposition. . . . By dual, *hierarchized* oppositions. . . . Logocentrism subjects thought—all of the concepts, the codes, the values—to a two-term system, related to 'the' couple man/woman." Everything, she continues,

elaborates the same systems . . . [based on] male privilege, which can be seen in the opposition by which it sustains itself, between *activity* and *passivity*. Traditionally, the question of sexual difference is coupled with the same opposition: activity/passivity. . . . In philosophy, woman is always on the side of passivity. . . . [T]here's no place at all for women in the operation! Either the woman is passive; or she doesn't exist. . . . And if you examine literary history, it's the same story. It all refers back to man to *his* torment, his desire to be (at) the origin. Back to the father. There is an intrinsic bond between the philosophical and the literary (to the extent that it signifies, literature is commanded by the philosophical) and phallocentrism. The philosophical constructs itself starting with the abasement of woman. Subordination of the feminine to the masculine order which appears to be the condition for the functioning of the machine.[64]

After explaining the background of woman's subordination, Cixous states that "the challenging of this solidarity of logocentrism and phallocentrism has today become insistent enough—the bringing to light of the fate which has been imposed upon woman, of her burial—to threaten the stability of the masculine edifice which passed itself off as eternal-natural; by bringing forth from the world of femininity reflection, hypotheses which are necessarily ruinous for the bastion which still holds the authority" (92). She then asks "what would become of logocentrism, of the great philosophical systems, of world order in general if the rock upon which they founded their church were to crumble? . . . If it were to come out in a new day that the logocentric project had always been, undeniable, to found (fund) phallocentrism, to insure for masculine order a rationale equal to history itself? . . . Then all stories would have to be told differently" (92–93). "For me," she concludes,

the question "What does she want?" that they ask of woman, a question that in fact woman asks herself because they ask it of her, because precisely there is so little place in society for her desire that she ends up by dint of not knowing what to do with it, no longer knowing where to put it, or if she has any, conceals the most immediate and the most urgent question: "How do I experience sexual pleasure? What is feminine *sexual pleasure,* where does it take place, how is it inscribed at the level of her body, of her unconscious? And then how is it put into writing?" (95).

It is not only by writing about female sexual pleasure that Cixous attempts to dethrone "phallocratic" culture, but also by challenging traditional literary forms and narrative modes and blurring the distinctions between fiction and essay. Also, in keeping with her injunction in *The Newly Born Woman,* she deconstructs the language of the father, and reconstructs it as "feminine writing," which, she states, frees, liberates language and word usage by posing plurality against unity and multitudes of meanings against single, fixed meanings.[65] Cixous's style has been characterized as "stream of the unconscious, flowing in long sentences full of hyperbolic metaphors about wombs and mother's milk which is generally equated with the 'encre blanche' (white ink) of 'écriture féminine.' "[66] As in the work of James Joyce—the subject of Cixous's 1968 doctoral thesis, *The Exile of James Joyce or the Art of Replacement*— there is in her work extravagant punning in several languages and an insistence on a plurality of tones and voices. Writing plays with and subverts linguistic signifiers. A further influence of Joyce can be seen in the fact that the action posits the development within the reader's mind of a new way of seeing.

It is virtually impossible to explicate Cixous's "novels"—a genre classification she abandoned after 1975 in favor of "fictions"—for, like poetry, Cixous's work is not description, but evocation, not linear demonstration but circular suggestion. It is Cixous's belief that a text cannot be read as an intellectual exercise, it must be felt by the reader. It must do so with a new language that is neither descriptive nor narrative. It is the playing with language, not the plot, that is important in her works. In fact, her novels have no linear plot. What is essential for Cixous is the dethroning of "phallic" language and ideas, as well as the exploring of the feminine unconscious and sexuality. "Instead of feminine writing, I speak of a decipherable libidinal femininity which can be read in a writing produced by a male or a female." This "feminine libidinal economy," according to Cixous, is "one that tolerates the movements of the other . . . one that tolerates the comings and goings, the movements, the *écart* [space, interval, gap]. So how is this going to work in a literary text? You will have literary texts that tolerate all kinds of freedom—unlike the more classical texts—which are not texts that delimit themselves, are not texts of territory with neat borders, with chapters, with beginnings and endings, etc., and which will be disquieting because you do not feel the arrest, the edge [the *arrêt* or the *arête*]." Cixous adds that

the ideal, or the dream, would be to arrive at a language that heals as much as it separates. Could one imagine a language sufficiently transparent, sufficiently supple, intense, faithful so that there would be reparation and not only separation?[67] I am attempting to write in that direction. I try to write on the side of a language as musical as possible. . . . I am not opposed to meaning, not at all, but I prefer to speak in terms of poetry. I prefer to say that I am a poet even if I do not write poems, because the phonic and oral dimensions of language are present in poetry, whereas in the banal, clichéd language, one is far removed from oral language.[68]

Dedans (Inside), 1969, Cixous's first novel, won the Prix Médicis. While it is labeled a novel, *Inside* is an autobiography of the unconscious, as is all her work, which, she declares,

is a single body in which no volume is an end in itself. You have to see the whole. Without a subject, that is to say without a story, they all set forth the adventure of the subject who goes in search of itself by examining either its inner being or its relationship with the Eternal Being or with others: history, ideologies. . . . I, in writing, use my personal experience—there are biographical reminiscences, dreams, things I have read. (I) reads *[sic]* the text which is being written. . . . One of the goals of writing is to establish limits: time and death, moral and social prohibitions, the traditional rules of narration.[69]

Inside is a meditation on the oedipal conflict from the perspective of the girl child. Cixous tells of her passionate love for her father and the violent suffering caused by his premature death. The "plot" tells of her efforts to fill the void caused by her father's absence. In a dreamlike recreation of her North African childhood, Cixous writes about her position in relationship to the family triangle made up of her brother, dead father, and German mother, a practicing midwife who introduced Cixous at an early age to "otherness" and the guttural sounds of another tongue. *Inside* conveys a feeling of enclosure and entrapment within her family and within her own body and her imagination. To liberate oneself is to be reborn, but it is also to die, for "outside" signifies absence, just as "inside" represents a community. Only language can build a bridge between the two places, between the two mutually destructive situations. The novel itself is also divided into two parts: in the first, the child wraps herself up in her love for her dead father. In the second part, the child, now a woman, wraps herself up in her love for her lover. It is because she is linked to the two men by a similar erotic drive that she has remained a prisoner of her past.

The three "novels" published between 1970 and 1972—*Le troisième corps* (The third body, 1970), *Les commencements* (The beginnings, 1970), and *Neutre* (Neuter, 1972)—are interrelated, although they can be read separately. In these works, Cixous questions genre, limits between self and other, and divisions between masculine and feminine. The title of *Le troisième corps* refers to the third body that emerges from the mingled bodies of the narrator and her lover in the bisexual relationship prescribed in *The Newly Born Woman,* in which one moves into the other without destroying the other. The novel, in the fashion of Cixous's mentor James Joyce, functions by association rather than by sequence. Here "a female 'narrator' writes with her phallus, a hollow phallus whose name is most unstable, T.t (Thod, thot, *t t*). With echoes from Thoth, the Egyptian god of writing, T.t can be filled with nouns and adjectives, thus subverting the sequence of subject and predicate, as well as the notion of character. The name does not name, it can be read across several languages at once. T.t, the writing phallus of the narrator,"[70] subverts the masculine pen (phallus) of phallocratic culture inscribing its message on the white, virginal page.

Portrait du soleil (Portrait of the sun, 1973) is again an autobiographical text whose title "mockingly carries echoes of Western heliocentrism. The sun is the origin, father, god, and capital. To make the portrait of the sun is to represent that which cannot be looked at, like death, to defy it, to make the impossible possible, to represent the impossible. . . . *Portrait* in a certain way is a feminine story of the eye, not one that beholds its object at a distance in a reappropriating manner but one that reinscribes the structure of the eye differentially."[71] *Portrait du soleil* is also a rewriting of Freud's Dora case from a feminine angle.[72] The hysteric, in the figure of Freud's Dora, occupies a privileged position in all Cixous's work because she turns against patriarchy its own prohibitions. In "The Laugh of the Medusa," Cixous writes of the "admirable hysterics who [haunted Freud] with their inaudible and thundering denunciations. . . . Those who, with a single word of the body, have inscribed the vertiginous immensity of a history which is sprung like an arrow from the whole history of men and from biblico-capitalist society. . . . You, Dora, you the indomitable, the poetic body, you are the true 'mistress' of the Signifier. Before long your efficacity will be seen at work when your speech is no longer suppressed, its point turned in against your breast, but written out over against the other" (257).

While *Préparatifs de noces au-delà de l'abîme* (Preparations for nuptials on the other side of the abyss, 1978) is classified a "fiction," it is an evocative prose poem, another episode in Cixous's autobiography of the unconscious. It is part of the literature that centers around women loving women, and also points the way towards a new, hitherto unknown love between women that differs from the militant lesbianism of Wittig. While Wittig seeks the power that has always belonged to males, and to repress all that has traditionally been classified as female, Cixous accepts only that female homosexuality that values the feminine and eschews power.

Le livre de Promethea (Promethea's book, 1983) also centers on women loving women. Cixous introduces it as a book about love: "I am a little bit afraid for this book. Because it is a book about love. It is a burning bush. It is better to throw yourself into it. Once in the fire, you are filled with sweetness. I am in it: I swear to you."[73] Here, as in *La bataille d'Arcachon* (The battle of Arcachon, 1986), we have a book about love without reference to the male. "Besides, it is Promethea's book. It is the book that Promethea lit like a fire in the soul of H" (21).

Le livre de Promethea is the diary of a burning passion in which two lovers swear eternal love. And the beloved Promethea, "the heroine of my life, of my imagination, of my book" (21), like the mythic hero

Prometheus, who gave fire to man, gives fire, light, and joy to woman. But, then, every true love is legendary. "It is easy to love and to sing of love," Cixous writes. "It is something I know how to do very well. It is even my art. But to be loved, that is true greatness. To be loved, to allow oneself to be loved, to enter into the magic and formidable circle of grace, to receive the gifts, to find the proper gratitude, that is the true labor of love" (29).

The bilingual text *Vivre l'orange (To Live the Orange)*, 1979, which Cixous designates as "fiction," is another of her works that blurs distinctions between fiction, essay, analysis, autobiography, and poetic evocation. Here Cixous celebrates the Brazilian writer Clarice Lispector for what she perceives to be specifically female empathetic attentiveness to people and objects and for her ability to represent them in a nurturing rather than dominating way. According to Cixous, "the typically feminine gesture, not culturally but libidinally, [is] to produce in order to bring about life, pleasure, not in order to accumulate."[74] Cixous explains in *Vivre l'orange* her affinity with Lispector: "I asked: 'What have I in common with women?' From Brazil a voice came . . . *The need to go to the sources. The easiness of forgetting the source. The possibility of being saved by a humid voice that has gone to the sources. The need to go further into the birth-voice.' "*[75] Cixous tells us that Lispector "gives us, not books, but the living saved from books, from narratives, from repressive constructions."[76] What she gives us is the orange, which becomes here a symbol for the concrete reality of women who must act against oppression.

And to all of the women whose voices are like hands that come to meet our souls when we are searching for the secret, we have needed, vitally, to leave to search for what is most secret in our being, I dedicate the gift of the orange. And to all of the women whose hands are like voices that go to meet the things in the dark, and that hold words out in the direction of things like infinitely attentive fingers, that don't catch, that attract and let come, I dedicate the orange's existence, as it has been given to me by a woman, according to the entire and infinite bringing-together of the thing, including all that is kin of the air and the earth, including all of the sense relations that every orange keeps alive and circulates, with life, death, women, forms, volume, movement, matter, the ways of metamorphoses, the invisible links between fruits and bodies, the destiny of perfumes, the theory of catastrophes, all of the thoughts that a woman can nourish, starting out from a given orange.[77]

Cixous found in Clarice Lispector a writer who echoes her own exhortations for women to write, to release the feminine potential of language and use it to effect the liberation of women. Giving a voice to the feminine in language is to give a voice to the whole woman— her body, her libidinal drive, and her unconscious—to silence the voice of the patriarchy in order to construct a new symbolic order.

Conclusion

In 1976 Simone de Beauvoir wrote that there had formerly been many female authors who rejected the notion of women's literature because they wanted to be free to discuss any subject in their works on an equal footing with men. "We still want it," she continued. "However, the recent evolution of feminism has made us understand that we occupy a unique position in this universe and that, far from denying that difference, we should assume it. . . . What we all want to express by means of very different works, is certainly not the feminine universe to which tradition formerly tried to confine us: it is all of contemporary society as we see it from our viewpoint as women."[1]

The diversity Beauvoir observed is manifest in the oeuvre of the French women authors of the twentieth century who have created a body of work that covers the entire spectrum of contemporary fiction, proving that there is no intrinsically female subject matter, style, or format. Colette, in over sixty works, including novels, short stories, plays, fictionalized reminiscences, and prose poems, brings a passionate love of the visible world into the domain of fiction; Simone de Beauvoir, in a series of psychological, social, metaphysical, and problem novels illustrates theses presented in her theoretical works; and Marguerite Yourcenar's novels reflect the classical restraint and the stylistic mastery of the great French literary tradition. Elsa Triolet's social and political documentary novels, in the aggregate, constitute a modern female bildungsroman; and Zoé Oldenbourg, one of the outstanding historical novelists of this century, seeks parallels in the past with our own situation in a civilization threatened by war, brutalities, and divided loyalties. The works of Geneviève Gennari remain within the framework of the traditional novel by virtue of the notion of causality and coherent chronology as well as by the idea of normative human behavior, even as they document the situation of French women in a changing society.

The novels of Françoise Sagan trace the development of the young woman of the post–World War II generation, and vary in style from the classical restraint and probing psychological analysis of *Bonjour Tristesse* to the romantic fairy tale, *The Painted Lady*. Françoise Mallet-Joris employs a wide variety of techniques and themes, from the

177

psychological probing of her first novels, to the metaphysical and spiritual preoccupations of her later works; Claire Etcherelli brings a consideration of the destiny of the working-class woman into the mainstream of the novel. Both Nathalie Sarraute and Marguerite Duras, practitioners of the experimental novel, have broken free from traditional plot structures and language in order to center their fictional exploration around previously unexplored mental and emotional states. The novels of Christiane Rochefort, Violette Leduc, Monique Wittig, and Hélène Cixous are predicated on the necessity to disrupt traditional patterns of thought and expression. Basic to their revolution is the subversion of male language and cultural forms.

But despite this diversity, the works, with very few exceptions, evidence an awakening feminine consciousness that informs the twentieth century women's novel and that leads finally to the poetic novels of Hélène Cixous, which represent the culmination of the movement away from the traditional novel. These novels would seem to fulfill, after one hundred years, Rimbaud's prophecy: "There will be poets! When woman's unmeasured bondage shall be broken, when she shall live for and through herself, man—hitherto detestable—having let her go, she, too, will be poet! Woman will find the unknown! Will her ideational worlds be different from ours? She will come upon strange, unfathomable, repellent, delightful things; we shall take them, we shall comprehend them."[2]

Notes and References

When the English edition of a work is listed, I have used the translation. When the French edition is listed, I have done the translation. The edition indicated is the one from which the notes have been taken; the edition listed in the bibliography is the first edition of the work.

Chapter One

1. Elaine Marks, *New French Feminisms*, ed. Elaine Marks and Isabelle de Courtivron (New York: Schocken Books, 1981), 36. Cf. pages on Rochefort, Wittig, Cixous in text.
2. Germaine Brée, *Women Writers in France* (New Brunswick, N.J.: Rutgers University Press, 1973), 48.
3. Henri Peyre, "Contemporary Feminine Literature in France," *Yale French Studies* 27 (Spring–Summer 1961):49.
4. Interview with Marguerite Duras, in *New French Feminisms*, 174.
5. Elaine Marks, "Lesbian Intertextuality," in *Homosexualities and French Literature*, ed. Elaine Marks and George Stambolian (Ithaca, N.Y.: Cornell University Press, 1979), 362.
6. Ibid., 364.
7. *La vagabonde* (Paris: Albin Michel, 1965), 30.
8. *Claudine at School*, in *The Complete Claudine*, trans. Antonia White (New York: Farrar, Straus & Giroux, 1976), 6.
9. See pp. 152–53.
10. See pp. 164–65.
11. Marks, "Lesbian Intertextuality," 363.
12. Many modern feminist critics object to the use of heroine because of its connotations and prefer to call the female protagonist hero.
13. *Claudine Married*, in *The Complete Claudine*, 367.
14. An interesting comparison can be made between Colette's view of the basic incompatibility between female and male sexuality and the same conclusion reached by Henry de Montherlant, expressed from the male point of view.
15. *Claudine Married*, 375.
16. Ibid., 419.
17. *La vagabonde*, 211–12.
18. *The Vagabond* (New York: Random House, Ballantine Books, 1982), 27.
19. Ibid., 28.
20. Virginia Woolf, *A Room of One's Own* (1929).

21. *The Vagabond,* 28.

22. This was the pet name Colette's father used for her.

23. A discussion of these novels follows, pp. 10–11, 13–14.

24. Maurice Goudeket, *Close to Colette* (New York: Farrar, Straus & Cudahy, 1957), 45.

25. See 29–30.

26. *The Other One* (New York: Farrar, Straus & Giroux, 1960), 140.

27. Ibid., 142.

28. On the former see pp. 146–48; on the latter, pp. 159–66.

29. The original title of this work was *Ces plaisirs,* and the pleasures to which Colette is referring are those "which are lightly called physical."

30. On the former see pp. 157–66; on the latter, pp. 167–76.

31. *The Pure and the Impure,* trans. Herma Briffault (New York: Farrar, Straus & Giroux, 1967), 102–3.

32. Ibid., 111.

33. Annis Pratt, *Archetypal Patterns in Women's Literature* (Bloomington: Indiana University Press, 1981), 112.

34. *The Second Sex,* trans. H. M. Parshley (New York: Random House, 1968), 267. Further references follow in the text.

35. "Les femmes s'entêtent," *Temps Modernes* (Paris: Gallimard, 1975); quoted in "Simone de Beauvoir et la lutte des femmes," *L'Arc* 61:1.

36. *Memoirs of a Dutiful Daughter* (New York: World Publishing Co., 1959), 366.

37. Cf. Konrad Bieber, *Simone de Beauvoir* (Boston: Twayne Publishers, 1979), 13.

38. *La force des choses* (Paris: Gallimard, 1963), 648.

39. Interview with Madeleine Chapsal, in *Les Ecrivains en personne* (Paris: René Juillard, 1960), 34.

40. Margaret Leighton, *Simone de Beauvoir on Women* (Rutherford, N.J.: Fairleigh Dickinson University Press, 1975), 32.

41. Anne Ophir, *Regards féminins* (Paris: Denoël-Gonthier, 1976), 11.

42. *La femme rompue* (Paris: Gallimard, 1967), flyleaf.

43. Interview with Pierre Viansson-Ponte, *Le Monde,* 11 January 1978, 2.

44. The phrase "des lendemains qui chantent" is from a Louis Aragon poem.

45. *La force des choses,* 648.

46. *L'Invitee* (Paris: Gallimard, 1943), 242.

47. It is interesting to note that of the fifteen novelists studied in this work, all of whom express either social, psychological, or aesthetic preoccupations, only Beauvoir and, to a lesser extent, Françoise Mallet-Joris address philosophical issues.

48. *La force de l'âge* (Paris: Gallimard, 1960), 599.

49. *The Blood of Others* (Harmondsworth, England: Penguin, 1964), 39.

50. *La force des choses*, 276.

51. Ibid., 288.

52. It is interesting to note that, while Anne and Henri are the same age, Henri is considered to be at the height of his sexual appeal, while Anne is deemed to be old and unattractive.

53. *The Mandarins* (New York: World Publishing Co., 1956), 610.

54. On the former see pp. 52–53; on the latter, pp. 139–42.

55. *Tout compte fait* (Paris: Gallimard, 1972), 139.

56. *Les Belles Images*, trans. Patrick O'Brian (New York: G. P. Putnam's, 1968), 223.

57. Ophir, *Regards féminins*, 12–13.

58. *The Woman Destroyed*, trans. Patrick O'Brian (New York: G. P. Putnam's, 1969), 73.

59. Ibid., 85.

60. Ibid., 253–54.

Chapter Two

1. Cf. Christiane Rochefort, Monique Wittig, Hélène Cixous, in chapter 7.

2. *Alexis*, trans. Walter Kaiser (New York: Farrar, Straus & Giroux, 1984), xi.

3. Ibid., 54.

4. In *L'Immoraliste* (1902), a novel by André Gide.

5. *Alexis*, 105.

6. Preface to *Denier du rêve*, rev. ed. (Paris: Gallimard, 1971), 8.

7. *Denier du rêve*, 144.

8. Preface to *Le coup de grâce* (Paris: Gallimard, 1971), 127.

9. Ibid., 246.

10. *Mémoires d'Hadrien* (Paris: Gallimard, 1974), 321.

11. *Memoirs of Hadrian*, trans. Grace Frick in collaboration with the author (New York: Farrar, Straus & Giroux, 1963), 21. Further references follow in the text.

12. *The Abyss*, trans. Grace Frick (New York: Farrar, Straus & Giroux, 1976), 361–62.

13. Ibid., 364–65.

14. Ibid., 137.

15. The Adamites were an ascetic sect noted for practicing ritual nakedness and dispensing with marriage on the basis of having entered a reborn state of heavenly innocence.

16. Pierre Horn, *Marguerite Yourcenar* (Boston: Twayne Publishers, 1985), 96.

Chapter Three

1. In Denise Bourdet, *Brèves rencontres* (Paris: Grasset, 1963), 251.
2. *La mise en mots* (Geneva: Editions d'Art Albert Skira, 1969), 21.
3. The theme of the woman alone is also developed by Geneviève Gennari, see pp. 71–72.
4. Jean-Paul Sartre, "Sur *Bonsoir Thérèse*," *Europe*, February 1939, 162.
5. *Bonsoir Thérèse* (Paris: Denoël, 1938), 107.
6. Sartre, "Sur *Bonsoir Thérèse*," 163.
7. Preface to *Le cheval blanc* (Paris: Gallimard, 1972), 18.
8. *Le cheval blanc*, 377.
9. Ibid., 421.
10. Ibid., 275.
11. In Dominique Dessanti, *Les clés d'Elsa* (Paris: Editions Ramsay, 1983), 340.
12. Preface to *Le cheval roux ou les intentions humaines* (Paris: Editeurs Français Réunis, 1953), 14.
13. Preface to Volume I, Aragon and Elsa Triolet, *Oeuvres romanesques croisées d'Elsa Triolet et d'Aragon* (Paris: Laffont, 1964), 1:13.
14. *Visages d'un autoportrait* (Paris: Gallimard, 1977), 113.
15. Ibid., 250; 253.
16. Ibid., 340.
17. *Le procès du rêve* (Paris: Gallimard, 1982), 142.
18. Ibid., 145.
19. Ibid., 157–58.
20. Léon-François Hoffmann, "Notes on Zoé Oldenbourg's *Destiny of Fire*," *Yale French Studies* 27 (Spring–Summer 1961):129.
21. *Destiny of Fire*, trans. Peter Green (New York: Pantheon Books, 1961), 15.
22. Ibid., 16.
23. Ibid.
24. *The Heirs of the Kingdom*, trans. Anne Carter (New York: Pantheon Books, 1971), 563.
25. *Catherine the Great*, trans. Anne Carter (New York: Pantheon Books, 1965), xiii–xiv.
26. *The Chains of Love*, trans. Michael Bullock (New York: Pantheon Books, 1959), 42.
27. Pratt, *Archetypal Patterns in Women's Literature*, 74.

Chapter Four

1. Jean Hardy Robinson, *Geneviève Gennari* (Boston: Twayne Publishers, 1984), 123.
2. See the similar reaction of Cottard in Albert Camus's *The Plague*.

3. The tragic consequences of racism figure most prominently in Claire Etcherelli's *Elise ou la vraie vie.*

4. Robinson, *Geneviève Gennari,* 60.

5. "La solitude des femmes sans hommes," in *Femmes* (Paris: Plon, 1967), 2:284–97.

6. *Journal d'une bourgeoise* (Paris: Grasset, 1959), 41.

7. Pratt, *Archetypal Patterns,* 134.

8. See pp. 29–30.

Chapter Five

1. *Bonjour Tristesse* (New York: E. P. Dutton & Co., 1955), 7.

2. Ibid., 53.

3. *A Certain Smile,* trans. Anne Green (New York: E. P. Dutton & Co., 1956), 28.

4. Ibid., 128.

5. Ibid., 14.

6. A month will come, a year will come, and we,
We shall be parted by a world of seas.
How shall we suffer when the day begins
And the sun climbs the sky and then declines,
And Titus will not see his Bérénice. . . . Jean Racine, *Bérénice.*

7. Madeleine Chapsal, *Les écrivains en personne* (Paris: René Juillard, 1960), 145.

8. Brigid Brophy, *Don't Never Forget* (New York: Holt Rinehart Winston, 1967), 274.

9. *Lost Profile* (New York: Delacorte, 1976), 60.

10. Ibid., 39.

11. Ibid., 174.

12. *La Chamade* (New York: E. P. Dutton & Co., 1966), 119.

13. Ibid., 146.

14. Ibid., 155.

15. See pp. 146–47.

16. *The Painted Lady,* trans. Lee Fahnestock (New York: E. P. Dutton & Co., 1983), 117.

17. *Lettre à moi-même* (Paris: Juillard, 1963), 67. Further references follow in the text.

18. Robert Kanters, "*La maison de papier:* Un journal qui dit nous," in Monique Detry, *Françoise Mallet-Joris* (Paris: Grasset, 1976), 91.

19. Lucille F. Becker, *Françoise Mallet-Joris* (Boston: Twayne Publishers, 1985), 2.

20. *Le rempart des béguines* (Paris: Juillard, 1951), 197.

21. Ibid., 201.

22. Becker, *Françoise Mallet-Joris,* 15.

23. *La chambre rouge* (Paris: Juillard, 1955), 23.

24. *Les mensonges* (Paris: Juillard, 1956), 335.

25. Charles Alva Hoyt, *Witchcraft* (Carbondale: Southern Illinois University Press, 1981), 50–51.

26. *J'aurais voulu jouer de l'accordéon* (Paris: Juillard, 1976), 61.

27. *Jeanne Guyon* (Paris: Flammarion, 1978), 62.

28. Ibid., 151.

29. Louis Barjon, "Les romans," *Etudes,* April 1967, 525.

30. *La maison de papier* (Paris: Grasset, 1970), 235.

31. Interview with Lucille F. Becker, January 1980.

32. *Allegra* (Paris: Grasset, 1976), 35. Further references follow in the text.

33. Ophir, *Regards féminins,* 153.

34. *Elise ou la vraie vie* (Paris: Denoël, 1967), 33. Further references follow in the text.

35. Ophir, *Regards féminins,* 164.

36. *A propos de Clémence* (Paris: Denoël, 1971), 24. Further references follow in the text.

37. *Un arbre voyageur* (Paris: Gallimard, 1978), 142. Further references follow in the text.

Chapter Six

1. Nathalie Sarraute, *L'Ere du soupçon* (Paris: Gallimard, 1956), 65.

2. Xavière Gauthier, excerpt in *New French Feminisms,* 163.

3. Ibid., 165.

4. "New Movements in French Literature: Nathalie Sarraute Explains Tropisms," *The Listener* 65, no. 1667 9 March 1961, 428.

5. In Roger Shattuck, *New York Times Book Review,* 1 April 1984, p. 1.

6. Gretchen Rous Besser, *Nathalie Sarraute* (Boston: Twayne Publishers, 1979), 20.

7. See pp. 160–63.

8. *L'Ere du soupçon,* 70.

9. *Portrait of a Man Unknown* (New York: George Braziller, 1958), 201.

10. Besser, *Nathalie Sarraute,* 76.

11. Ibid., 100.

12. Ibid., 112–13.

13. Interview with Bettina Knapp, *Kentucky Romance Quarterly* 14, no. 3 (1969):286.

14. *L'Usage de la parole* (Paris: Gallimard, 1980), 49.

15. Ibid., 98–99.

16. In Rosette C. Lamont, "Probing the Drama of the Commonplace," *New York Times,* 20 May 1985, 16.

17. Excerpt in *New French Feminisms,* 174.

18. Carol J. Murphy, *Alienation and Absence in the Novels of Marguerite Duras* (Lexington, Ky.: French Forum Publishers, 1982), 25–26.

19. *Les parleuses* (Paris: Minuit, 1974), 62.

20. The name she adopted, Duras, is the name of a village in a province in the south of France where her father once owned property. It is probably this region that provided the setting for her first two novels.

21. *Outside: papiers d'un jour* (Paris: Albin Michel, 1981), 277–78.

22. Jean Pierrot, *Marguerite Duras* (Paris: José Corti, 1986), 199.

23. *Un barrage contre le Pacifique* (Paris: Gallimard, 1950), 184.

24. *The Lover,* trans. Barbara Bray (New York: Pantheon Books, 1985), 25. Further references follow in the text.

25. Francine du Plessix Gray, "*The War* by Marguerite Duras," *New York Times Book Review,* 4 May 1986, 1.

26. The other three stories in the collection are "Le boa," "Le chantier," and "Madame Dodin."

27. *Days in the Trees* is the title of the theatrical version of 1966.

28. Interview with Bettina Knapp, "Interviews avec Marguerite Duras et Gabriel Cousin," *French Review* 45 (1971):659.

29. *The Square* (New York: Grove Press, 1959), 55–56.

30. *Les parleuses,* 59.

31. Xavière Gauthier, "Marguerite Duras et la lutte des femmes," *Magazine littéraire* 158 (March 1980):17.

32. The port area here, as in Mallet-Joris's *The Illusionist,* represents a liberation from bourgeois sexual constraints.

33. Interview with Madeleine Chapsal, in Madeleine Chapsal, *Quinze écrivains, entretiens* (Paris: Juillard, 1963), 59.

34. *Les parleuses,* 100.

35. Interview with Knapp, 656.

36. Ibid.

37. Ibid.

38. Ibid.

39. Interview with Colette Godard, "Marguerite Duras tourne *India song,*" in Marcelle Mariani, *Territories du féminin avec Marguerite Duras* (Paris: Minuit, 1977), 142.

40. Ibid., 75.

41. *L'Amante Anglaise,* (New York: Grove Press, 1968), 92–94.

42. Suzanne Horer and Jeanne Socquet, "Marguerite Duras: Interview," in *La création étouffée* (Paris: Pierre Horay Editions, 1973), 177.

Chapter Seven

1. Shoshanna Felman, "Women and Madness: The Critical Phallacy," *Diacritics* (Winter 1975):3.

2. It won the Prix de la Nouvelle Vague (New wave prize).

3. In "The Privilege of Consciousness," in *Homosexualities and French Literature*, 103.

4. Isabelle de Courtivron, "*Le repos du guerrier:* New Perspectives on Rochefort's Warrior," *L'Esprit créateur* 19, no. 2 (Summer 1979):26.

5. *The Warrior's Rest* (New York: David McKay, 1959), 29.

6. Ibid., 3.

7. The novel won the Prix du Roman Populiste (Populist novel prize).

8. Money provided by the government to buy consumer goods in exchange for each baby produced.

9. *Children of Heaven*, trans. Linda Asher (New York: David McKay, 1962), 1.

10. Marianne Hirsch, Mary Jean Green, and Lynn Higgins, "Rochefort and Godard: Two or Three Things about Prostitution," *French Review* 52, no. 3 (February 1979):440.

11. *Children of Heaven*, 62–63.

12. Interview with Monique Y. Crochet, *French Review* 54, LIV, no. 3 (February 1981):432–33. See also Colette, pp. 5–6.

13. *Une rose pour Morrison* (Paris: Grasset, 1966), 62.

14. *Cats Don't Care for Money* (New York: David McKay, 1964), 158.

15. Ibid., 160.

16. Ibid., 85.

17. Pratt, *Archetypal Patterns*, 45.

18. *Cats Don't Care for Money*, 60.

19. *Une rose pour Morrison*, 64.

20. "Privilege of Consciousness," 104–6.

21. Ibid., 106.

22. *Une rose pour Morrison*, 219.

23. *Printemps au parking* (Paris: Grasset, 1969), 270.

24. Interview with Marianne Hirsch, Mary Jean Green, and Lynn Higgins, *L'Esprit créateur* 19, no. 2 (Summer 1979):114.

25. *Archaos ou le jardin étincelant* (Paris: Grasset, 1972), 5. Further references follow in the text.

26. While *Archaos* in a take off on the oedipal myth, *The Warrior's Rest* is a reworking of "Beauty and the Beast."

27. Interview with Hirsch, Green, and Higgins, 114–15.

28. Ibid., 113.

29. Courtivron, "*Le repos du guerrier*," 23–24.

30. "Le chemin de la connaissance c'est la sexualité": Propos recueillis par Philippe Venault," *Magazine littéraire* 30 (July 1969):44.

31. *L'Asphyxie* (Paris: Gallimard, 1946), 5.

32. *La Bâtarde*, trans. Derek Coltman (New York: Farrar, Straus & Giroux, 1965), p. 3. Further references follow in the text.

33. Marks, "Lesbian Intertextuality," 373.

34. *Trésors à prendre* (Paris: Gallimard, 1960), 112.

35. *In the Prison of Her Skin,* trans. Derek Coltman (New York: Farrar, Straus & Giroux, 1971), 114.

36. Marks, "Lesbian Intertextuality," 361–62.

37. *The Woman with the Little Fox Fur: Three Novellas,* trans. Derek Coltman (New York: Farrar, Straus & Giroux, 1966). The protagonist of Flaubert's novella *A Simple Heart* (1877).

38. Adrienne Rich, quoted by Michele Wallace in "Blood, Bread, and Poetry—*Selected Prose 1979–1985," New York Times Book Review,* 15 March 1987, 18.

39. Hélène Vivienne Wenzel, "The Text as Body/Politics: An Appreciation of Monique Wittig's Writings in Context," *Feminist Studies* 7, no. 2 (Summer 1981):284–85.

40. *The Opoponax,* trans. Helen Weaver (New York: Simon & Schuster, 1966), 5.

41. Ibid., 256.

42. This is also the title of a speech given by Monique Wittig at the City University of New York Graduate Center, September 1979, and reprinted in *Feminist Issues,* 1, no. 2 (1981): 47–54.

43. Mary McCarthy, "Everybody's Childhood," in *The Writing on the Wall and Other Literary Essays* (New York: Harcourt, Brace & World, 1970), 110.

44. Wenzel, "Text as Body," 279.

45. *Les Guérillères,* trans. David LeVay (New York: Viking, 1971), 5. Further references follow in the text.

46. Wenzel, "Text as Body," 280–81.

47. *The Lesbian Body,* trans. David LeVay (New York: Avon, 1975), ix.

48. Marks, "Lesbian Intertextualities," 377.

49. Ibid., 376.

50. *The Lesbian Body,* 26.

51. Ibid., ix–x.

52. Diane Griffin Crowder, "Amazons and Mothers? Monique Wittig, Hélène Cixous and Theories of Women's Writing," *Contemporary Literature* 24, No. 2 (1983):121–22.

53. *The Lesbian Body,* x.

54. Wenzel, "Text as Body," 281.

55. *Lesbian Peoples Material for a Dictionary,* trans. Wittig and Zeig (New York: Avon, 1979), 5.

56. "One is Not Born a Woman," *Feminist Issues* 1, no. 2 (1981):47–54.

57. "The Laugh of the Medusa," in *New French Feminisms,* 255. Further references follow in the text.

58. "Castration or Decapitation," trans. Annette Kuhn, *Signs* 7, no. 1 (Autumn 1981):55.

59. Marks, *New French Feminisms,* 36.

60. Ibid., 36

61. Interview with Christine Makward, trans. Ann Liddle and Beatrice Cameron, *Sub-Stance* 13 (1976):28.

62. Recall Françoise Mallet-Joris's treatment of this issue. See above 93–95.

63. "Castration or Decapitation," 55.

64. "Sorties," in *New French Feminisms,* 90–92. Further references follow in the text.

65. Verena Andermatt Conley, *Hélène Cixous: Writing the Feminine* (Lincoln: University of Nebraska Press, 1984), 138.

66. Wenzel, "Text as Body," 268.

67. Cf. Baudelaire preface to *Petits poèmes en prose:* "Quel est celui de nous qui n'a pas dans ses jours d'ambition rêvé le miracle d'une prose poétique musicale sans rythme et sans rime, assez souple et assez heurtée pour s'adapter aux mouvements lyriques de l'âme, aux ondulations de la rêverie, aux soubresauts de la conscience?"

68. Conley, *Hélène Cixous,* 129, 137, 146.

69. *Littérature de notre temps,* no. 5 (Paris: Casterman, 1974), 61.

70. Conley, *Hélène Cixous,* 27.

71. Ibid., 40.

72. Dora is the name Freud gives to the heroine of his "Fragment of an Analysis of a Case of Hysteria," published in 1905.

73. *Le livre de Promethea* (Paris: Gallimard, 1983), 9. Further references follow in the text.

74. Quoted by Ann Rosalind Jones, "Writing the Body: Toward an Understanding of *l'écriture féminine*," *Feminist Studies* 7, no. 2 (Summer 1981):251.

75. *Vivre l'orange* (Paris: des femmes, 1979), 16.

76. Carol Armbruster, "Hélène Clarice: Nouvelle voix," *Contemporary Literature,* 24, no. 2 (1983):150.

77. *Vivre l'orange,* 16.

Conclusion

1. Ophir, *Regards féminins,* 11–12.

2. Arthur Rimbaud, letter to Pierre Demeny, 15 May 1871.

Selected Bibliography

Primary works are listed chronologically; secondary works are listed alphabetically.

COLETTE

Primary Works

Novels

Claudine à l'école. Paris: Albin Michel, 1900. (*Claudine at School.* In *The Complete Claudine.* New York: Farrar, Straus & Giroux, 1976.)

Claudine à Paris. Paris: Albin Michel, 1901. (*Claudine in Paris.* In *The Complete Claudine.* New York: Farrar, Straus & Giroux, 1976.)

Claudine en ménage. Paris: Mercure de France, 1902. (*Claudine Marrried.* In *The Complete Claudine.* New York: Farrar, Straus & Giroux, 1976.)

Claudine s'en va. Paris: Albin Michel, 1903. (*Claudine and Annie.* In *The Complete Claudine.* New York: Farrar, Straus & Giroux, 1976.)

La retraite sentimentale. Paris: Mercure de France, 1907. (*The Retreat from Love.* New York: Harcourt, Brace, Jovanovich, 1980.)

Les vrilles de la vigne. Paris: Ferenczi, 1908.

L'Ingénue libertine. Paris: Albin Michel, 1909. (*The Innocent Libertine.* New York: Farrar, Straus & Giroux, 1978.)

La vagabonde. Paris: Flammarion, 1910. (*The Vagabond.* New York: Random House, Ballantine Books, 1982.)

L'Entrave. Paris: Flammarion, 1913. (*The Shackle.* New York: Farrar, Straus & Giroux, 1976.)

Mitsou ou comment l'esprit vient aux filles. Paris: Fayard, 1919. (*Mitsou and Music-Hall Sidelights.* New York: Farrar, Straus & Giroux, 1957.)

Chéri. Paris: Fayard, 1920. (*Chéri.* In *Chéri and The Last of Chéri.* Baltimore: Penguin, 1974.)

Le blé en herbe. Paris: Flammarion, 1923. (*The Ripening Seed.* New York: Farrar, Straus & Giroux, 1978.)

La fin de Chéri. Paris: Flammarion, 1926. (*The Last of Chéri.* In *Chéri and The Last of Chéri.* Baltimore: Penguin, 1974.)

La seconde. Paris: Ferenczi, 1929. (*The Other One.* New York: Farrar, Straus & Giroux, 1960.)

La chatte. Paris: Grasset, 1933. (*The Cat.* In *Seven by Colette.* New York: Farrar, Straus & Giroux, 1955.)

Duo. Paris: Ferenczi, 1934. (*Duo.* In *Duo and Le Toutounier.* New York: Dell, 1974).
Le toutounier. Paris: Ferenczi, 1939. (*Le Toutounier.* In *Duo and Le Toutounier.* New York: Dell, 1974.)
Julie de Carneilhan. Paris: Fayard, 1941. (*Julie de Carneilhan.* In *Julie de Carneilhan and Chance Acquaintances.* London: Secker & Warburg, 1952.)
Trois . . . six . . . neuf. Paris: Corrêa, 1943. (Selections in *Places.* New York: Bobbs-Merrill, 1971.)
L'Etoile vesper. Paris: Milieu du monde, 1946. (*The Evening Star.* London: Peter Owen, 1973.)
Le fanal bleu. Paris: Ferenczi, 1949. (*The Blue Lantern.* New York: Farrar, Straus & Giroux, 1963.)
La fleur de l'âge. Paris: Editions Le Fleuron, 1949.

Short Story Collections
Bella-Vista. Paris: Ferenczi, 1937. (In *The Tender Shoot and Other Stories.* New York: Farrar, Straus & Giroux, 1958.)
Chambre d'hôtel. Paris: Fayard, 1940. (*Chance Acquaintances.* In *Julie de Carneilhan and Chance Acquaintances.* London: Secker & Warburg, 1952.)
Le képi. Paris: Fayard, 1943. (In *The Tender Shoot and Other Stories.* New York: Farrar, Straus & Giroux, 1958.)
Gigi et autres nouvelles. Paris: Ferenczi, 1943. (*Gigi.* In *Gigi and Selected Writings.* New York: New American Library [Signet], 1963.)

Autobiographical–Fictional Works
L'Envers du music-hall. Paris: Flammarion, 1913. (*Mitsou and Music-Hall Sidelights.* New York: Farrar, Straus & Giroux, 1957.)
La maison de Claudine. Paris: Ferenczi, 1922. (*My Mother's House.* In *My Mother's House and Sido.* New York: Farrar, Straus & Giroux, 1979.)
La naissance du jour. Paris: Flammarion, 1928. (*Break of Day.* New York: Farrar, Straus & Giroux, 1979.)
Sido. Paris: Ferenczi, 1928. (*Sido.* In *My Mother's House and Sido.* New York: Farrar, Straus & Giroux, 1979.)
Ces plaisirs. Paris: Ferenczi, 1932. Title changed to *Le pur et l'impur.* Paris: Ferenczi, 1941. (*The Pure and the Impure.* New York: Farrar, Straus & Giroux, 1967.)

Secondary Works

Biolley-Godino, Marcelle. *L'Homme objet chez Colette.* Paris: Klincksieck, 1972.
Cottrell, Robert D. *Colette.* New York: Frederick Ungar, 1974.
Davies, Margaret. *Colette.* New York: Grove Press, 1961.

Eisinger, Erica M., and Mari Ward McCarty, eds. *Colette: The Woman, The Writer.* University Park: Pennsylvania State University Press, 1981.

Goudeket, Maurice. *Près de Colette.* Paris: Flammarion, 1956. (*Close to Colette.* New York: Farrar, Straus & Cudahy, 1957.)

Marks, Elaine. *Colette.* New Brunswick, N.J.: Rutgers University Press, 1960.

Phelps, Robert. *Earthly Paradise: Colette's Autobiography Drawn from the Writings of Her Lifetime.* New York: Farrar, Straus & Giroux, 1966.)

Resch, Yannick. *Corps féminin, corps textuel: Essai sur le personnage féminin dans l'oeuvre de Colette.* Paris: Klincksieck, 1973.

Richardson, Joanna. *Colette.* London: Methuen, 1983.

Sarde, Michèle. *Colette libre et entravée.* Paris: Stock, 1978. (*Colette: Free and Fettered.* New York: Morrow, 1980.)

Ward Jouve, Nicole. *Colette.* Bloomington: Indiana University Press, 1987.

SIMONE DE BEAUVOIR

Primary Works

Novels and Short Stories

L'Invitée. Paris: Gallimard, 1943. (*She Came to Stay.* Cleveland: World Publishing Co., 1954.)

Le sang des autres. Paris: Gallimard, 1945. (*The Blood of Others.* New York: Knopf, 1948.)

Tous les hommes sont mortels. Paris: Gallimard, 1946. (*All Men are Mortal.* Cleveland: World Publishing Co., 1955.)

Les mandarins. Paris: Gallimard, 1954. (*The Mandarins.* Cleveland: World Publishing Co., 1956.)

Les belles images. Paris: Gallimard, 1966. (*Les Belles Images.* New York: G. P. Putnam, 1968.)

La femme rompue, Monologue, L'Age de discrétion [novellas]. Paris: Gallimard, 1968. (*The Woman Destroyed.* New York: Putnam, 1969.)

Quand prime le spirituel [stories]. Paris: Gallimard, 1980. (*When Things of the Spirit Come First.* New York: Pantheon, 1982.)

Autobiographical Works

Mémoires d'une jeune fille rangée. Paris: Gallimard, 1958. (*Memoirs of a Dutiful Daughter.* Cleveland: World Publishing Co., 1959.)

La force de l'âge. Paris: Gallimard, 1960. (*The Prime of Life.* Cleveland: World Publishing Co., 1962.)

La force des choses. Paris: Gallimard, 1963. (*Force of Circumstance.* New York: G. P. Putnam's, 1965.)

Tout compte fait. Paris: Gallimard, 1970. *All Said and Done.* New York: G. P. Putnam's, 1974.)

Nonfiction

Pyrrhus et Cinéas. Paris: Gallimard, 1944. ("Pyrrhus and Cineas" [selections], *Partisan Review* 3, no. 3 (1946):430–37.)

Pour une morale de l'ambiguité. Paris: Gallimard, 1947. (*The Ethics of Ambiguity*. New York: Philosophical Library, 1948.)

Le deuxième sexe. Paris: Gallimard, 1949. (*The Second Sex*. New York: Knopf, 1953.)

Djamila Boupacha [coauthor, Gisèle Halimi]. Paris: Gallimard, 1962. (*Djamila Boupacha*. New York: Macmillan, 1962.)

Une mort très douce. Paris: Gallimard, 1964. (*A Very Easy Death*. New York: G. P. Putnam's, 1966.)

La vieillesse. Paris: Gallimard, 1970. (*The Coming of Age*. New York: G. P. Putnam's, 1972.)

Secondary Works

Asher, Carole, *Simone de Beauvoir: A Life of Freedom*. Boston: Beacon Press, 1981.

Bieber, Konrad. *Simone de Beauvoir*. Boston: Twayne Publishers, 1979.

Cottrell, Robert D. *Simone de Beauvoir*. New York: Frederick Ungar, 1975.

Francis, Claude, and Fernande Gontier. *Simone de Beauvoir*. Paris: Librairie Académique Perrin, 1985. (*Simone de Beauvoir: A Life . . . A Love Story*. New York: St. Martin's Press, 1987.)

Gennari, Geneviève. *Simone de Beauvoir*. Paris: Editions Universitaires, 1959.

Leighton, Margaret. *Simone de Beauvoir on Women*. Rutherford, N.J.: Fairleigh Dickinson University Press, 1975.

Marks, Elaine. *Simone de Beauvoir: Encounters with Death*. New Brunswick, N.J.: Rutgers University Press, 1973.

Ophir, Anne. *Regards féminins*. Paris: Denoël-Gonthier, 1976.

Reck, Rima Drell. *Literature and Responsibility*. Baton Rouge: Louisiana State University Press, 1969.

Schwarzer, Alice. *Simone de Beauvoir aujourd'hui*. [six conversations]. Paris: Mercure de France, 1983. (*After "The Second Sex": Conversations with Simone de Beauvoir*. New York: Pantheon Books, 1984.)

"Simone de Beauvoir et la lutte des femmes," *L'Arc* 61 (1975).

Zéphir, Jacques. *Le néo-feminisme de Simone de Beauvoir*. Paris: Denoël-Gonthier, 1982.

MARGUERITE YOURCENAR

Primary Works

Novels and Short Stories

Alexis ou le traité du vain combat. Paris: Au Sans Pareil, 1929. (*Alexis*. New York: Farrar, Straus & Giroux, 1984.)

La nouvelle Eurydice. Paris: Grasset, 1931.

La mort conduit l'attelage. Paris: Grasset, 1934.

Denier du rêve. Paris: Grasset, 1934. Rev. enl. ed. Paris: Gallimard, 1971. (*A Coin in Nine Hands.* New York: Farrar, Straus & Giroux, 1982.)

Nouvelles orientales. Paris: Gallimard, 1939. Definitive ed. Paris: Gallimard, 1978. (*Oriental Tales.* New York: Farrar, Straus & Giroux, 1985.)

Le coup de grâce. Paris: Gallimard, 1939. (*Coup de Grâce.* New York: Farrar, Straus & Giroux, 1957.)

Mémoires d'Hadrien. Paris: Plon, 1951. Rev. Ed. with "Carnets de notes des *Mémoires d'Hadrien.*" Paris: Plon, 1958. Reprint. Paris: Gallimard, 1971. (*Memoirs of Hadrian and Reflections on the Composition of Memoirs of Hadrian.* New York: Farrar, Straus & Giroux, 1963.)

L'Oeuvre au noir. Paris: Gallimard, 1968. (*The Abyss.* New York: Farrar, Straus & Giroux, 1976.)

Comme l'eau qui coule. Paris: Gallimard, 1982. (*Two Lives and a Dream.* New York: Farrar, Straus & Giroux, 1987.)

Un homme obscur; Une belle matinée. Paris: Gallimard, 1985. (*Two Lives and a Dream.* New York: Farrar, Straus & Giroux, 1987.)

Autobiographical Works

Feux. Paris: Grasset, 1936. (*Fires.* New York: Farrar, Straus & Giroux, 1981.)

Le labyrinthe du monde [*Souvenirs pieux* and *Archives du nord*]. Paris: Gallimard, 1974–77.

Les yeux ouverts: Entretiens avec Matthieu Galey. Paris: Le Centurion, 1980. (*With Open Eyes.* Boston: Beacon Press, 1984.)

Quoi? L'Eternité. Paris: Gallimard, 1988.

Nonfiction

Sous bénéfice d'inventaire. Paris: Gallimard, 1962. Rev. enl. ed. Paris: Gallimard, 1978. (*The Dark Brain of Piranesi and Other Essays.* New York: Farrar, Straus & Giroux, 1984.)

Mishima ou la vision du vide. Paris: Gallimard, 1980. (*Mishima. A Vision of the Void.* New York: Farrar, Straus & Giroux, 1986.)

Discours de réception à l'Académie Française. Paris: Gallimard, 1981.

Secondary Works

Blot, Jean. *Marguerite Yourcenar.* Paris: Seghers, 1971. Reprint. Paris: Seghers 1980.

Farrell, C. Frederick, Jr., and Edith Farrell. *Marguerite Yourcenar in Counterpoint.* Latham, Md.: University Press of America, 1983.

Horn, Pierre. *Marguerite Yourcenar.* Boston: Twayne Publishers, 1985.

ELSA TRIOLET

Primary Works

Novels and Short Story Collections in French

Bonsoir Thérèse. Paris: Denoël, 1938.

Mille regrets. Paris: Denoël, 1942.

Le cheval blanc. Paris: Denoël, 1943.

Les amants d'Avignon [under pseudonym Laurent Daniel]. Paris: Editions de Minuit, 1943.

Yvette [under pseudonym Laurent Daniel]. Paris: Bibliothèque Française, 1944.

Qui est cette étrangère qui n'est pas d'ici? ou le mythe de la baronne Mélanie. Paris: Seghers, 1944.

Le premier accroc coûte deux cents francs. Paris: Denoël, 1945. (*A Fine of Two Hundred Francs*. New York: Virago/Penguin, 1985.)

Personne ne m'aime. Paris: Bibliothèque Française, 1946.

Les fantômes armés. Paris: Bibliothèque Française, 1947.

Anne-Marie [*Personne ne m'aime* and *Les fantômes armés*]. Paris: Bibliothèque Française, 1952.

L'Inspecteur des ruines. Paris: Editeurs Français Réunis, 1948.

Le cheval roux ou les intentions humaines. Paris: Editeurs Français Réunis, 1953.

Le rendez-vous des étrangers. Paris: Gallimard, 1956.

Le monument. Paris: Gallimard, 1957.

L'Age de nylon:

    I. *Roses à crédit*. Paris: Gallimard, 1959.

    II. *Luna-Park*. Paris: Gallimard, 1959.

    III. *L'Ame*. Paris: Gallimard, 1963.

Les manigances. Paris: Gallimard, 1962.

Le grand jamais. Paris: Gallimard, 1965.

Ecoutez-voir. Paris: Gallimard, 1968.

Le rossignol se tait à l'aube. Paris: Gallimard, 1970.

Secondary Works

Adereth, Max, "L'Oeuvre d'Elsa Triolet." *Pensée* 153 (September-October 1970):81–94.

Aragon, Louis. Preface to *Elsa Triolet choisie par Aragon*. Paris: Gallimard, 1960.

Aragon, Louis. Introduction and prefaces to *Oeuvres romanesques croisées d'Elsa Triolet et d'Aragon*. Paris: Laffont, 1964–68.

Becker, Lucille F. *Louis Aragon*. New York: Twayne Publishers, 1971.

Desanti, Dominique. *Elsa Triolet*. Paris: Editions Ramsay, 1983.

Madaule, Jacques. *Ce que dit Elsa*. Paris: Denoël, 1961.

Europe 454–55 (February-March 1967) [special issue on Elsa Triolet and Aragon].
Europe 506 (June 1971) [special issue on Elsa Triolet].

ZOÉ OLDENBOURG

Primary Works

Novels

Argile et cendres. Paris: Gallimard, 1946. (*The World is Not Enough.* New York: Pantheon Books, 1948.)
La pierre angulaire. Paris: Gallimard, 1953. (*The Cornerstone.* New York: Pantheon Books, 1955.)
Réveillés de la vie. Paris: Gallimard, 1956. (*The Awakened.* New York: Pantheon, 1957.)
Les irréductibles. Paris: Gallimard, 1958. (*The Chains of Love.* New York: Pantheon, 1959.)
Les brûlés. Paris: Gallimard, 1960 (*Destiny of Fire.* New York: Pantheon, 1961.)
Les cités charnelles: ou, L'Histoire de Roger de Montbrun. Paris: Gallimard, 1961. (*Cities of the Flesh: Or, The Story of Roger de Montbrun.* New York: Pantheon, 1963.)
La joie des pauvres. Paris: Gallimard, 1970. (*The Heirs of the Kingdom.* New York: Pantheon, 1971.)
La joie-souffrance. Paris: Gallimard, 1980.
Les amours égarés. Paris: Gallimard, 1987.

Autobiographical Works

Visages d'un autoportrait. Paris: Gallimard, 1977.
Les procès du rêve. Paris: Gallimard, 1982.

Historical Works

Le bûcher de Montségur. Paris: Gallimard, 1959. (*Massacre at Montségur: A History of the Albigensian Crusade.* New York: Pantheon, 1962.)
Les croisades. Paris: Gallimard, 1965. (*The Crusades.* New York: Pantheon, 1966.)
Catherine de Russie. Paris: Gallimard, 1966. (*Catherine the Great.* New York: Pantheon, 1965.)
Saint Bernard. Paris: Albin Michel, 1970.
L'Epopée des cathédrales. Paris: Réalités/Hachette, 1972.

Nonfiction

Que vous a donc fait Israël? Paris: Gallimard, 1974.
Que nous est Hécube? ou un plaidoyer pour l'humain. Paris: Gallimard, 1984.

Secondary Works

Hoffmann, Léon-François. "Notes on Zoé Oldenbourg's *Destiny of Fire*." *Yale French Studies* 27 (Spring-Summer 1961):127–30.
Nélod, Gilles. *Panorama du roman historique.* Paris: Sodi, 1969.

GENEVIÈVE GENNARI

Primary Works

Novels

Les cousines Muller. Paris: Horay-Flore, 1949. (*The Restless Heart.* New York: Abelard-Schuman, 1955.)
La fontaine scellée. Paris: Horay-Flore, 1950.
J'éveillerai l'aurore. Paris: Horay-Flore, 1952.
L'Etoile Napoléon. Paris: Horay-Flore, 1954. (*The Riven Heart.* New York: David McKay, 1956.)
Le plus triste plaisir. Paris: La Palatine, 1956.
Le rideau de sable. Paris: Pierre Horay, 1957.
Journal d'une bourgeoise. Paris: Grasset, 1959. (*The Other Woman I am.* New York: David McKay, 1961.)
Les nostalgiques. Paris: Grasset, 1963. (*Nostalgia.* New York: David McKay, 1964.)
La fugue irlandaise. Paris: Juillard, 1973.
Un mois d'août à Paris. Paris: Tchou, 1977.
La neuvième vague. Paris: Juillard, 1980.

Autobiographical Works

J'avais vingt ans: Journal 1940–45. Paris: Grasset, 1961.
La robe rouge. Paris: Tchou, 1978.

Nonfiction

Simone de Beauvoir. Paris: Editions Universitaires, 1958.
Le dossier de la femme. Paris: Librairie Académique Perrin, 1965.
Ce monde où je vis. Paris: Grasset, 1972.

Secondary Works

Lamoureux, Agnès. "Comment écrivent les femmes: Geneviève Gennari." *Revue des deux mondes,* 1 August 1964, 384–93.
Robinson, Jean Hardy. *Geneviève Gennari.* Boston: Twayne Publishers, 1984.

FRANÇOISE SAGAN

Primary Sources

Novels

Bonjour tristesse. Paris: Juillard, 1954. (*Bonjour Tristesse.* New York: E. P. Dutton & Co., 1955.)

Un certain sourire. Paris: Juillard, 1956. (*A Certain Smile.* New York: E. P. Dutton & Co., 1956.)

Dans un mois, dans un an. Paris: Juillard, 1957. (*Those without Shadows.* New York: E. P. Dutton & Co., 1957.)

Aimez-vous Brahms. . . . Paris: Juillard, 1959. (*Aimez-vous Brahms. . . .* New York: E. P. Dutton & Co., 1960.)

Les merveilleux nuages. Paris: Juillard, 1961. (*The Wonderful Clouds.* New York: E. P. Dutton & Co., 1962.)

La chamade. Paris: Juillard, 1965. (*La Chamade.* New York: E. P. Dutton & Co., 1966.)

Le garde du coeur. Paris: Juillard, 1968. (*The Heart-Keeper.* New York: E. P. Dutton & Co., 1968.)

Un peu de soleil dans l'eau froide. Paris: Flammarion, 1969. (*A Few Hours of Sunlight.* New York: Harper & Row, 1971.)

Des bleus à l'âme. Paris: Flammarion, 1972. (*Scars on the Soul.* New York: McGraw Hill, 1975.)

Un profil perdu. Paris: Flammarion, 1974. (*Lost Profile.* New York: Delacorte: 1976.)

Des yeux de soie [stories]. Paris: Flammarion, 1976. (*Silken Eyes.* New York: Delacorte, 1977.)

Le lit défait. Paris: Flammarion, 1977. (*The Unmade Bed.* New York: Delacorte, 1978.)

Le chien couchant. Paris: Flammarion, 1980. (*Salad Days.* New York: E. P. Dutton & Co., 1984.)

La femme fardée. Paris: Ramsay, 1981. (*The Painted Lady.* New York: E. P. Dutton & Co., 1983.)

Un orage immobile. Paris: Juillard, 1983. (*The Still Storm.* London: E. P. Dutton & Co., 1986.)

De guerre lasse. Paris: Gallimard, 1985. (*A Reluctant Hero.* New York: E. P. Dutton & Co., 1985.)

Un sang d'aquarelle. Paris: Gallimard, 1987.

Autobiographical Works

Réponses: 1954–1974. Paris: J. J. Pauvert, 1974. (*Responses: The Autobiography of Françoise Sagan.* Godalming, England: Black Sheep Books, 1979.)

Avec mon meilleur souvenir. Paris: Gallimard, 1984. (*With Fondest Memories.* New York: E. P. Dutton & Co., 1985.)

Nonfiction

Sarah Bernhardt. Paris: Laffont, 1987.

Secondary Works

Brophy, Brigid. *Don't Never Forget.* New York: Holt Rinehart Winston, 1967.

Hourdin, Georges. *Le cas Françoise Sagan*. Paris: Editions du Cerf, 1958.
Miller, Judith Graves. *Françoise Sagan*. Boston: Twayne Publishers, 1988.
Moeller, Charles. *Littérature du XXe siècle et christianisme*. Paris: Casterman, 1975.
Mourgue, Gérard. *Françoise Sagan*. Paris: Editions Universitaires, 1958.
Vandromme, Pol. *Françoise Sagan et l'élégance de survivre*. Paris: R. Desforges, 1977.

FRANÇOISE MALLET-JORIS

Primary Works

Novels and Short Story Collections
Le rempart des béguines. Paris: Juillard, 1951. (*The Illusionist*. New York: Farrar, Straus & Cudahy, 1952.)
La chambre rouge. Paris: Juillard, 1955. (*The Red Room*. New York: Farrar, Straus & Cudahy, 1956.)
Cordélia. Paris: Juillard, 1956. (*Cordelia and Other Stories*. New York: Farrar, Straus & Giroux, 1965.)
Les mensonges. Paris: Juillard, 1956. (*House of Lies*. New York: Farrar, Straus & Cudahy, 1957.)
L'Empire céleste. Paris: Juillard, 1958. (*Café Céleste*. New York: Farrar, Straus & Cudahy, 1962.)
Les personnages. Paris: Juillard, 1961. (*The Favorite*. New York: Farrar, Straus & Cudahy, 1962.)
Les signes et les prodiges. Paris: Grasset, 1966. (*Signs and Wonders*. New York: Farrar, Straus & Giroux, 1967.)
Trois âges de la nuit. Paris: Grasset, 1968. (*The Witches*. New York: Farrar, Straus & Giroux, 1967.)
Le jeu du souterrain. Paris: Grasset, 1973. (*The Underground Game*. New York: E. P. Dutton & Co., 1975.)
Allegra. Paris: Grasset, 1976.
Dickie-Roi. Paris: Grasset, 1979.
Un chagrin d'amour et d'ailleurs. Paris: Grasset, 1981.
Le clin d'oeil de l'ange [stories]. Paris: Gallimard, 1983.
Le rire de Laura. Paris: Gallimard, 1985.
La tristesse du cerf-volant. Paris: Flammarion, 1988.

Autobiographical Works
Lettre à moi-même. Paris: Juillard, 1963. (*A Letter to Myself*. New York: Farrar, Straus & Co., 1964.)
La maison de papier. Paris: Grasset, 1970. (*The Paper House*. New York: Farrar, Straus & Giroux, 1971.)
J'aurais voulu jouer de l'accordéon. Paris: Juillard, 1976.

Biographical Works
Marie Mancini, le premier amour de Louis XIV. Paris: Hachette, 1964. (*The Uncompromising Heart.* New York: Farrar, Straus & Giroux, 1966.)
Jeanne Guyon. Paris: Flammarion, 1978.

Secondary Works
Becker, Lucille F. *Françoise Mallet-Joris.* Boston: Twayne Publishers, 1985.
Détry, Monique. *Françoise Mallet-Joris: Dossier critique et inédits* and *Le Miroir, le voyage et la fête.* Paris: Grasset, 1976.
Géoris, Michel. *Françoise Mallet-Joris.* Brussels: P. de Méyère, 1964.

CLAIRE ETCHERELLI

Primary Works

Novels
Elise ou la vraie vie. Paris: Denoël, 1967.
A propos de Clémence. Paris: Denoël, 1971.
Un arbre voyageur. Paris: Gallimard, 1978.

Secondary Works
Ophir, Anne. *Regards féminins.* Paris: Denoël-Gonthier, 1976.
Ragon, Michel. *Histoire de la littérature prolétarienne en France.* Paris: Albin Michel, 1974.

NATHALIE SARRAUTE

Primary Works

Novels
Tropismes. Paris: Denoël, 1939. (*Tropisms.* New York: George Braziller, 1963.)
Portrait d'un inconnu. Paris: Robert Marin, 1948. (*Portrait of a Man Unknown.* New York: George Braziller, 1958.)
Martereau. Paris: Gallimard, 1953. (*Martereau.* New York: George Braziller, 1959.)
Le planétarium. Paris: Gallimard, 1959. (*The Planetarium.* New York: George Braziller, 1960.)
Les fruits d'or. Paris: Gallimard, 1963. (*The Golden Fruits.* New York: George Braziller, 1964.)
Entre la vie et la mort. Paris: Gallimard, 1968. (*Between Life and Death.* New York: George Braziller, 1969.)

Vous les entendez? Paris: Gallimard, 1972. (*Do You Hear Them?* New York: George Braziller, 1973.)

"disent les imbéciles." Paris: Gallimard, 1976. (*"fools say."* New York: George Braziller, 1977.)

L'Usage de la parole. Paris: Gallimard, 1980.

Enfance. Paris: Gallimard, 1983. (*Childhood.* New York: George Braziller, 1984.)

Nonfiction

L'Ere du soupçon. Paris: Gallimard, 1956. (*The Age of Suspicion.* New York: George Braziller, 1963.)

Secondary Works

Besser, Gretchen Rous. *Nathalie Sarraute.* Boston: Twayne Publishers, 1979.

Calin, Françoise. *La vie retrouvée: Etude de l'oeuvre romanesque de Nathalie Sarraute.* Paris: Minard, 1976.

Munley, Ellen W. "I'm Dying but It's Only Your Story: Sarraute's Reader on Stage." *Contemporary Literature* 24, no. 2 (1983):233–58.

Roudiez, Leon. *French Fiction Today: A New Direction.* New Brunswick, N.J.: Rutgers University Press, 1972.

Temple, Ruth Z. *Nathalie Sarraute.* Columbia Essays on Modern Writers, no. 33. New York: Columbia University Press, 1968.

Tison-Braun, Micheline. *Nathalie Sarraute ou la recherche de l'authenticité.* Paris: Gallimard, 1971.

MARGUERITE DURAS

Primary Works

Novels and *Récits*

Les impudents. Paris: Plon, 1943.

La vie tranquille. Paris: Gallimard, 1944.

Un barrage contre le Pacifique. Paris: Gallimard, 1950. (*The Sea Wall.* New York: Pellegrini & Cudahy, 1952.)

Le marin de Gibraltar. Paris: Gallimard, 1952. (*The Sailor from Gibraltar.* New York: Grove Press, 1966.)

Les petits chevaux de Tarquinia. Paris: Gallimard, 1953. (*The Little Horses of Tarquinia.* London: Calder, 1960.)

Des journées entières dans les arbres. Paris: Gallimard, 1954.

Le square. Paris: Gallimard, 1955. (*The Square.* New York: Grove Press, 1959.)

Moderato cantabile. Paris: Minuit, 1958. (*Moderato Cantabile.* New York: Grove Press, 1960.)

Dix heures et demie du soir en été. Paris: Gallimard, 1960. (*Ten-Thirty on a Summer Night.* In *Four Novels by Marguerite Duras.* New York: Grove Press, 1965.)

L'Après-midi de Monsieur Andesmas. Paris: Gallimard, 1962. (*The Afternoon of Monsieur Andesmas.* In *Four Novels by Marguerite Duras.* New York: Grove Press, 1965.)

Le ravissement de Lol V. Stein. Paris: Gallimard, 1964. (*The Ravishing of Lol V. Stein.* New York: Grove Press, 1966.)

Le vice-consul. Paris: Gallimard, 1965. (*The Vice-Consul.* London: Hamish Hamilton, 1968.)

L'Amante anglaise. Paris: Gallimard, 1967. (*L'Amante Anglaise.* New York: Grove Press, 1968.)

Détruire, dit-elle. Paris: Minuit, 1969. (*Destroy, she said.* New York: Grove Press, 1968.)

Abahn Sabana David. Paris: Gallimard, 1970.

L'Amour. Paris: Gallimard, 1971.

India Song. Paris: Gallimard, 1973.

L'Homme assis dans le couloir. Paris: Minuit, 1980.

Agatha. Paris: Minuit, 1981.

L'Homme atlantique. Paris: Minuit, 1982.

L'Amant. Paris: Minuit, 1984. (*The Lover.* New York: Pantheon, 1985.)

Les yeux bleus cheveux noirs. Paris: Minuit, 1986.

Emily L. Paris: Minuit, 1987.

Autobiographical Works and Memoirs

Les parleuses [interviews with Xavière Gauthier]. Paris: Minuit, 1974. (*Woman to Woman.* Lincoln: University of Nebraska Press, 1987.)

Les lieux de Marguerite Duras [interview with Michelle Porte]. Paris: Minuit, 1977.

Outside: papiers d'un jour. Paris: Albin Michel, 1981. (*Outside.* Boston: Beacon Press, 1986.)

La maladie de la mort. Paris: Minuit, 1982. (*The Malady of Death.* New York: Grove, 1983.)

La douleur. Paris: P. O. L., 1985. (*The War: A Memoir.* New York: Pantheon, 1986.)

Secondary Works

Brée, Germaine. "An Interview with Marguerite Duras." *Contemporary Literature* 13 (1972):401–23.

Cismaru, Alfred. *Marguerite Duras.* New York: Twayne Publishers, 1971.

Horer, Suzanne, and Jeanne Soquet. "Marguerite Duras: Interview." In *La création étouffée.* Paris: Pierre Horay Editions, 1973.

Marini, Marcelle. *Territoires du féminin avec Marguerite Duras*. Paris: Minuit, 1977.
Murphy, Carol J. *Alienation and Absence in the Novels of Marguerite Duras*. Lexington, Ky.: French Forum Publishers, 1982.
Pierrot, Jean. *Marguerite Duras*. Paris: Corti, 1986.
Tison-Braun, Micheline. *Marguerite Duras*. Amsterdam: Rodopi, 1985.
Vircondelet, Alain. *Marguerite Duras*. Paris: Seghers, 1972.

CHRISTIANE ROCHEFORT

Primary Works

Novels
Le repos du guerrier. Paris: Grasset, 1958. (*The Warrior's Rest*. New York: David McKay, 1959.)
Les petits enfants du siècle. Paris: Grasset, 1961. (*Children of Heaven*. New York: David McKay, 1962.)
Les stances à Sophie. Paris: Grasset, 1963. (*Cats Don't Care for Money*. New York: David McKay, 1964.)
Une rose pour Morrison. Paris: Grasset, 1966.
Printemps au parking. Paris: Grasset, 1969.
Archaos ou le jardin étincelant. Paris: Grasset, 1972.
Encore heureux qu'on va vers l'été. Paris: Grasset, 1975.
Quand tu vas chez les femmes. Paris: Grasset, 1982.
La porte du fond. Paris: Grasset, 1988.

Nonfiction
C'est bizarre l'écriture. Paris: Grasset, 1970.
Les enfants d'abord. Paris: Grasset, 1976.
Ma vie revue et corrigée [with Maurice Chavardès]. Paris: Stock: 1978.
Le monde est comme deux chevaux. Paris: Grasset, 1984.

Secondary Works

Arsène, Cécile. "The Privilege of Consciousness: An Interview." In *Homosexualities and French Literature,* edited by Elaine Marks and George Stambolian, 101–13. Ithaca: Cornell University Press, 1979.
Courtivron, Isabelle de. "*Le Repos du guerrier:* New Perspectives on Rochefort's Warrior." *L'Esprit créateur* 19, no. 2 (Summer 1979):23–33.
Hirsch, Marianne, Mary Jean Green, and Lynn Higgins. "Rochefort and Godard: Two or Three Things about Prostitution." *French Review* 52, no. 3 (February 1979):440–48.
———. "An Interview with Christiane Rochefort." *L'Esprit créateur* 19, no. 2 (Summer 1979):107–20.

VIOLETTE LEDUC

Primary Works

Novels and Novellas

L'Asphyxie. Paris: Gallimard, 1946. (*In the Prison of Her Skin.* New York: Farrar, Straus & Giroux, 1971.)

L'Affamée. Paris: Gallimard, 1948.

Ravages. Paris: Gallimard, 1955. (*Ravages.* London: Panther Books, 1969.)

La vieille fille et le mort: Les boutons dorés. Paris: Gallimard, 1964. (*The Old Maid and the Dead Man: The Golden Buttons.* In *The Woman with the Little Fox Fur: Three Novellas.* New York: Farrar, Straus & Giroux, 1966.)

La femme au petit renard. Paris: Gallimard, 1965. (*The Woman with the Little Fox Fur: Three Novellas.* New York: Farrar, Straus & Giroux, 1966.)

Thérèse et Isabelle. Paris: Gallimard, 1966. (*Thérèse and Isabelle.* New York: Farrar, Straus & Giroux, 1967.)

Le taxi. Paris: Gallimard, 1971. (*The Taxi.* New York: Farrar, Straus & Giroux, 1972.)

Autobiographical Works

La bâtarde. Paris: Gallimard, 1964. (*La Bâtarde.* New York: Farrar, Straus & Giroux, 1965.)

La folie en tête. Paris: Gallimard, 1971. (*Mad in Pursuit.* New York: Farrar, Straus & Giroux, 1971.)

La chasse à l'amour. Paris: Gallimard, 1973.

Nonfiction

Trésors à prendre. Paris: Gallimard, 1960.

Secondary Works

Beauvoir, Simone de. Preface to *La Bâtarde.* New York: Farrar, Straus & Giroux, 1965.

Courtivron, Isabelle de. *Violette Leduc.* Boston: Twayne Publishers, 1985.

Marks, Elaine. "Lesbian Intertextuality." In *Homosexualities and French Literature,* edited by Elaine Marks and George Stambolian. Ithaca: Cornell University Press, 1979.

Rule, Jane. "Violet Leduc." In *Lesbian Images.* Garden City, N.Y.: Doubleday, 1975.

MONIQUE WITTIG

Primary Works

Novels and Fictional Works

L'Opoponax. Paris: Minuit, 1964. (*The Opoponax.* New York: Simon & Schuster, 1966.)

Les guérillères. Paris: Minuit, 1969. (*Les Guérillères.* New York: Viking, 1971.)

Le corps lesbien. Paris: Minuit, 1973. (*The Lesbian Body.* New York: Avon, 1975.)

Brouillon pour un dictionnaire des amantes [with Sande Zeig]. Paris: Grasset, 1975. (*Lesbian Peoples Material for a Dictionary.* New York: Avon, 1979.)

Virgile, non. Paris: Minuit, 1985

Nonfiction

"One is Not Born a Woman." *Feminist Issues* 1, no. 2 (1981):47–54.

Secondary Works

Crowder, Diane Griffin. "Amazons and Mothers? Monique Wittig, Hélène Cixous and Theories of Women's Writing." *Contemporary Literature* 24, no. 2 (1983):117–44.

Jones, Ann Rosalind. "Writing the Body: Toward an Understanding of *L'Écriture féminine.*" *Feminist Studies* 7, no. 2 (Summer 1981):247–64.

Lindsay, Cecile. "Body/Language: French Feminist Utopias." *French Review* 60, no. 1 (October 1986):46–55.

Marks, Elaine. "Lesbian Intertextuality." In *Homosexualities and French Literature,* edited by Elaine Marks and George Stambolian. Ithaca: Cornell University Press, 1979.

McCarthy, Mary. "Everybody's Childhood." In *The Writing on the Wall and Other Literary Essays.* New York: Harcourt, Brace & World, 1970.

Ostrovsky, Erika. "A Cosmogony of O: Wittig's *Les guérillères.* In *Twentieth Century French Fiction: Essays for Germaine Brée,* ed. George Stambolian. New Brunswick, N.J.: Rutgers University Press, 1975.

Wenzel, Hélène Vivienne. "The Text as Body/Politics: An Appreciation of Monique Wittig's Writings in Context." *Feminist Studies* 7, no. 2 (Summer 1981):266–86.

HÉLÈNE CIXOUS

Primary Works

Novels, Stories, and "Fictions"

Le prénom de Dieu. Paris: Grasset, 1967.

Dedans. Paris: Grasset, 1969. (*Inside.* New York: Schocken Books, 1986.)

Les commencements. Paris: Grasset, 1970.

Le troisième corps. Paris: Grasset, 1970.

Un vrai jardin. Paris: Editions de l'Herne, 1971.

Neutre. Paris: Grasset, 1972.

Portrait du soleil. Paris: Denoël, 1973.
Tombe. Paris: Seuil, 1974.
Révolutions pour plus d'un Faust. Paris: Seuil, 1975.
Souffles. Paris: des femmes, 1975.
LA. Paris: Gallimard, 1976.
Partie. Paris: des femmes, 1976.
Angst. Paris: des femmes, 1977.
Chant du corps interdit, le nom d'Oedipe. Paris: des femmes, 1978.
Préparatifs de noces au-delà de l'abîme. Paris: des femmes, 1978.
Ananké. Paris: des femmes, 1979.
Vivre l'orange. Paris: des femmes, 1979.
Illa. Paris: des femmes, 1980.
With, ou l'art de l'innocence. Paris: des femmes, 1981.
Limonade tout était si infini. Paris: des femmes, 1982.
Le livre de Promethea. Paris: Gallimard, 1983.
La bataille d'Arcachon. Paris: Gallimard, 1986.

Nonfiction

L'Exil de James Joyce ou l'art du remplacement. Paris: Grasset, 1968. (*The Exile of James Joyce or the Art of Replacement.* New York: David Lewis, 1972.)
Prénoms de personne. Paris: Seuil, 1974.
La jeune née [with Catherine Clément]. Paris: Union Générale d'Editions, Collection "10/18," 1975. (*The Newly Born Woman.* Minneapolis: University of Minnesota, 1986.)
Un K. incompréhensible: Pierre Goldman. Paris: Christian Bourgeois, 1975.
"Le rire de la Méduse." *L'Arc* 61 (1975). ("The Laugh of the Medusa." In *New French Feminisms,* edited by Elaine Marks and Isabelle de Courtivron. New York: Schocken Books, 1981.)
"La missexualité, où jouis-je?" *Poétique* 26 (1976):240–49.
"Le sexe ou la tête?. *Cahiers du GRIF* 13 (1976):5–15.
"Castration or Decapitation," *Signs* 7, no. 1 (Autumn 1981):41–55.
La venue à l'écriture [with Annie Leclerc and Madeleine Gagnon] Paris: Union Générale d'Editions, Collection "10/18," 1977.

Secondary Works

Armbruster, Carol. "Hélène-Clarice: Nouvelle voix." *Contemporary Literature* 24, no. 2 (1983):145–57.
Conley, Verena Andermatt. *Hélène Cixous: Writing the Feminine.* Lincoln: University of Nebraska Press, 1984.
Crowder, Diane Griffin. "Amazons and Mothers? Monique Wittig, Hélène Cixous and Theories of Women's Writing." *Contemporary Literature* 24, no. 2 (1983):117–44.

Gallop, Jane. *The Daughter's Seduction: Feminism and Psychoanalysis.* Ithaca, N.Y.: Cornell University Press, 1982.

Jones, Ann Rosalind. "Writing the Body: Toward an Understanding of *L'Écriture féminine.*" *Feminist Studies* 7, no. 2 (Summer 1981):247–64.

Kuhn, Annette. "Introduction to Hélène Cixous's 'Castration or Decapitation?'" *Signs* 7, no. 1 (Autumn 1981):36–40.

Lindsay, Cecile. "Body/Language: French Feminist Utopias." *French Review* 60, no. 1 (October 1986):46–55.

GENERAL BIBLIOGRAPHY

Albistur, Maïté, and Daniel Armogathe. *Histoire du féminisme français du moyen-âge à nos jours.* Paris: des femmes, 1977.

Brée, Germaine. *Women Writers in France: Variations on a Theme.* New Brunswick, N.J.: Rutgers University Press, 1973.

Eisenstein, Hester, and Alice Jardine, eds. *The Future of Difference.* Boston: G. K. Hall, 1980.

Gelfand, Elissa D., and Virginia Thorndike Hules. *French Feminist Criticism: Women, Language and Literature.* New York: Garland, 1985.

Irigaray, Luce. *Speculum de l'autre femme.* Paris: Minuit, 1974. (*Speculum of the Other Woman.* Ithaca: Cornell University Press, 1985.)

Marks, Elaine, and George Stambolian, eds. *Homosexualities and French Literature.* Ithaca: Cornell University Press, 1979.

Marks, Elaine, and Isabelle de Courtivron, eds. *New French Feminisms.* New York: Schocken Books, 1981.

Moi, Toril. *Sexual/Textual Politics: Feminist Literary Theory.* London: Methuen, 1985.

Pratt, Annis. *Archetypal Patterns in Women's Literature.* Bloomington: Indiana University Press, 1981.

Index